Cambridge University Oriental Publications
NO. 22

The Commentary of
RABBI DAVID KIMHI
ON PSALMS CXX–CL

Edited and translated by
JOSHUA BAKER
Sometime Lecturer in Hebrew, Trinity College, Dublin
and
ERNEST W. NICHOLSON
Lecturer in Divinity at the University of Cambridge

A critically edited text and a translation of Rabbi David Kimhi's Commentary on Psalms CXX–CL.

David Kimhi was one of the most illustrious of medieval Jewish experts and his Biblical commentaries have been and remain an important source for both Jewish and Christian Students of the Bible. The editors have here made part of his famous commentary on the Psalms more widely available with a translation and explanatory notes together with an introduction to Kimhi's place in and contribution to medieval Jewish exegesis. This edition will serve as an introduction not only to Kimhi's commentary on Psalms but also to his work in general.

UNIVERSITY OF CAMBRIDGE
ORIENTAL PUBLICATIONS

NO. 22

THE COMMENTARY OF RABBI DAVID KIMḤI ON PSALMS CXX-CL

THE COMMENTARY OF
RABBI DAVID KIMḤI ON
PSALMS CXX-CL

EDITED AND TRANSLATED

BY

JOSHUA BAKER

Sometime Lecturer in Hebrew
Trinity College Dublin

AND

ERNEST W. NICHOLSON

Fellow of Pembroke College and
Lecturer in Divinity at the
University of Cambridge

CAMBRIDGE
AT THE UNIVERSITY PRESS
1973

Published by the Syndics of the Cambridge University Press
Bentley House, 200 Euston Road, London NW1 2DB
American Branch: 32 East 57th Street, New York, N.Y.10022

© Faculty of Oriental Studies, University of Cambridge 1973

Library of Congress Catalogue Card Number: 72–78889

ISBN: 0 521 08670 1

Printed in Great Britain
at the University Printing House, Cambridge
(Brooke Crutchley, University Printer)

CONTENTS

PREFACE

This edition of Kimḥi's commentary on Psalms cxx–cl has its basis in a doctoral thesis submitted to Trinity College Dublin in 1931. At that time I had hoped to develop the thesis as a whole for publication but was prevented from doing so by various commitments in other directions, although I did manage sporadically over the years to extend my research. In 1964 I suggested to my colleague Dr Nicholson, then a lecturer in Trinity College Dublin, that he collaborate with me to produce this present work for publication. The Introduction is essentially the product of my own research into Kimḥi's place in mediaeval Rabbinic exegesis, whilst the text and critical apparatus as well as the translation here published are the product of our combined labours over the past few years.

Our intention has been to produce not only a critical edition of Kimḥi's commentary on these Psalms as well as a discussion of his contribution to Biblical exegesis, but also by including a translation and glossary to provide in effect a text book for students seeking an introduction to mediaeval Hebrew commentaries.

We are both deeply indebted to Dr E. I. J. Rosenthal and Professor J. Weingreen for many valuable suggestions and much encouragement in the final preparation of this work. We also record our gratitude to the Publications Committee of the Faculty of Oriental Studies, Cambridge University, and in particular to Mr E. B. Ceadel, for including this volume in its series. We wish also to express our appreciation to Professor J. A. Emerton for his advice and constant encouragement.

JOSHUA BAKER

Dublin
August 1972

INTRODUCTION

I. KIMḤI AS A BIBLICAL EXEGETE

In the history of Biblical exegesis the name of Rabbi David Kimḥi (*ca.* 1160–1235 C.E.) occupies a very distinguished place. He wrote commentaries on Chronicles, Psalms, the Former Prophets, the Latter Prophets, and Genesis.[1] His commentaries on Genesis and Ezekiel are supplemented by philosophic-allegorical treatises on certain chapters of these books.[2] Kimḥi is also the author of the celebrated *Miklol* which comprises two parts, the one lexicographical and the other a detailed exposition of the principles of Hebrew grammar.[3] Both parts of this monumental work have enjoyed great popularity among both Jewish and Christian scholars down the centuries and indeed remain standard reference books on grammar and lexicography. Kimḥi also composed *Et Sofer* which is a short treatise in which are set forth the rules for the correct punctuation of scriptural scrolls. All other works ascribed to him, however, are probably not authentic.[4]

Unfortunately we know very little about the life of Kimḥi, least of all

---

[1] Of all these only the following have been critically edited: *Commentar zur Genesis von R. David Kimchi*, edit. from a manuscript in the Royal Library of Paris by A. Ginzburg (Pressburg 1842); S. Schiller-Szinessy, *The First Book of Psalms with the Longer Commentary of R. David Qimchi* (Cambridge 1883); L. Finkelstein, *The Commentary of David Kimḥi on Isaiah* (Isaiah i–xxxix) (New York 1926); W. Windfuhr, *Der Kommentar des David Qimchi zum Propheten Nahum* (Giessen 1927); H. Cohen, *The Commentary of Rabbi David Kimḥi on Hosea* (New York 1929); S. I. Esterson, 'The Commentary of Rabbi David Kimḥi on Psalms 42–72', *Hebrew Union College Annual*, x (1935); J. Bosniak, *The Commentary of David Kimḥi on the Fifth Book of the Psalms* (New York 1954). The only translations into English of his commentaries are: A. McCaul, *Rabbi David Kimchi's Commentary upon the Prophecies of Zechariah* (London 1837); A. W. Greenup, *Commentary of David Kimchi on the Book of Psalms* (Psalms i–viii only) (London 1918); R. G. Finch, *The Longer Commentary of R. David Kimḥi on the First Book of Psalms* (i–x, xv–xvii, xix, xxii, xxiv) (London 1919).

[2] The allegorical commentary on Ezekiel chapter i is found in standard Rabbinical Bibles, whilst that on Genesis ii 7 – v 11 was first published as an appendix in L. Finkelstein, *op. cit.* pp. liii–lxxiv.

[3] The title *Miklol* is usually reserved for the grammatical section, whilst the dictionary is generally known as *Sefer Ha-Shorashim* ('The Book of Roots'). The latter was edited by J. H. R. Biesenthal and F. Lebrecht (Berlin 1847). On the grammar see W. Chomsky, *David Kimḥi's Hebrew Grammar (Mikhlol) Systematically Presented and Critically Annotated* (New York 1952); J. Tauber, *Standpunkt und Leistung des R. David Kimchi als Grammatiker* (Breslau 1867).

[4] L. Finkelstein, *op. cit.* p. xx, notes the following: the commentary on the *Moreh Nebukim*, the commentary on *Pittum Haqqᵉtoreth* (published in *Kobez Debarim Neḥmadim*, Husiatyn 1902), a polemical work ascribed to him in *Milḥemeth Ḥobah* (Constantinople 1710), a commentary on the ritual of *Sheḥitah* and a commentary on Ruth. The commentary on Ruth was published by Robertus Stephanus (there is a copy of it in the library of Trinity College Dublin) but there can be no doubt that this commentary bears none of the marks of Kimḥi's style.

about his early life.[1] He was born in Provence about 1160 C.E. and was a son of a distinguished father, Rabbi Joseph Kimḥi (ca. 1105–65 C.E.) who had come from Spain and settled in Narbonne some years before David's birth.[2] Joseph Kimḥi died when David was a boy of probably no more than five years old and David received his education from his elder brother, Moses Kimḥi (ca. 1130–90 C.E.), himself already a scholar and commentator of repute. In his early years David Kimḥi was a keen student of the Talmud, but his written works, all of which were composed in the period after he was forty, are devoted to grammar and exegesis in which his father had acquired acclaim.[3] In his old age, when he had long been widely renowned, Kimḥi engaged vigorously in the defence of the works of Maimonides (ca. 1135–1204 C.E.) against the anti-Maimonists in connection with which he journeyed to Spain where he disputed with Rabbi Judah Alfakhar, one of the leaders of Spanish Jewry at that time.[4] The correspondence between Kimḥi and Alfakhar in connection with the anti-Maimonist controversy provides us with very valuable insights into the character of Kimḥi who, in spite of considerable abuse levelled against him, is revealed in the letters he wrote to have been a man of great patience and humility.[5] A few years after this controversy, which took place in 1232 C.E., Kimḥi died. But the widespread renown and acclaim which he had achieved during his life continued, and his voluminous writings became revered and standard works not only among Spanish Jews to whose exegetical tradition he was deeply indebted, but also among the French, German and Italian Jews.

It was at the request of one of his father's old pupils that Kimḥi's first commentary, that on Chronicles, was written, and in all his exegetical works he shows the care and patience of a very conscientious teacher. An even style is for the most part maintained throughout and if, as a consequence,

[1] For the few facts available about Kimḥi's life the work of A. Geiger remains standard: *Ozar Neḥmad*, II, pp. 153–73, reprinted in his *Kebusat Ma'amarim* (Breslau 1877), pp. 30–77 and also in his *Gesammelte Abhandlungen in hebräischen Sprache*, ed. S. Poznanski (Warsaw 1910), pp. 231–53 (Hebrew). See also L. Finkelstein, *op. cit.* pp. xviff. and the popular survey of Rabbinic literature in W. O. E. Oesterley and G. H. Box, *A Short Survey of the Literature of Rabbinical and Mediaeval Judaism* (London 1920), pp. 225ff.

[2] On Joseph Kimḥi see W. O. E. Oesterley and G. H. Box, *op. cit.* pp. 224f. Cf. H. J. Mathews, *Sepher Ha-Galuj von R. Joseph Kimchi* (Berlin 1887); W. Bacher, *Sepher Sikkaron: Grammatik der hebräischen Sprache von R. Joseph Kimchi* (Berlin 1888).

[3] David Kimḥi's works are spiced with quotations from and references to his father's works which are cited more often than any other source employed by him. For the sources cited by Kimḥi see H. Cohen, *op. cit.* pp. xx–xxvi.

[4] On the controversy see most recently D. J. Silver, *Maimonidean Criticism and the Maimonidean Controversy 1180–1240* (Leiden 1965); F. Talmage, 'David Kimḥi and the Rationalist Tradition', *Hebrew Union College Annual*, xxxix (1968), 177–218 where also further works are cited.

[5] The correspondence has been printed in *Kobez Teshuboth ha-Rambam* (Leipzig 1859).

it lacks artistic finish, at least it has the advantage of logical and systematic presentation.

While he draws largely upon the works of his predecessors, Kimḥi's own contribution is distinctly unique. The foundations of Hebrew grammar had been firmly laid by Judah Ḥayyuj (*ca.* 950–1000 C.E.) and Jonah Ibn Janaḥ (*ca.* 990–1050 C.E.), but to Kimḥi was left the task of summing up and ordering the results of their research.[1] This was accomplished with inexorable exactness and precision. But Kimḥi was no ordinary compiler, for in the arrangement and selection of the material employed by him he exhibits rare skill and judgement. There is no hesitation in criticising the opinions of earlier authorities and occasionally he offers an interpretation which is unmistakably original.

Of all the mediaeval Jewish exegetes, none was more thorough or methodical than Kimḥi. In his work not only is most careful attention given to separate verses, phrases and words, but his primary aim is always to present a lucid and systematic account of the context in relation to the book to which it belongs and also in its bearing upon the rest of the Old Testament. The introductions to his commentaries are full of interesting material. In addition, each chapter is prefaced with an outline of the central theme of the text. In dealing with a historical passage in the Bible, he makes a point of giving a thorough account of all the events and circumstances relevant to the passage in question. The method is also well exemplified in the commentary on the Psalms. The authorship and titles of the separate Psalms are discussed. Noteworthy too are his comments on their chronological order, as for example in Psalm ii 1:[2]

'The reason why this Psalm follows immediately the other is not known to us; nor why he arranged them in the order in which they are connected, for they are not arranged in historical order. For instance, the third Psalm is concerned with the affair of Absalom, and after it occur many Psalms whose subject-matter is earlier by a considerable period than the incident of Absalom.'

Kimḥi makes extensive use of parallel passages to illustrate an interpretation, but never hesitates to draw attention to difficulties arising from divergent accounts of the same incident. His attitude is frank and open as contrasted with the sophistry and subterfuge resorted to by the more erudite

---

[1] For an introduction to the contribution of these early Hebrew grammarians, see W. Bacher, 'Die hebräische Sprachwissenschaft vom 10. bis zum 16. Jahrhundert', in J. Winter and A. Wünsche, *Die jüdische Literatur seit dem Abschluss des Kanons*, II (Trier 1894), pp. 135–235. Brief discussions are also contained in Gesenius-Kautzsch, *Hebrew Grammar*, ed. A. E. Cowley (London 1910), pp. 17ff.; H. Bauer and P. Leander, *Historische Grammatik der hebräischen Sprache* (Halle 1922, reprinted Hildesheim 1965), pp. 36ff.

[2] Translated by R. G. Finch, *op. cit.* p. 12.

Abraham Ibn Ezra.[1] In his attempt to reconcile such divergences he relies for the most part on the evidence supplied by the Old Testament itself, using only as a secondary source historical material contained in the *Seder Olam*.[2]

Kimḥi's suggested interpretation of texts and words which are difficult or obscure from the linguistic point of view has been of particular importance. The Authorised Version bears ample testimony to this.[3] His suggestions are also frequently consulted by modern scholars, and often adopted, usually by express citation, though occasionally without the least acknowledgement.[4] In addition, it seems evident, as we shall see presently, that he anticipated the comparatively modern theory of the feature of Hebrew poetry known as *parallelismus membrorum*.[5]

Kimḥi was very much concerned with the establishment of a correct reading of the Biblical texts. He makes a number of citations from 'correct texts', refers to the *Sefer Hilleli*, the work *Oklah we-Oklah*, *Codex Severus*, a *Sefer Babli* and a *Codex Damascus*. The readings of *Ben Asher* and *Ben Naphtali* are also given in a few cases.

As for the sources used by Kimhi in his exegesis, there are numerous quotations from the Talmud and Midrashim and, from the massive list given by Cohen,[6] it appears that he employed as many as one hundred and

---

[1] See, for instance, the observation of Ibn Ezra in his comment on Isaiah xxxvi concerning the comparison of the text with the parallel passage in 2 Kings xviii: 'they are in meaning the same, although the one contains some additional words which the other has not; the words may be compared to instruments, their meaning to workmen' (ET by M. Friedländer, *The Commentary of Ibn Ezra on Isaiah*, London 1877).

[2] Cf. H. Cohen, *op. cit.* p. xxv.

[3] For the influence of Kimḥi and other mediaeval Jewish commentators on Reformation translations of the Old Testament see E. I. J. Rosenthal, 'Rashi and the English Bible', *Bulletin of the John Rylands Library*, xxiv, 1 (1940); 'Sebastian Münster's Knowledge and Use of Jewish Exegesis', *Essays presented to Dr J. H. Hertz*, ed. I. Epstein, E. Levine and C. Roth (London 1943); 'Edward Lively: Cambridge Hebraist', *Essays and Studies presented to Stanley A. Cook*, ed. D. W. Thomas (London 1950); 'Mediaeval Jewish Exegesis: Its Character and Significance', *Journal of Semitic Studies*, ix (1964), 271ff. See also B. Smalley, *The Study of the Bible in the Middle Ages*, 2nd ed. (Oxford 1952). The translators of the Authorised Version were well versed in Kimḥi, but much of his influence on their translation came via the Genevan version which was heavily dependent upon the Latin translations of Münster and Pagninus which in turn were very largely based on Kimḥi. Cf. H. Cohen, *op. cit.* p. x; E. I. J. Rosenthal, 'Mediaeval Jewish Exegesis: Its Character and Significance', p. 278 and his article on Sebastian Münster referred to above.

[4] Cf. M. H. Segal, 'Studies in the Books of Samuel', *Jewish Quarterly Review*, N.S. x (1919–20), 421–33.

[5] Synonymous parallelism had, however, been recognised by Menahem ben Saruk (*ca.* 910–70 C.E.). Cf. E. I. J. Rosenthal, 'Mediaeval Jewish Exegesis: Its Character and Significance', p. 269.

[6] H. Cohen, *op. cit.* pp. xx–xxvi. It should be noted, however, that Moses Ibn Ezra is in fact cited in *Sefer Ha-Shorashim* (under בד and עצב).

fifty other sources. The commentaries of his father and those of Ibn Ezra
are cited more frequently than any other exegete. But more important than
the matter of his dependence on any single commentator is the question
of determining the more general trends in his exegesis. Two distinct
influences are seen in operation here and we must now turn to a brief
discussion of this.

2. KIMḤI IN RELATION TO THE FRENCH AND SPANISH SCHOOLS OF EXEGESIS

Living as he did in Provence, which is situated between France and Spain,
Kimḥi came under the influence of two sharply distinguished Jewish
cultures, the one represented by the French school and the other by the
Spanish. In France scholarship consisted – for the greater part – of a
profound study of the Talmud and, while producing such outstanding
Halakists as Rashi (1040–1105 C.E.) and Rabbenu Tam (1100–71 C.E.), it
was singularly limited in its contribution to the field of Biblical exegesis.
With the exception of the commentaries of Rabbi Joseph Kara (*ca.* 1070–
1140 C.E.) and Rashbam (1100–60 C.E.),[1] it might be said that the achieve-
ments of the French scholars represented almost no advance upon the
incoherent mass of exegetical material embedded in the earlier Rabbinic[2]
literature. At all events, considerations of grammar and philology are
secondary, indeed, almost of no consequence in their work. In contrast to
this Talmudic and traditional approach of the French scholars there had
developed in Spain an exegetical method which is best characterised as
philosophical and philological.

There was, on the one hand, widespread effort to harmonise the contents
of Scripture with the postulates of contemporary science and philosophy.
This type of exegesis, exemplified in the writings of Maimonides, is just
as unsatisfactory as the earlier Rabbinic method which, as we have noted,
continued to flourish in the French school. Both systems are vitiated by
the absence of an objective approach to the study of the Bible. However,
Kimḥi generally succeeds in avoiding the digressions of the philosophical
Midrash – with the exception only of his allegorical commentary on parts

---

[1] We do not include Rashi's commentaries as having the same merit from the
standpoint of plain interpretation of the Biblical text. His commentaries have
enjoyed popularity and have exerted great influence throughout the ages, but their
importance lies not in their contribution to plain exegesis but rather in their
function of transmitting the material derived from the Talmud and the Midrashim.
For a slightly different view see I. Abrahams, *Chapters on Jewish Literature*
(Philadelphia 1899), pp. 123f. But see below, p. xviii n. 1.

[2] In the subsequent discussions the term 'Rabbinic' is strictly limited to Talmudic
and Midrashic literature. When we speak of a Rabbinic point of view we mean
one reflected in this literature.

of Genesis and Ezekiel and a number of passages in the Psalms. On the other hand, beginning with Saadya (*ca.* 882–942 C.E.)[1] there had grown up in Spain a distinguished line of grammarians, philologists and lexicographers from whose works much of what is important in Kimḥi's exegesis is derived. The origin of this emphasis upon grammar and philology in Biblical exegesis is best understood as a reaction to the Karaite movement.[2] Founded in the eighth century, this sect 'boldly challenged the claims of the current exegetical tradition, and indeed the authority of Rabbinical traditions generally, and insisted that the sole fount of authority for the religious life was to be found in the plain text of Scripture'.[3] In their controversy with the Karaites, Saadya and his successors adopted the Karaite's own emphasis on the *Peshat* – the plain meaning of the Biblical text as against the *Derash* or free, *Haggadic* exposition – and upon grammar and philology in their exegesis.[4] In his general adherence to the *Peshat* and his keen grammatical and textual work in his exegesis, Kimḥi is clearly strongly influenced by this anti-Karaite school of thought in Spain.

Besides these broad classifications, we should also note the beginnings of a more historical method. In particular the name of Moses Ibn Gikatilla (eleventh century C.E.) must be mentioned. His claim to importance rests upon the fact that he was the first commentator to advance purely historical explanations of prophecies in Isaiah and the Minor Prophets.[5] He is quoted by Kimḥi in at least fourteen instances,[6] though this hardly represents the full degree of his influence.

While the more permanent and objective features of Kimḥi's exegesis were derived from the Spanish schools, it is a matter for regret that most students of Kimḥi dwell almost solely upon this particular aspect of his works. For it cannot be sufficiently emphasised that no estimate of Kimḥi's system of interpretation is adequate which fails to take into account the influence exerted upon him by the earlier Rabbinic exegesis. In what follows some attempt is made to assess this influence.

---

[1] On Saadya see especially, E. I. J. Rosenthal, 'Saadya Gaon: An Appreciation of his Biblical Exegesis', *Bulletin of the John Rylands Library*, xxvii, 1 (1942); *Saadya Studies*, ed. E. I. J. Rosenthal (Manchester 1942); S. L. Skoss, *Saadia Gaon, the Earliest Hebrew Grammarian* (Philadelphia 1955).

[2] On the Karaites see W. O. E. Oesterley and G. H. Box, *op. cit.* pp. 215ff.

[3] *Ibid.* p. 215.

[4] *Ibid.* pp. 212ff. On this characteristic of mediaeval Jewish exegesis see the admirable survey of E. I. J. Rosenthal, 'Mediaeval Jewish Exegesis: Its Character and Significance' and the discussion by J. Weingreen, 'The Rabbinic Approach to the Study of the Old Testament', *Bulletin of the John Rylands Library*, xxxiv, 1 (1951).

[5] Cf. W. O. E. Oesterley and G. H. Box, *op. cit.* p. 218 n. 3.

[6] Cf. H. Cohen, *op. cit.* p. xxi.

3. KIMḤI AND THE RABBINIC EXEGESIS

If we were to select a commentator whose works best exemplify the union of the two streams of Jewish thought represented by the Spanish and French schools respectively it would not be David Kimḥi but his father Joseph. There is a peculiar flair and subtlety about the exegetical writings of Joseph Kimḥi. On the one hand we have grammar and philology, on the other Rabbinic dialectic and homily. The two elements combine to form a compound which is not easily resolved into its constituent parts. But with the younger Kimḥi no such difficulty arises. There is really no fusion; it is as though the two streams meet and run in the same channel without their waters actually mixing. And it is for this reason that the investigation of the relation between Kimḥi and the Rabbinic sources is not as difficult as might otherwise appear.

Kimḥi quotes more frequently from the Rabbinic sources than any other commentator. Quite apart from their bearing upon his interpretation, they are occasionally of considerable importance in establishing a correct text of these sources. In some instances he had probably a reading different from ours and his lengthy quotations from the Midrash are very useful for textual purposes. But, as a general rule, it must be borne in mind that it is the immediate purpose of the quotation rather than accuracy which is Kimḥi's primary concern. Several supposedly 'loose' quotations are in fact deliberate; parts of a passage are intentionally omitted as being irrelevant for the particular point requiring illustration.[1]

Of greater importance is the consideration of the degree of authority accorded by Kimḥi to the Rabbinic sources, especially when we bear in mind that they consist mainly of *Derash* as distinct from *Peshat*. Generally speaking, it may be fairly stated that he takes an intermediate standpoint between that of Rashi on the one hand and Abraham Ibn Ezra (1092–1167 C.E.) on the other. The latter had no use for *Derash* when it is opposed to the plain meaning of a text and at times is almost contemptuous in his reference to that kind of exegesis.[2] Rashi, however, attaches great importance to the Rabbinic exegesis upon which he draws very widely and, although occasionally criticising a Rabbinic interpretation,[3] he displays on the whole an attitude of profound respect for and unquestioned reliance

---

[1] See, for example, his quotation from *Sabbath* 25a included by Finkelstein in the list of 'loose' citations (*op. cit.* pp. xxxf.). The omission is in fact deliberate. Cf. also Kimḥi's comment on Psalm cxlv 10 where his quotation from *Baba Kama* 30a, a very celebrated passage, is considerably shorter than the text in question.

[2] Cf. for example Ibn Ezra's remark on Exodus xiii 8 'it is merely a Midrash and therefore of no authority' (trans. by M. Friedländer, *Essays on the Writings of Abraham Ibn Ezra* (London 1877), p. 95 n. 2). Cf. his critical observation in his comment on Genesis xxv 34 'let him not refute it with the reed of Midrash'.

[3] See Rashi's comments on 1 Sam. i 25; Isa. xxvi 11; Nah. i 8; Zech. i 12.

on the Rabbinic sources. As a general rule he fails to distinguish between *Peshat* and *Derash*, frequently presenting the latter as the correct understanding of a text, and occasionally without even stating that it is derived from a Rabbinic source.[1] Kimḥi's approach is fundamentally different. Side by side with the plain interpretation of a text he frequently gives the Rabbinic interpretation, but invariably makes it quite clear that he is quoting a Rabbinic source. Furthermore, he usually draws a clear line of demarcation between *Peshat* and *Derash*, showing a marked preference for the former method of exegesis. Where, as in 1 Kings vii 24, the Rabbinic interpretation appears to Kimḥi to be in accord with the plain meaning of the text, he notes the interpretation with express approval: 'Thus our teachers, of blessed memory, have expounded the text and such would appear to be the interpretation according to the plain meaning of the verse.' On the other hand, where the Rabbinic interpretation does not appeal to him, he does not hesitate to reject it. Thus, for example, of the Rabbinic interpretation of 2 Samuel iii 15 he states: 'The foregoing (interpretation) is altogether remote from the plain meaning of the text', whilst of the Rabbinic interpretation of Ezekiel iv 6 he says: 'This Midrashic comment is far-fetched.' In his comment on 1 Samuel i 25 he states: 'It is unnecessary to mention the Midrashic comment, which is as well known as it is far-fetched.' Similar observations are to be found in his comments on several other passages.[2]

Independently of such passages, it is abundantly clear from the tenor of all his works that Kimḥi's primary aim is to give the clear and simple meaning of the text in preference to any free or fanciful interpretation. His general approach is well exemplified in a statement made by him in the course of his Introduction to his commentary on Chronicles:

'I am not aware of any exegetes who have made a serious attempt to interpret it (Chronicles). I have found here in Narbonne different commentaries on this book written by various authors whose names are unknown here, but I observe that all these commentaries proceed for the most part along the lines of *Derash*. A scholar from Geronah, a pupil of my revered father, has asked me to write a commentary. I have thought fit to accede to his request.'

[1] Cf. for example Rashi's comments on 1 Sam. xxii 18; 2 Sam. vii 23, viii 13, ix 14. It would be incorrect to claim that *Peshat* finds no place in Rashi's exegesis and it can be said that the stress on *Peshat* in later French exegetes, especially Rashi's grandson Rashbam, owes its origins, slight though they be, to Rashi's work. But, as stated above, *as a general rule* Rashi's exegesis may be characterised as *Derash* and the claim of J. Pereira-Mendoza, *Rashi as Philologist* (Manchester 1940), p. 63, that he 'just as often said he preferred the Peshat' is questionable.

[2] See his comments on Josh. v 16; Jud. xvi 16; 1 Sam. xxii 18, xxv 38, xxvi 5; 2 Kings viii 25, xxii 10; Ps. cxxxii 5.

A more important statement is to be found in the Introduction to the commentary on the Former Prophets: 'I will also cite the words of our Rabbis, of blessed memory, in regard to passages where we require their interpretation, especially where they had a "tradition". In addition, I will cite some of the Midrashic interpretations for those who prefer *Derash*.' The concluding remark confirms us in the view that Kimḥi preferred the method of *Peshat*.[1] Nevertheless, despite such remarks, it is difficult to account for the numerous Midrashic quotations to be found in his works without assuming that consciously or subconsciously Kimḥi did attach importance to *Derash* as a means of interpretation. And indeed, we should not be surprised to find that that method of exegesis which had flourished for so many generations exercised over our author a subtle influence of which he himself may have been unaware.

Where the Rabbis had a 'tradition' with regard to a Biblical text, Kimḥi adopts their interpretation. In his comment on Judges xi 31, referring to the incident of Jephthah's daughter, he states: 'As for the statement of our Rabbis, if they had a tradition to that effect, we must accept it.' In this and in a number of other passages[2] Kimḥi accepts unreservedly the authority of the Rabbis, however far-fetched the comment may be. But such instances are exceptional and it appears that the sanction of antiquity with which such interpretations had become invested rendered these traditions of fundamental importance for later generations. The position is well summed up in a remark by Abraham Ibn Ezra: 'If the statement be based on tradition, we will accept it; if on reasoning, we hold a different opinion.'[3]

In the absence of a binding 'tradition', however, Kimḥi's attitude to the Midrashic citations cannot be precisely determined. The frequency with which they occur suggest a *prima facie* argument for supposing that he considered them to be fairly reliable interpretations of the Biblical text. On the other hand, the statement in the Introduction to the Former Prophets, cited above, may be construed as supporting a contrary opinion. At all events the cumulative effect of the direct testimony of his various pronouncements upon the passages used is inconclusive. In his comment on 1 Samuel xxviii 24 he quotes a dictum of Rabbi Samuel ben Ḥophni (d. *ca.* 1034 C.E.) to the effect that the opinions of the Rabbinic authorities are not to be accepted if opposed to the dictates of reason. But this principle, like the contrary tendency observed in the deference shown by Kimḥi to interpretations based on a 'tradition', represents only an extreme point of view and is not to be taken as characteristic of the general line of approach adopted by him.

---

[1] Cf. J. Weingreen, *op. cit.* pp. 169ff.
[2] Cf. his comments on Josh. iv 11; Jud. xii 8, xiii 4; 1 Sam. ii 8 2 Sam. xiv 26; Isa. xxxvi 22; Jer. i 13.
[3] Cf. Friedländer, *Essays on the Writings of Abraham Ibn Ezra*, p. 95 n. 2.

When, however, we come to consider the influence of the Rabbinic sources, not as expressed in actual quotations but rather in their more indirect consequences, we may succeed in achieving more satisfactory results. For their influence is to be traced in many comments and discussions in Kimḥi's works which, though not derived from the Talmudic and Midrashic literature, are essentially Rabbinic in character. This is particularly well in evidence in some of the lengthy *Halakic* digressions contained in Kimḥi's commentaries. The following two examples[1] will serve to illustrate the point we wish to make here.

(1) *1 Samuel xxv 44*. 'Saul had given Michal his daughter, David's wife, to Palti son of Laish from Gallim.' In commenting on this verse Kimḥi raises the following questions: (*a*) Since Michal was David's wife, how could Saul have given her to Palti? (*b*) How could Palti have taken Michal as his wife knowing as he did that she was married to David? (*c*) If Michal had wilfully sinned by having connections with another man while she was still David's wife, how is the fact that David subsequently took her again as his wife to be explained? These matters, which involve intricate points of the Rabbinic law of marriage and divorce, are discussed in the Rabbinic literature, though not with the elaborate detail found in Kimḥi. He notes a number of solutions, including those of the Rabbinic authorities, and then proceeds to explain that David was compelled by Saul to give Michal a divorce so that she should not 'be tied to an absent husband'. But it is not all as simple as this, for our author continues in *Halakic* fashion with a further series of questions and answers:

> *Question:* Having given Michal a divorce, how did David come to take her back, seeing that in the meantime she had already become married to Palti?
> *Answer:* In the absence of reality of consent on David's part, the divorce was invalid.
> *Question:* But surely David ran away of his own accord, thereby intimating the intention of deserting his wife?
> *Answer:* He really did not intend to desert her altogether, since we find that he would return occasionally to Saul's court. (Cf. 1 Sam. xx 6.)
> *Question:* Was the Beth Din not aware of the invalidity of the divorce obtained from David?
> *Answer:* David did not make public the circumstances of the divorce, but in the presence of two faithful friends he made the following declaration: 'You are witnesses to the fact that this divorce was obtained from me under duress. But do not divulge the matter to

---

[1] For further examples see Kimḥi's comments on 1 Sam. xxi 7, xxvi 5; 2 Sam. ix 2, 7, xi 4, xii 3, 6, 9.

anyone.' But neither Michal nor Palti were aware of these circumstances and they both understood the divorce to be valid.

(2) 2 *Samuel i 11*. 'And she made a vow and said . . . then I will give him to the Lord all the days of his life and no razor shall touch his head.' Kimḥi sees two difficulties in this verse: (*a*) According to Rabbinic law a vow of this kind, if made before the child is born, cannot take effect; (*b*) even in the case of a child already born, only a father has authority to make his (minor) son a Nazarite, no such authority being given to the mother. Kimḥi suggests that Elkanah may have subsequently joined in the vow, but it is evident that he does not regard this explanation as satisfactory. His concluding remark on this is significant: 'I am all the more surprised that our teachers, of blessed memory, did not discuss this matter, for I find no statement in either the Midrash or the Talmud containing a reference thereto.'

In these discussions, as indeed in a number of other passages in Kimḥi's works, one striking feature of Rabbinic theology is to be noted, viz. the doctrine of the Oral Law and its repercussions upon the Rabbinic concept of ancient Israel. It is assumed that alongside the Written Law the Oral Law was given to Moses on Mount Sinai and transmitted throughout all generations. The Pentateuch, the Written Law, contains general rules and principles; the Oral Law explains the mode and manner of their application. This doctrine provided a convenient fiction for the development of the Pentateuchal laws (in this respect Jewish law partakes of a phenomenon paralleled in other legal systems). But the idea of *Torah* as developed in Rabbinic literature is something much wider, more comprehensive than the concept of law as ordinarily understood. For *Torah* embraces civil and religious laws, institutions, ideas, ethical and moral values; in short, it includes the whole range of ideology and civilisation of Rabbinic Judaism. Accordingly, in its full implications the doctrine of the Oral Law results in a very definite attitude in the treatment and interpretation of the early history of Israel. The civilisation and culture of Rabbinic Judaism are projected back into the remote past, its laws, customs and institutions being assumed to have been already in existence in ancient Israel. Such, in brief, is the Rabbinic point of view.

This attitude is a marked feature of Rabbinic exegesis. That it exercised a profound effect upon the subsequent exegesis of the Middle Ages need therefore occasion no surprise. It occupies a central position in the exegetical systems of all mediaeval Jewish commentators. Kimḥi is no exception to this, though the effect of the doctrine of the Oral Law does not emerge as clearly in his work as in those of the traditional Rabbinic commentators of the French schools. Certainly, however, it is only in the light of this doctrine that the passages in Kimḥi outlined above assume a definite meaning and purpose. Thus in the fundamental issues Kimḥi follows the trend of the Rabbinic exegesis.

As a direct outcome of the belief in the antiquity of tradition is the veneration shown by the ancient Rabbis for the illustrious heroes and leaders in Israel's history. They elaborate and extol their virtues and weave round the Biblical narrative of their lives a religious, ethical or moral teaching. Correspondingly, there is a tendency to explain away any ostensible wrongdoing or conduct falling short of the Rabbinic standard. These features of Rabbinic literature are particularly conspicuous in Haggadic Midrashim. A similar attitude is frequently adopted by Kimḥi – one could hardly expect otherwise. Thus, in his comment on Judges xiv 2 he is evidently perplexed at Samson's marriage with a Philistine woman in disregard of the Biblical injunction against intermarriage (cf. Deut. vii 3). He says that it is impossible to believe that one of the Judges of Israel could have ignored such a stringent injunction, and he then solves the difficulty to his complete satisfaction by the assumption that Samson proselytised his Philistine women, 'converting them to the religion of Israel'!

In his comment on 1 Samuel xix 13, he is obviously unhappy about the Biblical narrative, and to explain away the presence of *teraphim* in David's household he cites a metaphysical exposition of the verse by Abraham Ibn Ezra. Similarly, in his comment on Judges vi 37–9, Kimḥi finds it necessary to deal with Gideon's apparent lack of faith in asking for a second Divine sign for the deliverance of his people. Adopting an interpretation by Saadya, Kimḥi explains that Gideon's request for a second sign was not prompted by any lack of faith, but by a desire to ascertain whether he himself was the person who would be worthy of being the instrument of such a great miracle.

One further observation may be made. The Haggadists, by the skilful use of proverb, parable and allegory, and particularly by free and ingenious treatment of the Biblical text, cultivated a form of popular discourse or sermon which made an immense appeal to the emotions of the people. Indeed, the *Haggadah* exerted a tremendous influence in moulding the character of traditional Judaism and has served as a storehouse of inspiration for Jews at all times. Although his commentaries are primarily directed to the simple interpretation of the text in accordance with his expressed purpose, occasionally Kimḥi adopts the role of guide and preacher to his people after the manner of *Haggadah*. This feature of his exegesis is well attested in his commentary on the Psalms and is frequently to be observed in that part of this commentary edited in the present volume.

All this indicates the strong influence upon Kimḥi of the broader aspects of Rabbinic exegesis. But in addition, there is also considerable evidence of the influence upon his works of some of the more detailed characteristics of that exegesis: we find, for example, elaborate treatment of metaphors, undue stress upon the significance of particles, loose connections of Biblical verses such as we are accustomed to find in the Midrashic literature.[1]

But while, on the one hand, Kimḥi's thorough acquaintance with the Rabbinic literature tends in some instances to lead him away from the plain interpretation of the text, on the other hand, in other instances he makes skilful use of the Rabbinic material as an aid to sound exegesis. Rabbinic literature is not an open book even for the more advanced student of the Bible, with the result that its bounteous legacy of knowledge and inspiration does not always receive the recognition it merits. Kimḥi's work brings out to some extent the importance of the contribution by the Rabbis to plain exegesis (*Peshat*), and not infrequently he is enabled to explain thereby a difficult word in the Old Testament. For, although Rabbinic literature cannot be said to deal with plain exegesis, there is to be found throughout its numerous tomes a wealth of objective exegetical material which still remains to be sifted.[2] Kimḥi frequently achieves important results by the use of these sources as the following few examples indicate.[3]

He explains פגרו in 1 Samuel xxx 10, 21 on the analogy of the use of the word in *Sabbath* 129a, where it has the meaning 'relax', 'take a holiday', 'be idle'. Similarly, he understands the difficult word וטאטאתיה in Isaiah xiv 23 from its occurrence in *Megillah* 18a, where reference is made to the colloquial use of the word: שקולי טאטיתא וטאטי ביתא 'take a broom and sweep the room'. Equally interesting is his reference to *Pesaḥim* 86a in discussing חומות וחל in Isaiah xxvi 1: 'What are the חל and the הומה? The wall proper and the minor wall.'[4]

Another aspect of traditional Rabbinic exegesis to be found in Kimḥi's commentaries is the unquestioned belief in the integrity of the Massoretic Text.[5] However, it is interesting to observe, as we shall now see, that

---

[1] See Kimḥi's comments on Ps. cxlviii 12. Cf. his remarks on Ps. xv 3, 5; 2 Sam. xii 24; Zech. v 3.

[2] For an important contribution on this aspect of Rabbinic exegesis see I. Frankel, *Peshat in Talmudic and Midrashic Literature* (Toronto 1956).

[3] For further examples see his explanations, by reference to Rabbinic sources, of צנמות (Gen. xli 23), והרעלות (Isa. iii 19), אדדה (Isa. xxxviii 15), וימתחם (Isa. xl 22), באגרף (Isa. lviii 4), כבד (Nah. ii 10. Cf. iii 15), בחלה (Zech. xi 8). See also his explanation of ראי in his comment on Nahum iii 6. AV, RV and RSV and some modern commentators translate the latter 'gazingstock', but more recently the word has been widely understood as 'excrement', which is the translation adopted in the New English Bible. Kimḥi clearly identifies the word with רעי 'excrement', 'dung'.

[4] Translated by W. Slokti in *The Babylonian Talmud*, ed. I. Epstein (Soncino Press, London 1938).

[5] Cf., for example, *Nedarim* 37b: 'The textual reading, as transmitted by the Soferim, their stylistic embellishments, (words) read (in the text) but not written, and words written but omitted in the reading, are all *halaka* from Moses at Sinai' (translated by H. Freedman, *The Babylonian Talmud*, ed. I. Epstein, London 1938). Cf. Kimḥi's remarks on Jud. i 24 and Hos. viii 13.

Kimḥi by his own methods succeeds in achieving the same results for the meaning of some difficult readings in the text as are obtained by modern scholars either by means of emendation or by reference to the ancient versions of the Old Testament.

4. KIMḤI AND THE MASSORETIC TEXT

Kimḥi's interpretation of the *qere* and *kethibh* is rather modern in tone. In the Introduction to his commentary on Joshua he states that

> 'in the course of the first exile the books were lost, the scholars dispersed and the students of the Torah dead, so that the men of the Great Synagogue who restored the Torah to its previous status found differences of reading among the manuscripts and they accepted the reading of the majority according to what they thought best. Where they could not determine the truth with certainty, they inserted the reading with the provision that it be not read, or they wrote it on the margin (so that it might be read) but omitted it from the main text. Likewise, they accepted one reading for the main text and put the other in the margin.'

Kimḥi regards both the *qere* and the *kethibh* as equally authoritative and sacrosanct. The dogged persistence with which he endeavours to interpret in all cases not only the *qere* but also the *kethibh* evidences this. For this purpose an ingenious casuistry is occasionally employed. Thus, for example, in Judges xi 34 where the *kethibh* is ממנו 'from him', Kimḥi explains that Jephthah's wife had no children by him. Thus he takes אין־לו ממנו בן או־בת to mean 'he had neither son nor daughter (left him) from him (i.e. her first husband) (except this one daughter)'.

In his treatment of a passage in which there is an evident omission, Kimḥi is guided by the principle of מקרא קצר 'elliptic text'.[1] The correctness of the text is not questioned, but the author of the Biblical work intends us to infer something more than is actually written down.[2] On the basis of this Kimḥi uses his knowledge of the Old Testament to remarkable effect. Examples of his method are given below and it is interesting to note that many of his conjectures agree almost verbatim with the readings suggested by the LXX.

(1) *1 Samuel x 21*. After 'and the family of Matri was picked' the LXX adds 'Then he presented the family of Matri man by man' (ויקרב את משפחת

---

[1] One of the thirty-two canons of Haggadic interpretation formulated by Rabbi José the Galilean.

[2] Cf. Kimḥi on Psalm cxlii 5: 'This is in the interests of brevity, in accordance with Biblical usage, because the one is easily understood from the other.' See also his comment on 2 Kgs. viii 16.

המטרי לגברים). Kimḥi achieves a similar result, stating: 'this text is elliptic, for to this end he had already presented the family of Matri man by man'.

(2) *Joshua ix 21.* On the basis of the LXX it appears that the verse originally read 'Let them live and become (והיו) hewers of wood and drawers of water to all the congregation.' Kimḥi comments: 'This text is elliptic, for (in the first place) the chiefs said: "Let them live and become (וְיִהְיוּ) hewers of wood and drawers of water." But the verse takes the elliptical course and says (simply) "they became", using *waw* consecutive for past tense (וַיִּהְיוּ).'

(3) *1 Samuel xiv 18.* The Massoretic Text reads, 'Bring forward the Ark.' The LXX reads, 'Bring forward the ephod.' Kimḥi comments: 'He means the ephod and the urim and thummim.'

(4) *1 Samuel xxx 9.* 'So David and his six hundred men set out and they came to the ravine of Besor. And those who were left over remained.' Kimḥi comments: 'The verse is elliptic, for he means that they all came to the ravine of Besor, that four hundred crossed over the ravine and that the remainder, who did not cross over, remained there' (cf. *v.* 10).

(5) *1 Samuel xiii 15.* 'And Samuel arose and went from Gilgal to Geba of Benjamin.' There is an obvious omission in the Massoretic Text, for in *v.* 16 we read that Saul is already in Geba of Benjamin. The addition is supplied by the LXX.[1] Kimḥi ingeniously comments: 'And Samuel arose *and Saul together with him.*'

(6) *Judges ii 3.* 'Sides' (לצדים). Kimḥi assumes that this is to be understood as לצנים לצדים 'thorns in your side' (cf. Num. xxxiii 55).[2]

(7) *2 Samuel xiii 39* (ותכל דוד). Kimḥi suggests that נפש 'soul' is to be supplied before דוד – giving the reading ותכל נפש דוד 'and David's soul longed'. S. R. Driver and R. P. Smith arrive at the same meaning on the basis of the Lucian Recension.[3]

The belief in the integrity of the Massoretic Text had also very important consequences upon Kimḥi's contribution to the study of Hebrew grammar. Evident mistakes such as the use of the wrong gender, number or person

---

[1] Cf. *Biblica Hebraica, in loc.*
[2] Cf. S. A. Cook, *Judges*, Cambridge Bible for Schools and Colleges (London 1913), *in loc.*
[3] See I. Frankel, *op. cit.* p. 163.

have to be accounted for.[1] The process is frequently accomplished by the device of explaining one irregularity by another. The same applies to the omission or meaningless addition of prepositions. Thus in one passage he states that the *litterae serviles* are occasionally omitted from the context where the sense is sufficiently clear. By the use of this principle he attempts to explain ודוד הגיד 'And David said' in 2 Samuel xv 31 which he considers to be equivalent to ולדוד הגיד 'And to David he said *or* it was told.'

Rules of commutation and transposition are occasionally applied by Kimḥi somewhat loosely, though he is more discriminate than Rashi. Furthermore, on rare occasions he even resorts to the adoption of such fanciful hermeneutical devices as Athbash[2] and Atbaḥ.[3] But it should be borne in mind that the foregoing are exceptions to the general character of his work; such exceptions apart, Kimḥi's exposition of Hebrew grammar is an achievement of great merit.

5. KIMḤI AND PARALLELISM

In conformity with the Rabbinic insistence upon the importance of every letter and every external peculiarity of the sacred text, parallel expressions would naturally come in for very forced treatment. Synonymous words and repetitions suggest a homiletical interpretation. Thus each member of the parallelism is regarded as of special significance.

As against such a method Kimḥi as a general rule explains parallelism by some such formula as 'he repeats the meaning with different words', 'he repeats the meaning', 'the verse gives the same meaning twice', 'the verse repeats itself in meaning according to the usage of the language'. Many examples of this are found in the text edited in the present volume. Not quite so frequently we find a formula indicating that the meaning is repeated for the sake of emphasis. All this is obviously a close approximation to the modern treatment of parallelism, but whether or not Kimḥi regarded the parallelism structure as a form of poetry is really beside the point, for in practice the result is in either case the same.

In view, however, of the extraordinary popularity of the Midrashic method of interpretation – Kimḥi's father uses it extensively – it would be strange and unexpected to find that Kimḥi altogether succeeds in avoiding it. And indeed, contrary to the view of Finkelstein,[4] it seems that this traditional method was not without its consequences upon David Kimḥi's

---

[1] See Kimḥi's comments on 2 Sam. iii 3, xvi 2; Isa. i 29; Ps. cxxi 1. See also the section in *Miklol* dealing with gender, number and person of verbs.

[2] For this word see M. Jastrow, *A Dictionary of the Targumin, the Talmud Babli and Yerushalmi, and the Midrashic Literature* (edition here consulted published in New York 1950), p. 131. Cf. Kimḥi's comments on Jer. xxv 26; Ps. xiv 3.

[3] On this word see M. Jastrow, *op. cit.* p. 42. Cf. Kimḥi's comment on Ezek. xxi 19.

[4] L. Finkelstein, *op. cit.* pp. xxivf.

exegesis. Some examples of this to be found in the text in the present work are given below.[1] As far as we are aware the comments are original, though there can be no certainty about this. But in any case what is particularly significant is that these comments are presented as the ordinary literal interpretation of the text without any suggestion of their Rabbinic origin, if such there be.

(1) *Psalm cxxv 5. But as for those who turn aside into their own crooked ways:* the expression refers to such evildoers as are in Israel. *The Lord will lead them away with the evildoers:* of the nations.

(2) *Psalm cxxvii 2. It is vain for you:* he says this concerning Absalom who was quick to rebel against his father to usurp the kingship. *Going late to rest:* he says this about Adonijah who waited until David became old and lay on his death-bed before he rebelled and attempted to usurp the royal office.

(3) *Psalm cxxviii 1. Blessed is every one who fears the Lord:* that is, the person who is careful to observe the negative commands. *Who walks in his ways:* that is, the person who performs the positive commands.

(4) *Psalm cxxx 5. I wait for the Lord:* I wait for him in this world that he may show me salvation. *My soul waits:* my soul will wait at death for him to gather unto himself my glory.

(5) *Psalm cxxxi 1. My heart is not proud:* in secret. *Nor are my eyes haughty:* in public.

(6) *Psalm cxlv 2. Every day I will praise thee:* in this world. *And I will extol thy name:* in the world to come.

These texts show unmistakably the influence of the traditional Rabbinic exegesis upon Kimḥi. As a general rule, however, he shows a very thorough understanding of the basic idea of parallelism. A typical example is provided in his comment on Hosea ii 5 (EVV 3):

> 'Lest I strip her naked,
> and make her as in the day she was born.'

Kimḥi understands this verse in the light of Job i 21, an interpretation later adopted by G. Buchanan Gray who had this to say of Kimḥi's comment:[2]

---

[1] For examples elsewhere see his comments on 1 Sam. xii 3; 2 Sam. xi 11, xii 24; Isa. xiv 1; Ezek. xviii 21; Zech. xi 10.

[2] G. Buchanan Gray, *The Forms of Hebrew Poetry* (London 1915), p. 21.

'Strangely enough, the modern commentators which I have consulted
do not give the really pertinent reference to Job i 21; and it was not until
I turned to Kimḥi that I found a commentator who did. He very correctly
paraphrases the second line: I will cause her to stand naked as on the
day of her birth, and regards it as repeating the meaning of the first line
by synonymous terms.'

6. KIMḤI'S COMMENTARY ON THE PSALMS

It is not possible to determine with certainty the precise order of Kimḥi's
commentaries. We know that the commentary on Chronicles is the earliest,
and it is likely that the next to follow was that on Genesis. It is also clear,
from its Introduction, that the commentary on Jeremiah was started after
the commentaries on the Former Prophets and Isaiah. But as to the commentary on the Psalms, no satisfactory evidence is forthcoming, but it
seems likely that it was written before the commentary on Kings. In that
commentary he quotes from the Targum on Psalms[1] but the latter is not
referred to in his commentary on the Psalms, all of which would suggest
that at the time of writing the commentary on the Psalms Kimḥi had not
yet acquired a copy of the Targum and that he had only acquired a copy
when later on composing his commentary on Kings. Finkelstein argues
that the commentary on Samuel preceded that on Psalms. His reasons are
as follows:[2]

(1) At the end of the comment on Psalm xviii 30 Kimḥi cites a Midrashic
interpretation which, it is argued, would certainly have been repeated in
the commentary on Samuel if this commentary had been written later.

(2) There is a long comment on Psalm xviii 8 but no note on the corresponding verse in Samuel.

(3) Comparing 1 Chronicles xviii 12, 2 Samuel viii 13, and Psalm lx 2,
Finkelstein states that in his comment on the last of these Kimḥi draws
attention to the bearing of the word בהצותו on the matter, and noting
that he does not mention this in his comments on the passages in Chronicles
and Samuel, Finkelstein concludes that the commentaries on both
Chronicles and Samuel were written before the commentary on the Psalms.

These arguments may, however, be questioned on the following grounds.
As to (1), an additional note or comment on a given text is not a sufficient
criterion for the relative lateness of a particular work. This also applies to

---

[1] L. Finkelstein, *op. cit.* p. xcv, cites his comment on 2 Kgs. xvii 31 where the
Targum on Psalm cv 10 is quoted.
[2] *Ibid.* xcvf.

(2). Thus, for example, in his commentary on Psalm xxvi 1, Kimḥi cites a Midrashic comment to explain the apparent inconsistency with Psalm cxliii 2. This comment is not, however, given in Psalm cxliii itself. As to (3), the comment involving the word in question is in fact inserted earlier in the long comment on the Samuel text. On balance, it seems more probable, therefore, that with the exception of the commentary on Chronicles, that on the Psalms is the earliest of Kimḥi's commentaries.

The contents of the commentary on the Psalms are very varied and provide good specimens of the different exegetical methods employed by Kimḥi. In contrast to his other works, the Psalms commentary is rather homiletical. Occasionally he abandons the role of commentator to become *Darshan*. This is particularly evident in passages where he refers to the trials and tribulations of his people, for like the masters of *Haggadah* he attempts to sustain their broken spirit with words of hope and comfort. The current digressive philosophical interpretations appear fairly frequently and in such passages he has been guided to a large extent by Abraham Ibn Ezra's comments. Also notable in the commentary on the Psalms are the polemical passages against Christianity. These passages have been collected and published as a separate work under the title *Answers to the Christians*.[1]

7. THE TEXT OF THE COMMENTARY

The first edition of the commentary on the Psalms was printed at Bologna in 1477 C.E. and the second at Naples in 1487 C.E. Other early editions are Venice 1517 C.E., Salonika 1522 C.E. and Isny 1542 C.E. In preparing the critically edited text of Kimḥi's commentary on the Psalms contained in the present volume, the two earliest editions and seven manuscripts have been used as follows:

Editions: Bologna 1477 C.E.
Naples 1487 C.E.

Manuscripts:[2] Mich. 381. Spanish Rabbinic characters. Name of scribe Eliah ben Joseph. Dated 1461 C.E.

---

[1] On this aspect of Kimḥi's work see, most recently, F. Talmage, 'A Hebrew Polemical Treatise', *Harvard Theological Review*, lx (1967), 323–48 and 'R. David Kimḥi as Polemicist', *Hebrew Union College Annual*, xxxviii (1967), 213–35, where also further bibliography is provided. On anti-Christian polemics in mediaeval Jewish exegesis generally see E. I. J. Rosenthal, 'Anti-Christian Polemics in Medieval Bible Commentaries', *Journal of Jewish Studies*, xi (1960), 115–35.

[2] The descriptions of the first four of these manuscripts are as in A. Neubauer, *Catalogue of the Hebrew Manuscripts in the Bodleian Library and in the College Libraries of Oxford* (Oxford 1886).

Poc. 213. Karaite Rabbinic characters.

Mich. 468. Spanish Rabbinic characters.

Can. Or. 68. Italian Rabbinic characters.

MS. Adler 1318. Spanish Rabbinic characters. Name of scribe Jacob ben Abraham. Dated 1515 C.E.

British Museum Or. 1018. Fifteenth century.

British Museum Or. 1489. Fifteenth century.

The manuscript Poc. 213 is really unique in the nature of its variants. Though in a few instances it yields better text than the other sources employed, it should be used sparingly. The following are some of its more important characteristics:

(1) It is somewhat briefer than the other manuscripts, with the possible exception of British Museum Or. 1018, and a very terse style is used (e.g. ש for אשר). Pronominal suffixes are lavishly employed, and unessential words are omitted (e.g. פירוש). In a few instances the order and arrangement of the content are at variance with the standard text.

(2) The abbreviation ע"ה (= עליו/עליהם השלום 'peace be upon him/them') is used instead of ז"ל when referring to the ancient Rabbis.

(3) Instead of citing the source of a particular comment, the scribe prefers to introduce it with the words ויש מפרשים 'and some interpret. . . .'.

(4) Biblical quotations are more accurately given than in the other manuscripts. In one case an altogether different verse is given, though it is equally satisfactory for illustrating the point under discussion.

The British Museum manuscript Or. 1018 is a considerably abbreviated text and is of limited value. But all other manuscripts are more reliable and on the whole carefully written,[1] vowel points being used in some in a few instances. The most reliable of all is Can. Or. 68. Mistakes are here corrected by the scribe and noted in the margin; in one instance, where he was in doubt, he has given both readings, the one on top of the other. References to Christianity as well as to the ruling temporal powers are, however, omitted.

In establishing our text the *editio princeps* has been taken as the norm, but where a better reading is clearly suggested by the others there has been no hesitation in accepting it. As a rule abbreviations are avoided, with the exception of the following: 'ית = יתברך 'blessed be he', or יתעלה = 'exalted be he'; ז"ל = זכרם/זכרונם לברכה or זכרו/זכרונו לברכה = 'of blessed memory' (lit. 'may his/their memory be for a blessing'); וגו = וגומר 'etc.' (גמר =

---

[1] British Museum Or. 1489 is particularly beautifully written.

'to finish', 'complete', 'end'). With regard to the addition of יּת after אל or האל 'God', we have been guided by its use in the Naples edition and the manuscripts Mich. 381, Mich. 468, Can. Or. 68, which agree in all cases in its retention or omission.[1] In the variant readings מ׳ = מוֹסִיף 'he adds' denotes an addition, and ח׳ = חסר 'lacking', 'wanting' denotes an omission.

In fixing the orthography our aim has been to secure uniformity as far as possible. In all cases unnecessary vowels due to the influence of Mishnaic or later Hebrew are dispensed with. Thus, for example, אבר is uniformly written without *yod*, and the *yod* and *waw* in the Piel and Pual forms respectively are also omitted. Where the retention of *scriptio plena* is sanctioned by usage in the Massoretic Text, it is inserted. Thus, for example, the *waw* of the imperfect, infinitive, and past participle appears in our text, whereas in כֻּלָּם it is always omitted. Where a verse is cited from the Bible, or being part of Kimḥi's text forms the subject of his comment, the Massoretic Text is rigidly adhered to, unless there are sufficient grounds for supposing that Kimḥi had a different reading.[2]

In the variant readings, the following abbreviations have been used to denote the source of the variants:

Bologna, B	MS Adler 1318, A
Naples, N	Can. Or. 68, C
Mich. 381, R	British Museum Or. 1018, D
Poc. 213, P	British Museum Or. 1489, S
Mich. 468, M	

The present edition of Kimḥi's commentary on Psalms cxx–cl has been made independently of J. Bosniak's edition of the commentary on the whole of the fifth book of Psalms.[3] Both editions have in common their use of the early editions of Bologna and Naples, though Bosniak also employed the Venice edition (1517 C.E.). Bosniak also used the manuscript Adler 1318. But the remaining sources employed by him are different from those utilised for the present edition. The manuscripts Adler 313 and Deinard, which he uses, do not cover Psalms cxx–cl. Of the remaining two,

---

[1] Poc. 213 inserts יּת in each case, a practice which is frequently followed by the *editio princeps*.

[2] It should be noted that properly speaking the verses from the Psalms which precede Kimḥi's comments are not an integral part of the commentary itself, being merely cited to indicate the word or words which are engaging his attention. The danger in translating them is that a translation may suggest an interpretation in advance. Every attempt has been made, however, to avoid this danger. In many instances the renderings in the standard English Versions have been used, including the New English Bible, though in many others it has been necessary to provide a fresh translation in order fully to bring out Kimḥi's interpretation.

[3] New York 1954.

Adler 2809, apart from being mutilated in places, has two major gaps, the folios containing the commentary on Psalms cxxvii 2–cxxviii 5 and cxlvii 5–cl being missing, whilst the manuscript designated H. G. Enelow presents a considerably abbreviated version of the commentary with in places the scribe's own free rendering of Kimḥi's comments, all of which reduces seriously its value.

Of those readings given by Bosniak which are not found in the sources we have employed, most are of only minor significance. A few more striking readings adopted by him and not present in our sources have been noted in our critical apparatus.

TEXT AND TRANSLATION

Psalm CXX

1. שיר המעלות אל ה׳ בצרתה לי קראתי ויענני. אלה שירי
המעלות הם חמשה עשר ואמרו כי היו אומרים אותם הלוים בחמש
עשרה מדרגות שהיו בהר הבית בין עזרת ישראל לעזרת נשים
שהיו עולים בהם מעזרת נשים לעזרת ישראל ואומרים שיר אחד
במעלה אחת.   ורבותינו ז״ל דרשו עוד ואמרו הני חמש עשרה
מעלות כנגד מי אמרן דוד אמרו בשעה שכרה דוד שתין פירושו
יסודות לבית המקדש עלה התהום ופחדו שיציף העולם כתב.
אחיתופל שם המפרש ונתנו בתהום וירד התהום שש עשרה אלפי
אמה.   אמרו טוב היה לעולם שלא ירד כל כך התהום כי המים
הם צרך העולם והארץ מתלחלחת מן התהום.   אמר חמש עשרה
מעלות והעלהו חמש עשרה אלפי אמה, והעמידו על אלף אמה.
והגאון רב סעדיה ז״ל פירש שירי המעלות שהיו נאמרים
השירים האלה בהגבהת קול מאד ובכל שיר מהם היו מעלים
הקול.   ויש לפרש עוד כי פירוש המעלות מעלות הגלות שעתידים
ישראל לעלות מארצות הגלות אל ארץ ישראל.   ואלה השירים
נאמרים על לשון בני הגלות וזכר בהם צרת הגלות וזכר בהם
תוחלת הישועה וההבטחה שתהיה על כל פנים.   אמר שיר המעלות
אל ה׳ בצרתה לי.   אומר על לשון בני הגלות בלשון יחיד
דרך כלל.   בצרתה.   התי׳ו לרב הצרה וכן ישועתה רב הישועה.
ויענני.   עבר במקום עתיד וכמוהו רבים ובדברי הנבואה
ברב;

4 BRMC	שהיו ... ישראל ח׳	13 NRD	בהגברת קול מאד
7 RC	שישטוף	14 M	כי כן פירוש
7 M	כל העולם	17 R	וההבטחה

PSALM CXX

1. A Song of Ascents. In my distress I cry to the Lord that he may answer me: These Songs of *ma'aloth* consist of fifteen psalms, and it has been said[1] that the Levites were wont to recite them on the fifteen steps which were in the Temple Mount separating the Men's Court from the Women's Court, for they used to go up by these steps (in passing) from the Women's Court to the Men's Court, chanting one such psalm on each step. Our teachers, of blessed memory, have further commented as follows:[2] These fifteen (Songs of) Ascents, in what connection did David compose them? And (in reply) they say: When David began to dig the foundations – the meaning of *shittin* is 'foundations' – for the Temple and the deep waters surged and they were afraid that it might inundate the world, Ahitophel wrote down the Tetragrammaton[3] and placed it in the deep, whereupon the deep descended sixteen thousand cubits. But the people said: 'Twere better for the world that the deep should not sink to such a low level, for the waters are necessary for the world, since the earth becomes moistened from the deep. And so David[4] recited these fifteen *ma'aloth* and (thereby) raised it up fifteen thousand cubits, thus reducing it to one thousand cubits (below the ordinary level). The Gaon, Rabbi Saadya, of blessed memory, takes *shir hamma'aloth* to mean that these songs were sung in a high key,[5] for in each one of these songs they raised their voices (to a high pitch). It is also possible to interpret the meaning of *hamma'aloth* as being *ma'aloth haggaluth* – the ascents from the exile – that is, the ascents whereby Israel will at some future time go up from the lands of the exile to the land of Israel, (in which case) all of these psalms represent the utterances of the exiles. Hence the psalmist speaks of the affliction of exile, the hope of deliverance, and the assurance that it will eventually come to pass. He says: *A Song of Ascents. In my distress . . . to the Lord*: he employs the singular collectively to represent the exiles. *Baṣṣarathah: tau* is added because of the magnitude of the distress, as in *y'shuathah* (Ps. iii 3; Jon. ii 10) where it indicates the greatness of the salvation. *Wayya'aneni*: perfect

---

[1] Lit. 'and they have said', that is, the Rabbis. (Cf. *Middoth* ii 5; *Succah* 51b; *Yoma* 16a. Unless otherwise indicated, references throughout are to the Babylonian Talmud.) It is doubtful whether the statement in the Talmud has been correctly interpreted by Kimḥi. It has been pointed out that the reference really says nothing about the singing of these psalms after the steps but merely compares the number of the psalms in question with that of the steps. Cf. A. F. Kirkpatrick, *The Book of Psalms* (Cambridge 1901), p. xxviii; C. A. Briggs, *The Book of Psalms*, i, International Critical Commentary (Edinburgh 1906), p. lxxix.

[2] *Succah* 53a and 53b.

[3] Lit. the 'separate' or 'distinct' name. From the pual of *parash* = 'to separate, specify, express clearly'.

[4] Lit. 'he said'.

[5] Lit. 'with an exceeding raising of the voice'.

2. ה׳ הצילה נפשי. הגוים שאנחנו בתוכם שהם אנשי שקר
ומרמה;

3. מה יתן לך ומה יסיף לך. אמר כנגד המדבר דברי שקר
ומשים עלילות דברים על ישראל בגלות מה תועלת יש לך בלשון
רמיה ומה יתן לך ומה יוסיף לך. ורמיה תאר בשקל עניה
סערה, שביה בת ציון. ובדרש אמר כנגד הלשון מה יתן לך
האל ומה יוסיף לך לשמרך שלא תדבר רע, הנה ברא כל האברים
זקופים ואתה מוטל כל האברים מבחוץ ואתה מבפנים ולא עוד
אלא שהקיף לך שתי חומות אחת של עצם ואחת של בשר ועם כל
זה לא נשמרת מה יתן לך ומה יוסיף לך;

4. חצי גבור. המשיל הדברים הרעים לחצי גבור שנונים
שמכים מכה בלתי סרה שהחצים שנונים ויוצאים מיד גבור. וכן
המשילם לגחלי רתמים שהם חמים מאד ולא יכבו לזמן רב אף
בעת שנראים כבים מבחוץ וידמו אפר הם מבפנים אש בוערה.
כן דברי לשון רמיה שמראה בפני אדם שאין לבו רע עליו כדי
שלא ישמר ממנו וכשיפרד ממנו ידבר עליו רעות ואמר עם כי
שניהם בו החצים והגחלים נכללים בו ביחד שניהם;

22 M	מהגוים אשר אנחנו בתוכם	35 BNM	אפילו
26 N	או מה יוסיף	36 N	בעת שנראים רפים
26 BNRM	ורמיה ... ציון ח׳	39 RC	החצים והגחלים שניהם נכללים בו ביחד
34 BNMA	שמכים ... מיד גבור ח׳		

instead of imperfect. There are many instances of this, mainly in the prophetic literature.[1]

2. Deliver me, O Lord: (from) the people in whose midst we are, for they are lying and deceitful men.

3. What will it give to you, and what more will it do for you?: he addresses these words to the person who utters false charges and lying accusations against Israel in exile[2] – what can the deceitful tongue accomplish for you? Or what can it give you or add to you? And *r^emiyyah* is an adjective in the form of (*'^aniyyah* in) *'^aniyyah so'^arah* (Isa. liv 11 'O afflicted one, storm-tossed') and (*sh^ebiyyah* as in) *sh^ebiyyah bath ṣion* (Isa. lii 2 'O captive daughter of Zion'). According to the Midrashic interpretation[3] he speaks of the tongue itself: What more can God give you or add to you to keep you from speaking evil? For he created all the organs upright in position[4] but you alone lie flat; all the organs are on the exterior (of the body) but you alone within it. And not only this, but he has also put two walls around you, the one of bone and the other of flesh. Yet notwithstanding all this, you have not been on your guard. And so, *what more can he give to you or what can he add to you?*

4. (Sharp) arrows of the mighty: he compares evil words with the sharp arrows of the mighty which inflict an irremediable[5] wound, for such arrows are sharp and, besides, are discharged from the hand of the strong. He also represents them metaphorically as *glowing coals of broom tree* since these are very hot and do not burn out for a long time. For even when they appear from the outside to be extinguished and like ashes, yet within they are as burning coals. So is it with the words of a deceitful tongue. He (who speaks thus) gives a person the impression that his heart is not evilly disposed towards him, so that he is not on his guard against him. But when he parts from him, he speaks maliciously about him. (For this reason the psalmist expressly) uses (the particle) 'together with', since in a sense the respective qualities of both – arrows and burning coals – find their counterpart in him, the distinguishing feature of both of them being included in his character.[6]

---

[1] Lit. 'the words of the prophets'.
[2] Lit. 'that speaks falsehood and imputes insidious charges against Israel in exile'.
[3] *Arakin* 15b.
[4] Lit. 'erect'.
[5] The expression is taken from Isaiah xiv 6 and rendered in RSV as 'with unceasing blows' and in NEB as 'with unerring blows'.
[6] Lit. 'both are in him – arrows and burning coal – they are included together in him'.

5. אויה לי כי גרתי משך. גרתי בגלות משך כלומר שנמשכה 40

גלותי מאד ושכנתי עם רעים עם אהלי קדר וזכר הגלות אשר

בישמעאל ולא זכר באדום כי רב גלות ישראל בין הישמעאלים

וזכר קדר כי הם המשפחות המיוחסות אשר בישמעאל והם ראש

המלכות. ויש מפרשים משך הוא קדר וקראם כן לפי שהם מושכי

קשת ופירושו גרתי עם משך וכפל הענין במלות שונות. ויש 45

מפרשים משך האומה אשר היא מבני יפת הנזכרת בתורה·ואמר

יוסף בן גוריון כי הם בני תושכאנה והם באמונת הנוצרים

וזכר משך בעבור מלכות אדום לפי שרומה היא במחוז תושכאנה

וקדר בעבור מלכות ישמעאל והנה זכר שתי המלכיות שישראל

גולים ביניהם; 50

6. רבת. התי׳ו במקום ה"א ואינה לסמיכות וכן רבת צררוני

רבת תעשרנה והדומים להם שכתבנו בספר מכלול. אמר רב לי

בגלות עם גוי שהוא שונא שלום;

7. אני. בפי שלום וכי אדבר שלום אליהם המה ידברו

למלחמה; 55

Psalm CXXI

1. שיר למעלות אשא עיני אל ההרים. זה לבדו עם למ׳ד

והלמ׳ד במקום ה׳א הידיעה והוא כמו המעלות וכן השליש

אשר למלך נשען על ידו כמו המלך עד לשמים הגיע כמו עד

5. Woe is me, that I sojourn (in) Meshek: for I have sojourned for a long time[1] (*meshek*), that is, my exile is prolonged[1] (*nimshᵉkah*) and I dwell with evil-doers among the tents of Kedar. He speaks of the dispersion in the lands of Ishmael, but does not mention that in Edom,[2] because the exiles are scattered for the greater part among the Ishmaelites. He refers particularly to Kedar, for these people belong to the most illustrious families in Ishmael, being the rulers of the kingdom. Some explain Meshek as being identical with (the people of) Kedar and that they are referred to as *meshek* because they 'draw the bow',[3] in which case the meaning (of the latter half of the verse) would likewise be *I dwell among the Moshki*, that is, he repeats the one idea in different words. Others consider *meshek* to be one of the races enumerated in the Torah (cf. Gen. x 2) as descended from the children of Japheth. And Joseph ben Gurion states that they are (none other than) the people of Tuscany, being of the Christian faith. Accordingly, the psalmist refers to Meshek as representing the kingdom of Edom, since Rome is situated in the province of Tuscany, (and similarly he mentions) Kedar because it represents the kingdom of Ishmael. Thus he speaks[4] of the two kingdoms in whose midst Israel is exiled.

6. Rabbath: *tau* is used in place of *he*, and not as an indication of the construct state, as in 'Greatly (*rabbath*) have they afflicted me' (Ps. cxxix 1, 2) and 'thou greatly (*rabbath*) enrichest it' (Ps. lxv 10). I have noted other examples of this in the book *Miklol*. What he means is: I have been too long in exile in the midst of a people who hate peace.

7. I am for peace with (the utterances of) my mouth, but when I speak words of peace to them they reply (with words) of war.

PSALM CXXI

1. A Song of Ascents. I lift up my eyes to the hills: *lammaʿᵃloth*: this is the only instance of *maʿᵃloth* with *lamed* (prefixed), the *lamed* being used in place of the *he* of the definite article. It is equivalent in meaning to *hammaʿᵃloth* 'the ascents', like 'the captain on whose hand the king (*lammelek*) leaned' (2 Kgs. vii 2) (where *lammelek* is the same in meaning) as *hammelek*; 'which has reached up to heaven (*lashshamayim*)' (2 Chron. xxviii 9) (where

---

[1] Kimḥi takes *meshek* from the root *mashak* = 'to draw, extend', hence, 'a *long* time', 'a prolonged time'.

[2] In Rabbinic literature Edom is frequently used in speaking of Rome. In later Jewish literature it also means Christianity, or Christian nations. Ishmael is used as a patronymic for the people of Ishmael, that is, the Arabs. It then has the secondary meaning of Muslim.

[3] Cf. n. 1 above.

[4] Lit. 'Behold!'

השמים ויש בו דרש שיר למעלות שיר למאה מעלות והוא
60 כענין הדרש שכתבנו למעלה ועוד דרשו בו שיר למי שהוא
עתיד לעשות מעלות לצדיקים לעתיד לבוא. אשא. כמו
המצפה עזר מרחוק שעולה על ההרים ונושא עיניו אילך
ואילך אם יבואו לו עוזרים. ואל ההרים כמו על ההרים
וכן אל ההרים לא אכל ויך את הפלשתי אל מצחו כמו על
65 מצחו;

2. עזרי. אני אם אשא עיני אל ההרים מאין יבא עזרי
לא יועיל לי כלום כי אין לי עזר אלא מעם ה׳ ואליו אשא
עיני כי הוא יעזרנו ויקבצנו מן הגוים כי הוא עושה שמים
וארץ והכל בידו ויכול לעשות מה שירצה כי כל הגוים כאין
70 נגדו;

3. אל יתן למוט רגליך. אומר כל אחד לחברו בגלות
דרך נחמה טוב הוא ששמת בטחונך באל שיהיה בעזרך כי כן
יעשה ואף על פי שהאריך הגלות לא יתן למוט רגלך. אל
ינום שומרך. כי בהיותנו בגלות דומה לישן כאלו לא
75 יראה בענינו כמו שאמר עורה למה תישן ה׳;

4. הנה לא ינום. התנומה פחותה מן השינה ואמר לא
ינום כל שכן לא יישן כי הוא שומר ישראל בכל עת אפילו
בגלות שומר אותנו שלא יעשו אותנו הגוים כלה והם
שונאים אותנו והאל לא יתנם להרע לנו כפי מחשבתם כי
80 לא יישן אפילו בעת שנתנו הוא שומרנו;

63 N	לראות אם יבאו אליו עוזרים	CS	שיהיה עזרך
63 RC	לו ח׳	76 RPMS	מהשינה
66 M	אם אני אשא	77 MAC	ואפילו
67 R	מעם ה׳ לבדו	78 B	שומר אותנו שלא יעשה ממנו כלה בגוים
72 R	שהוא עזרך	N	שומר אותם שלא יעשו אותנו הגוים כלה

the meaning is the same) as *hashshamayim*. And there is a Midrashic interpretation (of this word) as follows:[1] *shir hamma'aloth* signifies *shir l'me'ah ma'aloth* 'a song of one hundred ascents' which is similar in meaning to the Midrashic (comment) which we noted above.[2] And others have further explained[3] *ma'aloth* (as meaning) a song to him who will in the future assign places on high[4] for the righteous in the world to come. *I lift up*: just as a person in expectation of help from afar goes up to the hills and lifts his eyes (looking) hither and thither to see if helpers are coming to him. And *'el heharim* is equivalent to *'al heharim* 'upon the hills', like 'he has not eaten upon the mountains (*'el heharim*)' (Ezek. xviii 6), and 'he struck the Philistine upon his forehead (*'el misho*)' (I Sam. xvii 49) (where *'el misho* has the same meaning) as *'al misho*.

2. My help: as for me, *if I lift up my eyes to the hills, whence does my help come?* It will in no wise avail me, for there is no help for me except from the Lord, and to him do I lift up my eyes, for he will remember us and gather us from the nations, since he it is who *made heaven and earth*: everything is in his power and he can do whatsoever he pleases, for 'all the nations are as nothing before him' (Isa. xl 17).

3. He will not let your foot be moved: this is what each person says to his companion in exile, by way of comforting him: It is well that you have put your trust in God that he may deliver you, for he will certainly do so. And though the exile is prolonged,[5] yet *He will not let your foot be moved. He who keeps you will not slumber*: for while we are in exile, (God) is likened as it were to one who sleeps, as though he does not see any of our afflictions, just as it says 'Awake! Why sleepest thou, O Lord?' (Ps. xliv 24).

4. Behold, he does not slumber: *t'numah* 'slumber' connotes a degree of somnolence not quite as intense as *shenah* 'sleep'.[6] Since he says *he does not slumber*, how much more so is it true to say that *he does not sleep*, for he preserves Israel at all times, watching over us even in exile so that the nations may not exterminate us. Though they hate us, yet God suffers them not to inflict hurt upon us according to their plans, for *he does not sleep*: even during the time when we are asleep, he keeps vigil over us.

[1] *Sifre Eqeb* 40: 7.
[2] Kimḥi is here possibly referring to the Rabbinic tradition concerning the number of steps leading from the Women's Court to the Men's Court which he mentions in his commentary on Psalm cxx 1.
[3] *Yalkut Shimeoni* on Ps. cxxi 1.
[4] Lit. 'to make gradations'.
[5] Lit. 'and though he has prolonged the exile'.
[6] Lit. 'slumber is less than sleep'.

5. ה׳ שמרך.‏ הוא צלך והוא על יד ימינך לעזרך בכל
מעשיך;

6. יומם השמש.‏ טעמו לצלך שזכר כלומר הוא צלך שלא יככה
חם השמש ביום וקר הירח בלילה כי חם השמש ייבש הלחה והירח
יוסיף הלחה יהיה ממנה הקרירות והחם והקר הם סבת התחלואים   85
והאל ישמרך מהם;

7. ה׳ ישמרך מכל רע.‏ שלא יזיקוך בני אדם וחיות השדה.‏
ישמור את נפשך.‏ אם יבואוך תחלואים יהיו מרוק עונות אבל
הוא ישמר את נפשך שלא תמות מתוך החלאים;

8. ה׳ ישמר.‏ בגלות ישמרך כמו שאמרנו.‏ ובצאתך מהגלות   90
תצא בשלום ותבוא אל ארץ ישראל בשלום וישמרך מעתה ועד
עולם;

Psalm CXXII

1. שיר המעלות לדוד שמחתי באמרים לי בית ה׳ נלך.‏ אפשר
כי שאר המעלות שלא נזכר בהם לדוד חברום המשוררים האחרים
ולא נזכרו שמות המחברים ואשר נאמר בהם לדוד חברם דוד.‏   95
והמזמור הזה מאמר בני הגלות ומרב תאותם לבנין בית המקדש
יזכרו עלות ישראל לרגלים וידברו על לשון האבות שהיו בזמן
הבית ואמר שמחתי.‏ אומר כל אחד ואחד שמחתי;

2. עמדות היו.‏ כי העולים ראשונים היו עומדים בשערים
מצפים הבאים אחריהם;   100

3. ירושלים הבנויה.‏ אומרים בני הגלות כשהיתה בנויה
ירושלים והיתה שכינה בתוכה כמה היתה מהללה ואנה תמצא

---

85 RP	כי יהיה ממנו הקרירות	99 R	הראשונים
91 R	וישמרך after מכל רע מ׳	102 B	השכינה
98 BR	כל אחד אומר שמחתי		

5. The Lord is your keeper: he is *your shade* and he is by *your right hand* to help you in all your doings.

6. The sun . . . by day: the meaning is best understood by connecting (this verse) with *ṣilᵉka* 'your shade' in the preceding verse. That is to say, he is *your shade* so that the heat of *the sun shall not strike you by day* nor the cold of *the moon by night.* For the heat of the sun dries up the moisture in the body, whilst the moon increases the moisture from which cold arises. And heat and cold are the causes of disease, but God will keep you from them.

7. The Lord will keep you from all evil: so that neither man nor beast (can) inflict any hurt upon you. *He will keep your soul*: for if any manner of sickness comes upon you, it shall so befall you only to purge you of your sins. But *he will keep your soul* so that you do not die in the throes of sickness.

8. The Lord will keep: in exile he will preserve you, as we have expounded (above). And when you go forth from captivity, you will go forth in peace and come to the land of Israel in peace, and he will keep you *from this time forth and for evermore.*

PSALM CXXII

1. A Song of Ascents. Of David. I was glad when they said to me, Let us go to the house of the Lord: It is possible that other (Songs of) Ascents which are not ascribed to David were composed by other poets without the names of the authors being recorded. But such as bear the superscription 'Of David' were composed by David himself. This psalm represents the thoughts of the exiles who out of their great desire for the rebuilding of the Temple call to mind the Ascent of Israel for the festivals and emulate the speech of their forefathers who lived during the period of the (first) Temple. Thus he says: *I was glad*: that is, every single person says *I was glad.*

2. Our feet are standing: the pilgrims who arrived first used to stand within the gates waiting for them that came after them.

3. O Jerusalem, built (as a city . . .): the exiles say: While Jerusalem was (still) established and the Shekinah[1] dwelt there, how greatly was it renowned! And where could one find a city to compare with it, in which

---

[1] That is, the 'Divine Presence' from *shakan* = 'to dwell'.

עיר כמוה שחברה לה עלת ישראל יחדו שלש פעמים בשנה מי
ראה עיר כמו אותה העיר;

105

4. ששם עלו. כי שם היו עולים ש_ים עשר שבטים שהיו
שבטי יה שומרי מצותיו וכלם היתה ירושלים מכילה אותם
זו היתה עדות לישראל שהאל בחר בהם להודות לשם ה' על
הנסים שהיה מראה להם וזה אחד מהם כמו שאמרו במשנה ולא
אמר אדם לחברו צר לי המקום כשאלין בירושלים ועוד נס

110

גדול מזה שהיו נקבצים כלם בעזרה עומדים צפופים ומשתחוים
רוחים או פירש עדות לישראל זה שהיו עולים שם השבטים
עדות ומצוה היתה להם לישראל שיעלו להודות לשם ה';

5. כי שמה ישבו כסאות. לשון רבים. למלכי בית דוד
כמו שמפרש. כסאות לבית דוד. היו שם ויהיו שם עוד;

115

6. שאלו. אומרים בני הגלות אלה לאלה שאלו מהאל שלום
ירושלים ושלום ירושלים הוא קבוץ גליות כי עד אזתה העת
לא יהיה לה שלום כי נלחמים עליה ערלים וישמעאלים ואמר
אחר כן כנגד ירושלים ישליו אהביך והם ישראל בגלות שהם
מתאבלים על חורבנה;

120

7. יהי שלום בחילך. החפירה שהיא סביב החומה תקרא
חיל. אמר יהי שלום שישובו ישראל אליך ועוד לא תהיה
מלחמה בחילך ובארמנותיך. וארמנות הם בתי המשגב בתוך
העיר;

8. למען אחי. אמר כל אחד מבני הגלות למען אחי ישראל
שגלו ממך למענם אדברה נא שלום בך שישובו להיות שוכנים

125

בך;

9. למען. ועוד למען בית אלהינו החרב אבקשה מהאל טוב
בעבורך;

106 B	מכילה אותם instead of מכל השבטים	116 MC	קבוץ הגלות BPSD
107 BN	בם להודות	118 B	והם ישראל בגלות שמתאבלים
113 B	לשון רבים חד לשכינה וחד למלכות בית דוד	120 BNRPMCDS	יקרא
		121 B	ושוב לא תהיה

קבוץ הגליות
והם ישראל בגלות שמתאבלים
יקרא
ושוב לא תהיה

the congregation of Israel was gathered together compactly on three
occasions in the year? Who has seen a city like that city?

4. To which the tribes go up: for the twelve tribes used to go up there,
that is, *the tribes of the Lord* that kept his commandments. And Jerusalem
contained them all. This was (indeed) *a testimony to Israel* that God had
chosen them *to give thanks to the name of the Lord* because of the miracles
which he had shown them. And this (indeed) was one of them, as it says
in the Mishnah:[1] Nor did any man ever say to his companion: This place
is too crowded[2] for me to lodge over night in Jerusalem. But a still greater
miracle than this was the fact that all of them were assembled within the
Temple Court, standing serried and yet (able to) bow down at ease.[3] Or
perhaps we may interpret *'eduth* as meaning that the pilgrimage made by
the tribes to that place was *a decree* and a command to Israel that they go
up there *to give thanks to the name of the Lord.*

5. For thrones are set there: (*thrones*) plural number (referring to) the
kings of *the house of David*, as he explicitly states: *thrones of the house of
David* which were there at that time and will be there again (at some future
time).

6. Pray: the exiles say to each other: *Pray* to God *for the peace of Jerusalem.*
And by *the peace of Jerusalem* the psalmist means the ingathering of the
exiles, for until that time she will have no peace, since the Gentiles[4] and
the Ishmaelites[5] fight with one another on her account. And then[6] he says
with regard to Jerusalem: *May those who love you prosper!* That is, the
people of Israel in exile, for they mourn her destruction.

7. Peace be within your ramparts: the rampart which is round about
the walls is called a *ḥel.* He says: *may there be peace*, meaning: may Israel
return to you and may there be no more war *within your ramparts and
fortifications. Arm^enoth* are the fortified buildings[7] in the interior of the city.

8. For the sake of my brethren: each one of the exiles says: *for the sake
of my brethren* Israel who are exiled from you, for their sake *I will say:
Peace be within you!* that they may return to dwell within you.

9. For the sake of: furthermore, for the sake of the Temple of our God
which is destroyed *I will seek good* from God for your sake.

---

[1] *Aboth* v: 5.   [2] Lit. 'this place is too narrow'.
[3] *Aboth* v: 5.
[4] Lit. 'the uncircumcised', referring here to Christians.
[5] See above, p. 7 n. 2.   [6] Lit. 'and afterwards he says'.
[7] Lit. 'the fortified houses'.

Psalm CXXIII

1. שיר המעלות אליך נשאתי את עיני. כשידבר על לשון
בני הגלות פעם ידבר לשון יחיד דרך כלל ופעם לשון רבים. 130
הישבי בשמים. היו׳ד נוספת והוא כמו היושב. אמר אין
לי עזר בארץ ואיני מקוה העזר אלא ממך;

2. הנה. שאין להם מחיה ופרנסה אלא מהם ואליהם תלויות
עיניהם ואדוני אבי ז"ל פירש אל יד אדוניהם. אל יד
גברתה. בעת שיכו אותם אין להם למי ישאו עין אלא להם 135
עצמם שירחמו עליהם וירפו ידם מהם כן אנחנו מי הכנו
ומי נתננו בגלות האל שהוא אדוננו ואנחנו עבדיו ואין
לנו למי נשא עין אלא אליו שנתננו בגלות שירחם עלינו
ויוציאנו ממנו;

3. חננו. הכפל לחזק הבקשה. כי רב. זמן ארוך שבענו 140
בוז הגלות;

4. רבת שבעה. פירשנוהו. הלעג השאננים. חסר הנסמך
כמו הארון הברית. אמר שבעה נפשנו הלעג לעג השאננים
שלועגים עלינו או יהיה ה'א השאננים במקום למ'ד שבענו
הלעג שאננו לשאנים ושבענו הבוז שאננו לגאיונים 145
והשאננים הם הגוים שהם שקטים ושאנים ואנחנו עניים
וכואבים ביניהם ילעגו לנו. לגאיונים. מלה אחת בכתוב
והוא כמו גאים אלא שנראתה בו למ'ד הפעל שהיא מומרת
ביו'ד והנו'ן נוספת והוא כמו עליונים במשקל אלא
שנשתנו תנועותיו מפני אות הגרון והוא בקרי שתי מלות 150
לגאי יונים והוסיף בו ענין בקרי כי גאי כמו גאים

PSALM CXXIII

1. A Song of Ascents. I lift up my eyes to thee: when he represents the people in captivity as speaking, sometimes he uses the singular number collectively and at other times he uses the plural. *O thou that dwellest in the heavens*: *hayyosh^ebi*: the *yod* is paragogic, the meaning being equivalent to *hayyosheb* 'the one who dwells'. He says: There is no help for me on earth, nor do I expect help from anyone but thee.

2. Behold: for they[1] receive their living and sustenance from none but them,[2] and to them their eyes are raised. My revered father, of blessed memory, explains *to the hand of their master* and *to the hand of her mistress* as follows: When they are punished[3] they have none to whom to raise their eyes (in supplication) except to those same people that they may have pity on them and withdraw their hands from them. So it is with us. Who has punished[3] us and placed us in exile? God who is our Lord and whose servants we are. Yet we have none to whom to raise our eyes but to him who has exiled us that he may have mercy on us and deliver us from (exile).

3. Have mercy on us: the repetition is to strengthen the entreaty. *For greatly*: (that is) for a long time *we have suffered*[4] *the scorn* of exile.

4. Too long we have suffered:[4] *rabbath shab^e'ah* as we have already explained. *The scorn of those who are at ease*: the substantive in the construct state (*la'ag*) is to be supplied[5] (after *halla'ag*) just as (*'^aron* is to be supplied in) *ha'^aron habb^erith* 'the ark (the ark of) the covenant' (Josh. iii 14). He says: *too long we have suffered*[4] *the scorn*, the scorn of *those who are at ease* and who mock us. Or possibly the *he* of *hashsha'^ananim* is used instead of *lamed*, (that is) *we have suffered*[4] *the scorn* with which we are regarded in the eyes of *those who are at ease, and suffered*[4] *the insults of the proud*.[6] As for *those who are at ease*, they are the nations that are at rest and ease whilst we are afflicted and grieved amongst them who mock us. *Lig^e'eyonim* is one word, according to the *kethibh*, and is equivalent to *ge'im* 'proud' except that the third[7] radical *waw*, for which *yod* is substituted, (also) appears, the *nun* being paragogic, on the analogy of *'elyonim* but (with this difference, that) the vowels are transposed because of the guttural letter. According to the *qere*, however, it comprises two words *lig^e'e yonim*. The *qere* gives additional force to the meaning, for *g^e'e* is the same as *ge'im* 'the

---

[1] That is, 'the slaves'.
[2] That is, 'the masters'.
[3] Lit. 'struck, smitten'.
[4] Lit. 'filled with'.
[5] Lit. 'is missing'.
[6] Lit. 'we are filled with the scorn which we are to those who are at ease, and filled with the contempt which we are to the proud'.
[7] Lit. 'the *lamed* (radical) of the root'.

ויונים מעניך העיר היונה שהוא עניך ולא תונו איש את
עמיתו ולא יונו נשיאי את עמי;

Psalm CXXIV

1.   שיר המעלות לדוד לולי ה׳ שהיה לנו. זה יאמר נא

155   ישראל בגלות ומהו;

2.   לולי. בקום עלינו אדם. בקום עלינו אויבים בגלות
לכלותנו לולי ה׳ שהיה לנו כמו עמנו;

3.   אזי. היו׳ד נוספת והוא כמו אז חיים בלעונו כמו
ולא יקח ממך בשר מבשל כי אם חי ואמר דרך משל חיים

160   בלעונו כי אין דרך האדם לאכול הבשר כי אם מבשל והם
מרב תאותם לבלענו חיים היו בולעים אותנו בחרות אפם
בנו לולי ה׳ שהיה לנו. וכן נבלעם כשאול חיים;

4.   אזי המים שטפונו. משל לצרות. נחלה עבר על נפשנו.
נחל שוטף והמלה קריאתה מלעיל הטעם בנו׳ן וה׳א נוספת

165   וההי׳ת בשוא לבדו וכן נחלה מצרים;

5.   אזי עבר על נפשנו המים הזידונים. אמר עבר ואמר
המים כמו מי נדה לא זרק עליו. או עבר טעמו לנחל שזכר
ר״ל נחל המים הזידונים ופירוש הזידונים ששוטפים בזדון
וברשע;

170 6.   ברוך ה׳ שלא נתננו טרף לשניהם. שלא הניח אותנו
בידיהם לטרפנו כמו שחשבו;

152	RPCS	חרב היונה מ׳	העיר היונה after	164	M	תנוע בנין
160	BNRMS	אדם		167	R	עליו after סמא הוא מ׳
160	R	בשר		168	N	ברשע ובזדון

proud', whilst *yonim* may be explained from *ha'ir hayyonah* 'the oppressing city' (Zeph. iii 1), the meaning of *hayyonah* being (as in) 'you shall not oppress (*tonu*) one another' (Lev. xxv 17) and 'my princes shall no more oppress (*yonu*) my people' (Ezek. xlv 8).

PSALM CXXIV

1. A Song of Ascents. Of David. If it had not been the Lord who was for us: this *let Israel say* in exile. And what is it (that they should say)?

2. If it had not been ... when men rose up against us: when enemies rose up against us in exile to exterminate us, *if it had not been the Lord who was with us*, taking *lanu* to be the same as *'immanu* 'with us'.

3. *'ᵃzay:* the *yod* is paragogic, (the word) being the same as *'az* 'then'. *They would have swallowed us raw,*[1] *hayyim* being understood as in 'for he will not accept stewed meat from you, but raw (*hay*)' (1 Sam. ii 15). He says metaphorically: *they would have swallowed us raw,* for it is not usual for men to eat flesh unless it is cooked. But because of their intense desire *to swallow us* they would have *swallowed us raw when their anger was roused against us, if it had not been the Lord who was with us.* Similarly (we have) 'Like Sheol let us swallow them raw (*hayyim*)' (Prov. i 12).

4. The flood would have swept us away: a figurative expression for persecutions. *The torrent would have gone over us:* (*nahᵉlah* means) a sweeping torrent. The word is to be accented *mil'el* – the accent is on the *nun* – the *he* being paragogic and the *heth* with *shewa* only. Similarly *nahᵉlah misrayim* 'the brook of Egypt' (Num. xxxiv 5).

5. Then the raging waters would have gone over us: he uses the singular *'abar* although he speaks of the waters (plural). Similarly (we may compare the use of the singular *zoraq* in) 'the water of purification has not been sprinkled (*zoraq*) upon him' (Num. xix 20). Or perhaps *'abar* is to be connected with *nahal* mentioned (in the previous verse), thus meaning '*the torrent* of raging waters (would have gone over us)'. And by *raging* he means: they sweep along with violence and wickedness.

6. Blessed be the Lord who has not left us as a prey to their teeth: for he has not abandoned us in their hands to tear us in pieces as they had intended to do.

---

[1] Lit. 'alive'.

‏7. נפשנו כצפור נמלטה מפח יוקשים. כי לא תוכל הצפור
להמלט אם לא ישבר הפח שהוא בתוכו כן אנחנו הגוים אשר
אנחנו בתוכם הם יכלו ויאבדו בעזרת האל שיעזרנו ואנחנו
נמלטנו;‏

175

‏8. עזרנו בשם ה׳ עשה שמים וארץ. כי הוא עושה שמים
וארץ ויש לו כח בעליונים ובתחתונים והוא יכול לעזרנו
ולהוציאנו מהפח שהוא הגלות;‏

Psalm CXXV

‏1. שיר המעלות הבוטחים בה׳ כהר ציון לא ימוט לעולם ישב.‏
180   ‏הבוטחים בה׳ לא ימוטו כמו הר ציון שלא ימוט. כי לעולם
ישב. בשוב הגלות לא ימוט ולא יחרב לעולם אלא לעולם ישב
ופירוש ישב יעמוד לעולם ויהיה קים וכן ואתה קדוש יושב
קים נצח וכן אתה ה׳ לעולם תשב;‏

‏2. ירושלים הרים. אף על פי שהרים סביב לה אין לה חזק
185   ‏וישלטו הגוים וילכדו אותה אלה מאלה ולא יהיה לה חזק עד
שיהיה עם ה׳ בתוכה שיהיה הוא סביב לעמו ושמו יהיה להם
חזק יותר מן ההרים ולא ישלוט בהם אויב מעתה ועד עולם;‏

‏3. כי לא ינוח. כמו שכתוב בנבואת ישעיה והיה הנשאר
בציון והנותר בירושלים קדוש יאמר לו. כי הרשעים כלם
190   ‏בין מישראל בין מ שאר הגוים יכלו וירושלים שהיא גורל
הצדיקים לא ינוח בה שבט הרשע כלומר חזק וכח הרשע כמו
שהוא היום הרשע לשבט ולמטה; למען לא ישלחו הצדיקים.
כלומר שלא ילמדו הצדיקים ממעשיהם אם ישארו רשעים בארץ.
וכן צוה האל בצאת ישראל ממצרים והביאם לארץ צוה להם‏

173	M	‏בתוך הגוים N הגוים אשר היינו בתוכם‏	183 RD ‏קים לנצח‏
174	RPMCDS	‏נמלטה B 175. הם ח׳‏	187 B ‏האויב‏
177	M	‏והוא יכול להוציאנו‏	189 M ‏כי הרשעים מאומת העולם‏
177	C	‏לעזרנו ולהושיענו ולהוציאנו‏	194 NRC ‏ובבואם לארץ‏
179	BM	‏בהר‏	194 MC ‏להם ח׳‏

(Cp. Biblia Hebraica Stuttgartensia)

7. We have escaped like a bird from the fowler's trap: for a bird cannot escape unless the trap in which it is (caught) be broken. So it is with us among the nations – by the help of God they will be destroyed and will perish, and (in this way) we shall escape.

8. Our help is in the name of the Lord, maker of heaven and earth: for he is the *maker of heaven and earth* and he has power over the higher and lower orders of creation and he can help us and deliver us from the snare, that is, the exile.

PSALM CXXV

1. A Song of Ascents. Those who trust in the Lord are like Mount Zion, which cannot be moved but abides for ever: *those who trust in the Lord* will not be moved even as Mount Zion which cannot be moved, for *it will abide for ever*: on the return of the exile it shall not be moved, nor shall it ever be destroyed but *will abide for ever*. The interpretation of *yesheb* is: it will stand for ever and be permanently established; similarly 'Holy art thou, that dwellest' (Ps. xxii 4) (where the meaning of *yosheb* is) 'existing for ever', and also 'but thou, O Lord, shalt abide (*tesheb*) for ever' (Ps. cii 13).

2. As the hills are round about Jerusalem: though *hills* be *round about her*, yet she has no (inherent) strength so that it is possible for the nations to gain mastery over her, capturing her from one another. She shall have no strength until such time as the people of the Lord will (return to dwell) in her, for then will he be *round about his people*: his name will be a greater strength for them than mountains, so that the enemy will no longer rule them *from this time forth and for evermore*.

3. For (the sceptre of wickedness) shall not remain: as it is written in the prophecy of Isaiah (iv 3): 'And he who is left in Zion and remains in Jerusalem shall be called holy', for all the wicked, both from among Israel and from among other nations, shall have been destroyed. And as for Jerusalem which is *the lot of the righteous, there shall not remain* there *the sceptre of wickedness*, that is, the force and power of wickedness, even as in our own time[1] wickedness (exercises) power and dominion. *So that the righteous will not set (their hands to injustice)*: that is to say, that the righteous may not learn from their (evil) deeds, should any of the wicked remain upon earth. A similar injunction[2] was given by God to Israel when they went forth from Egypt and he brought them to the (promised) land. He commanded them to drive out the nations and to put them to death, as it

[1] Lit. 'today'.
[2] Lit. 'likewise God commanded'.

195 לגרש הגוים ולהמיתם ואמר למען לא ילמדו אתכם לעשות ככל
תועבתם וגו׳. ולא עשו כן ובזה נכשלו אבל לעתיד לבא
לא יהיה שם מכשול עון כי כל הרשעים יכלו;

4. היטיבה. לטובים. במעשיהם ולישרים בלבותם;

5. והמטים עקלקלותם. בישראל כלומר שמטים דרכיהם
200 בעקלקלותם. יוליכם ה׳ את פעלי האון. מן הגוים. ויש
לפרש והמטים עקלקלותם בלבותם שאין תוכם כברם יוליכם
ה׳ את פעלי האון בגלוי כנגד מה שאמר לטובים ולישרים
בלבותם. שלום על ישראל. כיון שיכלו הרשעים מישראל
שלום על ישראל הנשארים כמו שנאמר בנבואת צפניה והשארתי
205 בקרבך עם עני ודל וחסו בשם ה׳. ואמר שארית ישראל לא
יעשו עולה וגו׳ כי המה ירעו ורבצו ואין מחריד. הנה
שלום על ישראל;

Psalm CXXVI

1. בשוב. ענין הנחה כמו שובה ה׳ רבבות אלפי ישראל
וגו׳. וכן ושב ה׳ אלהיך את שבותך וגו׳. או יהיה ענין
210 תשובה ויהיה פעל יוצא. שיבת. ענין תשובה שישובו בני
ציון לה. היינו כחולמים. כחלום יעוף יהיו בעינינו
צרות הגלות מרב השמחה שתהיה לנו בשובנו לארצנו כן פירשו
אדוני אבי ז"ל והחכם רבי אברהם בן עזרא פירש. כן
יאמרו ישראל בשוב האל שבותם אין אדם רואה בעיניו בפלא
215 הזה רק בחלום;

197 MC לא יהיה שום מכשול   209 R את שבותך ורחמך
206 R עולה after ידברו כזב מ׳   212 C שמחה
208 C כמו שכתוב

says: 'that they may not teach you to do according to all their abominable practices' (Deut. xx 18). But they did not do so and as a result were made to stumble. In the future to come, however, there will be no (such) stumbling block of iniquity, for all the wicked will have been destroyed.

4. Do good (O Lord) to those who are good: in their deeds and *to those who are upright in their hearts.*

5. But as for those who turn aside into their own crooked ways: (the expression refers to such evildoers as are) in Israel. The meaning is: such as turn aside the path of others into their own crooked ways.[1] *The Lord will lead them away with the evildoers:* of the nations. It is also possible to interpret *'ªqalqallotham* (of the duplicity) of their hearts, since their inner thoughts do not correspond to their outward acts.[2] *The Lord will lead them away with the evildoers:* into exile, in contrast to what he says of *those who are good* and of *those who are upright in their hearts. Peace be upon Israel:* since the wicked shall have been destroyed from the midst of Israel, there will be peace for such as remain in Israel, as it is said in the prophecy of Zephaniah (iii 12): 'For I will leave in the midst of you a people humble and lowly and they shall seek refuge in the name of the Lord.' And it says further (Zeph. iii 13): 'Those who are left in Israel shall do no wrong . . . for they shall feed and lie down, with none to terrify them.' And so! *Peace* shall be upon Israel!

PSALM CXXVI

1. *Bᵉshub* (expresses) the idea of causing to rest (*hªnaḥah*) as (in the phrase) 'Give rest (*shubah*), O Lord, to the ten thousand thousands of Israel!' (Num. x 36), and also 'and the Lord your God will cause to cease (*wᵉshab*) your captivity' (Deut. xxx 3). Or it may have the (ordinary) meaning of *tᵉshubah* 'returning', being used as a transitive verb in the context.[3] *Shibath* has the sense of 'returning', for the children of Zion will return to her. *We were like those who dream:* just like a fleeting dream will the sorrows of exile appear to us because of the great happiness which we shall later enjoy on returning to our land. Such is the interpretation of my revered father, of blessed memory. But the learned Abraham Ibn Ezra has commented as follows: Thus will Israel say when God turns back their captivity: No man has ever seen for himself a miracle such as this except in a dream!

---

[1] Lit. 'who turn aside their paths into their crooked ways'.
[2] Lit. 'whose inside is not as their outside'. Cf. *Yoma* 72b.
[3] In his comment on Nahum ii 3 as well as in *Sefer Ha-Shorashim* (under *shub*) Kimḥi cites Rabbi Judah Ḥayyuj and Rabbi Jonah Ibn Janaḥ respectively as the authors of the two suggestions noted in this passage.

2. אז ימלא. הגדיל ה׳. יתמהו בגוים ויאמרו פלא
גדול; הגדיל ה׳ לעשות עם אלה. כלומר עם ישראל.
הגדיל. ואומרים ישראל;

3. הגדיל ה׳ לעשות עמנו. לפיכך היינו שמחים כלומר
זו השמחה הגדולה שתראו בנו ושימלא שחוק פינו מפני
שהגדיל ה׳ לעשות עמנו פלא גדול וטובה גדולה;

4. שובה. יאמרו ישראל בעודם בגלות שובה ופירושו
כמו שפירשנו הניח או כמו השיבה. שבותנו. גלותנו
וכתוב בו׳ו וקרי ביו׳ד והענין אחד. כאפיקים בנגב.
נגב היא ארץ יבשה כמו ארץ הנגב נתתני והיא צמאה למים
ואם יעברו בה אפיקי מים יהיה חדוש גדול וטובה גדולה
כן תהיה תשובת גלותנו. דמה הגלות לנגב והישועה לאפיקי
מים;

5. הזרעים. לפי שדמה הגלות לארץ הנגב שהזורע בה
יזרע בה בדמעה כי בזרעו בוכה ומתחנן לאל שימטיר עליה
ויקצור מה שזורע בברכה. והדבר רחוק שהזורע בה יקצור
ממנה אם לא יהיו רחמי האל כן ישראל בגלות עם כל צרתם
זורעים והזריעה היא מעשה המצות ועושים אותם בדמעה
מפני צרת הגלות מיחלים לאל שיוציאם מהגלות ויקצרו ברנה
מה שזרעו בדמעה והקציר הוא הגמול הטוב;

6. הלוך ילך משך הזרע. פירושו יקר הזרע וכן ומשך חכמה
מפנינים יקר החכמה ונקרא הדבר היקר משך לפי ששמו נמשך
למרחוק והזרע יקר בארץ הנגב והעני הנושא אותו והולך אל
השדה לזרעו הולך ובוכה מפחדו שמא יאבד ולא יצמח מפני
יבשות הארץ והאל רואה דמעיו ומרחם עליו וממטיר על הארץ
ובעת הקציר יבוא אל ביתו ברנה תחת אשר היה הולך ובוכה

2. Then (our mouth) was filled ... the Lord has done great things: the nations will be amazed and will say: A great miracle! *The Lord has done great things for them,* that is, for Israel. *He has done great things*: the people of Israel say:

3. The Lord has done great things for us: therefore we are now *glad,* that is, the great rejoicing which you see among us and which fills *our mouth with laughter* is due to the fact that the Lord has magnificently made manifest for us a great miracle and abundant kindness.

4. Give rest: let Israel say (this) whilst in exile. The meaning of *shubah* is as we have (already) explained, viz. 'cause to rest' or 'return'. *Sh^ebuthenu* (means) our exile. It is written with *waw* and is to be read with *yod,* but the meaning is the same.[1] *Like watercourses in the dry land: negeb* is dry land as (in the passage) 'you have set me in the dry land (*'ereṣ hannegeb*)' (Josh. xv 19). Such a land is parched for lack of water. But if streams of water were to run through it, there would be a great revival of nature and great blessing. So shall it be with the return of our exile. Thus he compares the exile to *the dry land* and the deliverance from it to streams of water.

5. They who sow (in tears): (he continues the metaphor) for he has described the exile (in the preceding verse) as *the dry land.* He who sows there sows in tears and as he sows he cries in supplication to God that he may cause it to rain upon it so that he may reap with blessing what he has sown. And it is far-fetched to suppose that the person thus sowing will reap (anything) from it except by the mercy of God. So also Israel in exile sow amidst all their trouble, the sowing being the performance of *Miṣwoth* which they perform in tears because of the affliction of exile, trusting in God that he will deliver them from exile. *They will reap with joy* what they sow in tears. And the reaping represents the good reward (which they shall receive).

6. He who goes forth ... precious seed: *meshek hazzara'* means 'precious seed', as in 'and the price (*meshek*) of wisdom is above pearls' (Job xxviii 18), that is, wisdom is precious. A precious thing is so termed *meshek* because its reputation is widespread (*nimsh^ekah*).[2] Now seed is a precious thing in *the dry land,* and the poor man who carries it as he goes into the field to sow, goes on his way *weeping,* fearing lest it perish and does not grow because of the dryness of the land. But God sees his tears and having mercy upon him sends rain upon the earth so that at harvest time he will come home *with joy* instead of going about weeping (as he did) in the

---

[1] Lit. 'but the meaning is one'.
[2] From the root *mashak* = 'to draw out, extend'.

בעת הזרע וישא ברנה אלומות קצירו אל ביתו כן ישראל

בגלות סובלים עול הגלות ונושאים משא המסים לקים התורה

והמצות שהוא הזרע במשל ובעת הגאולה שהוא עת הקציר יבואו

245   אל ארץ ישראל ברנה וישאו אלומות הטובות שייטיב עמהם האל

ויצאו מן הגלות בכסף ובזהב;

Psalm CXXVII

1. שיר המעלות לשלמה אם ה' לא יבנה בית. זה המזמור נאמר

על שלמה ולמ'ד לשלמה ענינה בעבור כמו אמרי לי אחי הוא

ונאמר על בנין הבית שחשב דוד לבנותו ואסף כסף וזהב ונחשת

250   למלאכה ולא עלתה בידו שקידתו ועמלו שיבנהו הוא אלא בנו

וגם כן זה הענין בשאר בני העולם שלא תעלה בידם מחשבתם

וגם יש בו רמז למלך המשיח כי גם הוא נקרא שלמה בשיר השירים

ונפרשהו על שלשת הענינים על שלמה תחלה. אמר אם ה' לא

יבנה בית שוא עמלו בניו בו אמר על בנין בית המקדש כי עמל

255   דוד לבנותו וכיון שלא רצה האל שיבנהו לא בנה אותו ופירוש

בניו המתעסקים בבנין. כן אמר על ירושלים לפי שהיא ראש

הממלכה ובה נבנה הבית אמר מי שיבנה הבית ברצון האל והוא

שלמה בני אותו הבנין לא יהיה לשוא אלא באמת יהיה נכון

הבית. כן עיר ירושלים אם ה' לא ישמרנה שוא שקדו השוקדים

260   אבל ה' ישמרנה שצוה להיות בני מלך בה וכיון שברצונו הוא

ישמור הבית והעיר. ושקד הוא ענין ההתעסקות וההשתדלות

על הדבר;

2. שוא לכם. אמר זה על אבשלום שהקדים למרוד באביו ולקחת

המלוכה ואמר עליו והשכים אבשלום ועמד על יד דרך השער וגו'

265   ואמר ויגנב אבשלום את לב אנשי ישראל ואמר כנגדו וכנגד

העוזרים אותו שוא לכם משכימי קום. מאחרי שבת. אמר כנגד

sowing season, for he will carry home with joy the sheaves of his harvest. So will it be with Israel in exile, for they endure the yoke of exile and bear the burden of taxes in order to fulfil the *Torah* and the *Miṣwoth*, which correspond to the seed in the metaphor. But at the time of Redemption, that is, the harvest time (so to speak), they will come to the land of Israel *with joy* and will bear the good sheaves which God will bountifully bestow upon them, and they will go forth from exile with silver and gold.

PSALM CXXVII

1. **A Song of Ascents. Of Solomon. Unless the Lord builds the house:** this psalm refers to Solomon, (the preposition) *lamed* in *lishᵉlomoʰ* meaning 'of' or 'concerning', as in 'say of me (*li*): he is my brother' (Gen. xx 13). It was composed in connection with the building of the Temple which David intended to build and for the construction of which he collected silver, gold and copper. But despite his diligence and labour it was not he but his son who succeeded in building it. The theme applies equally well in the case of all human beings whose plans do not succeed. In addition there is present in it an allusion to the Messianic King, for he too is called Solomon in the Song of Songs.[1] Hence we may interpret it in any one of these three senses. Firstly, as referring to Solomon, he says: *Unless the Lord build the house, its builders toil in vain*: he speaks here of the building of the Temple, for David laboured to build it but since God did not wish him to build it he did not (succeed in) building it. The meaning of *bonaw* is those who engage in the (work of) building. He speaks similarly about Jerusalem, since it was the capital of the kingdom and the place where the Temple was to be built. He says: if he who builds the Temple does so with the consent of God – as in the case of Solomon my son – that building will not be in vain but in truth the Temple will be firmly established. And so also with regard to Jerusalem he says: *unless the Lord guards it, the watchman's vigilance is in vain*. But the Lord will guard it since he has decreed that the children of Israel[2] are to (dwell) there. And because all this is in accordance with his will, he will guard the Temple and the city. *Shaqad* means to busy oneself with or strive after something.

2. **It is vain for you:** he says this about Absalom who was quick to rebel against his father to usurp the kingship. Of him it is said: 'And Absalom used to rise up early and stand beside the way of the gate etc.' (2 Sam. xv 2). And it is also said: 'So Absalom stole away the hearts of the men of Israel' (*ibid. v.* 6). And he states concerning him and those who helped him: *it is in vain that you rise up early. Going late to rest:* he says this about Adonijah

---

[1] Possibly referring to Midrash Rabba Song of Songs iii 7, 9, 11.

[2] Lit. 'the children of the king'. The expression is used of Israel. Cf. *Sabbath* 67a.

אדוניה שאחר לעשות המרד ולשבת בכסא המלוכה עד שזקן דוד

והיה שוכב על המטה ושניהם. אכלי לחם העצבים. כי עמלו

לקנות המלוכה ולא עלתה בידם. עצבים. מן העצבון תאכלנה

270 ואומר אכלי לחם כי כמו שעמל האדם על הלחם כן עמלו על

המלוכה ולא הועילו ואמר. כן יתן לידידו שנא. שלמה הוא

ידידו ידיד האל כמו שכתוב ויקרא שמו ידידיה בעבור ה׳

ופירושו כן כמו שהיו הם חושבים לקחת המלוכה בעמלם כן

נתן האל המלוכה בלא עמל לשלמה וזהו שנא במנוחה בלא עמל

275 כאדם הישן או בעודנו ישן ולא היה יודע בדבר המלוכה דבר

האל היה מתקן לו המלוכה. ושנא כתוב באל״ף והוא כמו בה״א.

3. הנה. אמר דוד הנה אני רואה כי נחלת ה׳ בנים. כלומר

הטוב שיתן האל לידידו בעולם הזה הם הבנים והם נחלתו כי

נחלה טובה יש לי בשלמה בני. שכר פרי הבטן. כפל הענין

280 במלות שונות רוצה לומר השכר שיתן האל בעולם הזה לאדם

שכר מעשיו הטובים הוא פרי הבטן;

4. כחצים. לפי ששלמה היה בן זקונים ורצה בו האל להיות

תחתיו אחריו אבל בחייו לא היה לו עזר. ואמר כן בני

הנעורים. רוצה לומר הבנים שיהיו לו לאדם בימי נעוריו

285 הם לאדם עזר גדול כמו החצים ביד הגבור, ודוד היו לו

בנים בני הנעורים טובים וחכמים וגבורים כמו שאמר ובני

דוד כהנים היו ואמר ובני דויד הראשנים ליד המלך שהיו

ראשנים לעזרתו. וכלם היו טובים לבד אבשלום ואדניה

שהתגאו ביפים ויצאו לתרבות רעה והיה מתפאר בטובים ואמר

290 כי כל אדם יש לו להתפאר על בנים טובים ולחשבם לעצמו

לחלק טוב ולנחלה טובה שנתן לו האל;

who waited until David was old and lay on his death-bed before he rebelled and attempted to usurp the royal office. Both of them (are referred to in the expression) *who eat the bread of toil*, for they strove hard to obtain the kingship but were not successful. *Ha'ăṣabim* (may be explained) from 'in toil (*be'iṣabon*) you shall eat of it' (Gen. iii 17). And thus he says *who eat the bread of toil*, for as a man labours for his (daily) bread, so did they labour for the kingship but to no avail. And he says *so he gives to his beloved sleep*: Solomon is his beloved, the beloved of God, as it is written 'So he called his name Jedidiah, because of the Lord' (2 Sam. xii 25). The interpretation of this is as follows: just as they intended by their (strenuous) labour to usurp the royal office, so did God grant the kingship to Solomon without any effort whatsoever (on his part). And this is the meaning of *shena'*: at ease and without exertion, just as when a man is asleep. Or (it may mean): while he was still insensible[1] and unaware of the affair of (the succession to) the monarchy, the word of God had secured the kingship for him. *Shena'* is written with *aleph* but it is the same as with *he*.

3. Behold: David says: *Behold, I see that sons are a heritage from the Lord*, as though to say, the blessing which God bestows upon his beloved in this world consists in sons and they are his *heritage*, for I have a good heritage in Solomon my son. *The fruit of the womb a reward*: he repeats the same idea in different words. He means to say that the reward which God gives to a man in this world – that is, the reward for his good works – is *the fruit of the womb*.

4. Like arrows: because Solomon was a son of his old age and, moreover, had been chosen by God as his successor, he was no help to him during his lifetime.[2] For this reason he says: *so are the sons of one's youth*, meaning that the sons which a man has in his youth are a great help to him, *like arrows in the hand of a warrior*. David too had sons who were *sons of youth*, being good, wise and strong, even as it says: 'And David's sons were chief ministers' (2 Sam. viii 18),[3] and 'David's sons were the chief officials (*hari'shonim*) in the service of the king' (1 Chron. xviii 17), (that is) they were the first (*hari'shonim*) to his assistance. And they were all good, with the exception of Absalom and Adonijah who became arrogant in their excellency and depraved. But he took pride in the good (sons). And so he tells us that every man has reason to take pride in good sons and to reckon them to himself as a good gift[4] and *heritage* which God has bestowed upon him.

---

[1] Lit. 'asleep'.

[2] Lit. 'because Solomon was a son of his old age and God had delighted in him to be in his place after him, but during his life he was no help to him'.

[3] In his commentary on 2 Samuel viii 18, Kimḥi takes *Koh͟nim* to mean not priests but chief ministers. Cf. 1 Chron. xviii 17 cited next in the text above.

[4] Lit. 'portion'.

5. אשרי הגבר. לפי שהמשיל אותם לחצים המשיל ביתו

לאשפה. לא יבשו. האב והבנים כשידברו בשער בפני

הזקנים כי הם רבים וטובים ויוכלו לדבר לפני

295 אויביהם. לא יבושו ולא יחתו מהם, ועל המשיח יתפרש

כך. אמר אם ה׳ לא יבנה בית. אמר על בית המקדש ועיר

אמר על ירושלים והנה מיום שחרב בית המקדש וגלו ישראל

וחרבה ירושלים היתה ירושלים פעם בנויה פעם חרבה כי

היתה ביד אדום וביד ישמעאל וכל השנים יתגרו מלחמה

300 עליה אלה יבנוה ואלה יחריבוה לפי שאין רצון האל בבנינם

ובשמירתם. שוא עמלו הבונים ושוא שקדו השומרים. ואמר

שוא לכם משכימי קום. אלו אדום שכבשו תחלה ירושלים.

מאחרי שבת. אלו הישמעאלים שבאו באחרונה והתגרו עם

הנוצרים ולקחו אותה מידם והם מידם וכל הימים עד בוא

305 הגואל עמלים וטורחים עליה. לפיכך קראם אכלי לחם העצבים.

ואמר כן יתן לידידו שנא. לידידו הוא המלך המשיח ויתן

לו האל ירושלים בלא עמל ואלה שעמלו עליה לא ישארו בה.

והפסוקים האחרים הם דברי דוד כמו שפירשנו, ויתפרשו גם

כן על כל אדם ומה שנפרשהו על בני העולם כך הוא. זכר

310 תחלה בנין הבית והוא קיום המלכות לאיזה מלך שיהיה לו

ולבניו אחריו כמו ובית יבנה לך ה׳ שפירושו המלכות.

ואמר כי אין ביכלת המלך להקים המלוכה לו ולבניו אחריו

אם לא ברצון האל ואחר כך זכר שמירת העיר מפחד האויבים

כי לא יועילו שומרי החומות שלא יכבשוה האויבים אם ה׳

315 לא ישמרנה. ואחר כך דבר על העוסקים בעסק העולם

ורודפים אחרי הממון והם משכימים למלאכה או לסחורה גם

מאחרים עד בוא השמש במלאכתם או בשבתם בחנויות למכור

סחורתם וכל ההשתדלות הזאת שוא להם אם לא יעזרם האל

295	B	ועל מלך המשיח	
299	CS ישמעאלים	היםמעאלים N	307 N לא ישארו עליה ולא ישכנו בה
299	NMCS התגרו	התגרו במלחמה N	309 BNR הוא כך
302	MC	שכבשו ירושלים תחלה	309 NMC על אדם.
303	MC ישמעאלים PD 303.	והתגברו על הנוצרים	309 N ומה שנבאר שהוא על בני העולם
304	NMC	ולקחו אותה מהם והם מהם	310 N בנין בית המקדש
304	N ויהיה ביניהם מלחמה היתה הימים כל וכן		315 RMS ואחר כן
304	BNRCDS עליה וטרחם עמלם הגואל בוא עד		316 BPAD אחר הממון
305	N קראם כן על		316 C המשכימים
306	BRS המשיח מלך		317 NRC שבתם
			318 RPMC ההשתדלות הזה

5. Happy is the man: since he has compared them to *arrows*, so now he compares his house to a *quiver*. *They will not be put to shame*: (that is) the father and the sons when they speak at the gate in the presence of the elders, seeing they are numerous and good and are able to parley with their enemies. They shall neither *be put to shame* nor dismayed by them.

As referring to the Messiah, the psalm may be interpreted as follows. He says: *Unless the Lord build the house*: he says this of the Temple, whilst by *city* he means Jerusalem. Now from the day that the Temple was destroyed, Israel exiled and Jerusalem laid in ruins, Jerusalem has been rebuilt on several occasions and in turn destroyed, for it has been under the rule of Edom or Ishmael who throughout all these years have warred with each other over it, the one building it anew and the other destroying it (once more). The reason for this is that God has no desire for their work of restoration or for their guarding it. They who build it *labour in vain* and *in vain* do the watchmen keep vigilance over it. And he says: *It is in vain that you rise up early*: (that is) the Edomites who were the first to capture Jerusalem. *Going late to rest*: (that is) the Ishmaelites who eventually came and fought the Christians and removed it from their power, the latter in turn recovering it from them. And so, until the Redeemer come they will (continue) to toil and moil on its account. Therefore he refers to them as those *who eat the bread of toil*. And he says: *So he gives to his beloved sleep*: meaning by *his beloved* the King Messiah, for God will deliver Jerusalem to him without any labour (on his part). But they that strive for it will not remain in it. The remaining verses are the words of David, as we have (already) explained.

The psalm may also be interpreted as referring to every human being, and in so far as we may interpret it as bearing upon mankind it is as follows. In the first place he speaks of the building of a house, by which is meant the establishment of a dynasty for a king – whoever he may be – both for himself and his sons after him. Similarly (we have) 'The Lord will build you a dynasty (*bayith*)' (1 Chron. xvii 10). Thus he says that it is not within the power of any king to establish a dynasty for himself and his sons unless it be by the will of God. Next he mentions the guarding of a city against the terror of enemies; those who guard the walls are powerless to prevent enemies from capturing it unless the Lord guards it. Subsequently he speaks of those engaged in earning their livelihood and in pursuit of wealth.[1] They get up early for their work or business, remaining even as late[2] as sunset at their (daily) labours or in attendance[3] at their stores to sell their merchandise. Yet all this striving is *vain* for them unless God helps them. For to him in whom God delights and whom he loves he gives wealth

---

[1] Lit. 'those who engage in the affairs of the world and pursue wealth'.
[2] Lit. 'delaying until sunset'.
[3] Lit. 'or in their sitting'.

כי למי שירצה בו האל ויאהבנו יתן לו הממון בלא יגיעה

320   ובלא עמל כאלו הוא ישן. ואחר כך זכר ענין הבנים שהוא

גם כן מתנה טובה מאת האל כשיהיו טובים;

Psalm CXXVIII

1. שיר המעלות אשרי כל ירא ה׳. שבח דרכי הירא את ה׳

שיעשה זה כל מי שהוא בגלות ויזכה לראות בטוב ירושלים

אם יתנהג בדרכי האל. וירא האל הוא שנזהר ממצות לא תעשה.

325   ההולך בדרכיו שזהיר במצות עשה. אחר כך ספר על הנהגת

מחיתו;

2. יגיע כפיך. כי הטובה היא שיחיה ממלאכתו ולא יהנה

מאחרים כל זמן שיוכל ליגע עצמו במלאכה ואם תחיה בזאת

ההנהגה אשריך וטוב לך. יאשרוך בני העולם ויהיה גמול

330   טוב לך מאת האל וזהו מה שפירשו רבותינו ז״ל אשריך בעולם

הזה וטוב לך לעולם הבא;

3. אשתך. בסגול האל״ף אמר גם זה מהנהגות הטובות בעולם

הזה שתצוה אשתך שתהיה כגפן פוריה בירכתי ביתך והמשיל

אותה לגפן כי אין לך עץ שנוטעים אותו בתוך הבית אלא

335   גפן שיש בני אדם נוטעים אותה בירכתי ביתם וכשתגדל

מוציאים אותה מחור הבית ולחוץ אל השמש והנה שרשה בתוך

הבית וענפיה חוץ לבית כן האשה תהיה צנועה בירכתי הבית

שלא תצא חוץ לביתה כי זה דרך אשה מנאפת כמו שאמר עליה

שלמה פעם בחוץ פעם ברחובות. ואמר בירכתי כי גם בביתה

340   תהיה צנועה שלא תשב בפתח ביתה שיראוה עוברים ושבים כי

זהו דרך אשה רעה כמו שאמר עליה וישבה לפתח ביתה אלא

תהיה תמיד בירכתי הבית שלא יראה אותה אלא בעלה ובני

ביתה אבל בניה יצאו חוץ למלאכתם ולצרך הבית כמו שיצאו

319	C	יתן לו בלא יגיעה הממון		334	R	שנוטעין
322	C	שבח דרך		338	RS	כמו שאמר שלמה המלך עליה
322	B	הירא את דבר ה׳			B	כמו שאמר המלך שלמה עליה
325	N	שהזהיר BR	שנזהר	341	R	כי כן דרך אשה זונה
	M	שיזהיר AC	שנזהר ממצות עשה	341	A	כמו שאמר עוד עליה שלמה
330	R	ויאשרוך בכל העולם		341	P	וחשב בפתח עינים
332	NPD	האל״ף בסגול				

without labour or toil, as though he were asleep. Finally, he makes mention
of the matter of children which also are a good gift from God (bestowed
upon men) if they be worthy.[1]

PSALM CXXVIII

1. A Song of Ascents. Blessed is every one who fears the Lord: he
commends the ways of him who fears the Lord so that every one should
do so in exile and (in this way) succeed in seeing the prosperity of Jerusalem
by regulating his conduct[2] in accordance with the precepts of God.[3] (And
by the words) *who fears the Lord* (is meant) the person who is careful to
observe the negative commands. *Who walks in his ways:* (and likewise)
performs the positive commands. Subsequently he describes how such a
person earns his livelihood.

2. The labour of your hands: for the good way for man (to follow) is
that he should live from his own work and not profit by that of others,
provided[4] he is in a fit condition to work hard in a trade.[5] And if you live
in such a manner *you will be happy, and it will be well with you:* men will
pronounce you happy and you will have a good reward from God. And
this is how our teachers, of blessed memory, have interpreted it:[6] *you will
be happy* in this world and *it will be well with you* in the world to come.

3. *'Esht^ekah* (is written) with *seghol* under the *aleph*. He says: this too is
a rule of good conduct in this world, viz. that you command *your wife* to
be *like a fruitful vine within your house:* he compares her to a vine, for no
tree is to be found[7] within the house except the vine, which some people
plant inside their house. As it begins to grow it is led through an aperture
in the house into the sunlight so that[8] its root is inside the house, whilst the
branches are outside. So should a woman be chaste, remaining within the
house and not going forth from the home. For such is the way of a lewd
woman, just as Solomon says of her 'Now she is in the street, now in the
market' (Prov. vii 12). He states (specifically) *within:* that is, even in her
home she is to be chaste and is not to sit at the door of her house to be seen
by those who pass to and fro. For such is the way of the evil woman, just
as it says of her 'she sits at the door of her house' (Prov. ix 14). She should
always be *within* the house so that none may see her except her husband
and the members of her household. But her children should go forth into

---

[1] Lit. 'if they are good'.   [2] Lit. 'if he conduct himself'.
[3] Lit. 'in the ways of God'.   [4] Lit. ' so long as'.
[5] Lit. 'provided he is able to exert himself in work'.
[6] *Berakoth* 8a; *Aboth* IV: 1, VI: 4; *Ḥullin* 44b.
[7] Lit. 'for you have not a tree'.   [8] Lit. 'and behold'.

לחוץ ענפי הגפן שיהיו פרים ורבים ממגד תבואות שמש ואם
345   תהיה אשתך בזה הדרך יהיו בניך כשתילי זיתים. והמשיל
אותם לזית כי עץ הזית אינו מקבל הרכבה מעץ׳ אחר והשתילים
טובים בני אביהם כך הבנים שיולדו מאשה זאת לא יהיה
בהם חשד ממזרות כי אמם צנועה ולא נזקקה אלא לבעלה, ועֹוד
המשילם לזיתים כי עץ הזית יהיה עלהו לח כל ימות השנה
350   כך הם יהיו בהדם וביפים במעשים טובים. ואמר סביב לשולחנך.
שיהיו לפניך לשרתך בעת שתאכל ויהיו תמיד סביב לשלחנך שלא
יהיו משלחים זוללים וסובאים אלא לא יאכלו ולא ישתו אלא
על שלחנך;

4. הנה כי כן. באלה המדות וההנהגות יברך הגבר שהוא
355   ירא ה׳;

5. יברכך ה׳ מציון. ממקום שכינתו שהוא ציון. וראה.
ותזכה לראות בטוב ירושלים כשישובו לה ישראל מהגלות.
כל ימי חייך. ותראה בטוב כל ימי חייך בין הגלות בין
בטוב ירושלים. וראה בטוב. שזכר עומד במקום שנים;

360   6. וראה. ותאריך ימים עד שתראה בנים לבניך ועד שתראה
שלום על ישראל וזהו ׳בקבוץ גליות אם יבוא הגואל בימיך
ואם לאו יחיך הבורא אז עם המתים הצדיקים שיחיו ותראה
שלום על ישראל;

Psalm CXXIX

1. שיר המעלות רבת צררוני מנעורי. המשיל ימי הגלות לימי
365   האדם והתחלת הגלות לימי הנעורים וארך ימי הגלות לימי הזקנה
ואומר כי מתחלת הגלות צררו אותנו האויבים צרה רבה וזה

347	N	שנולדו	352	N	אלא לא instead of ולא
349	R	כי עץ הזית יהיו עליו ירוקים ולחים	353	C	על before סביב מ׳
		כל ימות השנה	366	A	אמרו A 366. צרות רבות
352	R	סובאים וזוללים			

the world[1] to their work and for the necessities of the home, just as the branches of the vine shoot forth fruitful and numerous 'with the choicest fruits of the sun' (Deut. xxxiii 14). And if your wife is of this disposition, then *your children will be like olive shoots*: he pictures them as olives because the olive tree does not lend itself to grafting[2] from any other tree. Such plants are goodly, being the legitimate offspring of the parent plant. So are the children born of a woman such as this; there can be no suspicion of illegitimacy,[3] for their mother is chaste and does not cohabit[4] with anyone other than her husband. And for a further reason he represents them as olives, viz. since the leaves of the olive tree are fresh throughout all the year,[5] so will they be (ever fresh) in their splendour and beauty as a result of their good deeds. And he says: *around your table*, (that is) they will be with you to attend to you when you eat and they will always be *around your table*, for they will not be scattered (away from home), nor gluttonous nor addicted to drink. Nor will they eat nor drink except at your table.

4. Behold, thus will (the man) be blessed: (that is to say) by such rules and norms of conduct *will the man be blessed who fears the Lord.*

5. May the Lord bless you from Zion: from the place of his Divine Glory,[6] which is Zion. *And may you see*: you will succeed in seeing *the prosperity of Jerusalem* when Israel returns to her from exile. *All the days of your life*: and you will see prosperity *all the days of your life*, both (the prosperity) in exile and *the prosperity of Jerusalem*. The expression *and see the prosperity* mentioned is to be understood again.[7]

6. And may you see: (that is) you will prolong your days until you see *your children's children* and until you see *peace upon Israel*, that is, at the ingathering of the exiles, if the Redeemer comes in your lifetime; but if not, the Creator will revive you at that time, together with the righteous (among the) dead, who are destined to be resurrected, and you will see peace upon Israel.

PSALM CXXIX

1. A Song of Ascents. Greatly have they afflicted me from my youth: he draws an analogy between the duration of exile and the course of human life, (representing) the beginning of exile as the period of youth and the prolonged stages of exile as the period of old age. He says that from the beginning of the exile our enemies have afflicted us with grievous oppression. And this is (what he means by) *let Israel now say*, viz. (that they

---

[1] Lit. 'go forth without'.
[2] Lit. 'does not receive grafting'.
[3] Cf. *Yerushalmi, Kilayim* i: 7.
[4] Lit. 'connected'.
[5] Lit. 'all the days of the year'.
[6] Lit. 'Shekinah'. See above, p. 11 n. 1.
[7] Lit. 'stands for twice'.

יאמר ישראל תהלה לאל שלא כלו בגלות כי מתחלת הגלות החלו
לצרור אותנו בצרות רבות ועד היום הזה כן עושים ועם כל
זה לא יוכלו לי לכלותי כמו שחשבו. ומה שכפל הענין לחזק
ההודאה לאל כמנהג הלשון;

370

2. רבת. פירשנוהו;

3. על גבי. משל לרב הסבלות והפרך הבזיון והקלון כמו
שאמר ותשימי כארץ גוך וכחוץ לעברים; האריכו למעניתם.
המענית הוא הקו שיחרוש החורש בשורים בשדה כשעור שירצה
בו ואחר כך יחזור ויעשהו אחר כמוהו וכן עד שיחרוש כל
השדה, וכל מה שיהיה ארוך המענית תהיה יגיעת השורים רבה
כי לא ינוחו עד ראש הקו. ובאמרו האריכו למעניתם רוצה
לומר שלא נתנו אותנו לנוח מעבודתם וסבלותם;

375

4. ה׳ צדיק קצץ. עבר במקום עתיד אמר ה׳ שהוא צדיק
וישר בדרכיו יקצץ ויכרות עבות רשעים ועבות הוא מיתרי
העל כלומר יסיר עלם מעלינו;

380

5. יבשו. כשיקצץ האל עבותם מעלינו אז יבשו ויסגו אחור
ממחשבתם הרעה עלינו. שנאי ציון. הגוים אינם שונאי
ציון אבל אוהבים אותה עד שנלחמים בעבורה גוי עם גוי
אלא פירושו. שנאי ציון. שונאי בני ציון והם ישראל;

385

6. יהיו כחציר גגות. עשב הצומח בגג שאין לו העמדה
וקיום עד שקודם שיצא ונראה יבש בחם השמש. ובאמרו
שקדמת הוא דרך הפלגה כי לא ייבש עד שיצא ויראה פני השמש

367	N	שלא כלינו	375	NP	ויעשה
369	RC	יכלו	383	NPA	אינם שונאים ציון
374	PMCDS	שירצו	387	NR	נראה יבש

should offer up) praise to God because they were not completely destroyed in exile. For from the outset of the exile they set about afflicting us with dire afflictions, and even to this day do likewise. Yet in spite of all this *they have not prevailed against* me to exterminate me as they had planned. And as for the repetition of the same idea (in the next verse), it is to emphasise the thanks (due) to God, being the usual method of expressing emphasis in the language.[1]

2. *Rabbath*: we have already explained this form.[2]

3. Upon my back: a figurative expression denoting their many burdens and the oppression, shame and contempt (to which they were subjected) just as it says: 'And you have made your back like the ground and like the street for them to pass over' (Isa. li 23). *They made long their furrows*: *ma'anith* is the furrow[3] which the ploughman ploughs with the oxen in the field over the distance he wishes, coming back again to make another one of the same length, and so forth until the whole field is ploughed. The longer the furrow, the greater is the fatigue of the oxen, for they have no rest until the end of the furrow.[3] And so when he says *they made long their furrows*, he means that they have allowed us no respite from their service and onerous exactions.

4. The Lord is righteous, he has cut: *qiṣṣeṣ*: past tense instead of the future. He says: the Lord who is *righteous* and upright in his ways will *cut* and destroy *the bonds of the wicked*. And *'aboth* denotes the ropes of the yoke. That is to say, he will remove their yoke from us.

5. May they be put to shame: when God will have *cut their bonds* from us, then *will they be put to shame and thrown back* from their evil design against us. *Those who hate Zion*: the nations do not hate Zion itself. On the contrary, they love her, so much so that they go to war on her account, nation with nation. The (correct) interpretation of *śon'e ṣion* is those who hate the children of Zion, that is, Israel.

6. Let them be like grass on the housetops: (the meaning is: let them be like) grass that grows on the housetops, which is transient and impermanent,[4] for before it has sprung forth it (already) looks withered from the heat of the sun. And when he says *which before*, (it is to be understood) by way of hyperbole since the grass does not (really) wither until it springs

---

[1] Lit. 'according to the custom of the language'.
[2] Cf. the commentary on Psalm cxx 6.
[3] Lit. 'line'.
[4] Lit. 'which has neither stability nor permanence'.

אבל מרב מהירותו ליבוש אמר כן דרך הפלגה כמו שאמר בבקר
יציץ וחלף ולערב ימולל ויבש. שלף. הוא ענין חליצת הדבר   390
ויציאתו ממקומו כמו שלף איש נעלו אלא שהוא יוצא וזה
עומד;

7.   שלא מלא. כלומר שלא יבוא לידי קצירה. וחצנו. זרועו
כמו והביאו בניך בחצן, חצני נערתי. מעמר. אוסף העמרים;

8.   ולא אמרו העברים. מנהג העברים לאמר לקוצרים ברכת   395
ה' עליכם כמו שאמר בעז לקוצרים ה' עמכם. ומה שאמר ברכנו
אתכם בשם ה' הוא כפל דבר ועל חציר גגות לא יאמר זה כי
אינו זרע ברכה ולא יבוא לידי קצירה, כן יהיו הגוים כי
כל תורתם ואמונתם הבל וריק כחציר גגות וכן יכלו כחציר
גגות אבל תורת ישראל המשיל לזרע ברכה כמו שפירשנו בפסוק   400
הזרעים בדמעה;

Psalm CXXX

1.   שיר המעלות ממעמקים קראתיך ה'. דמה הגלות למעמקי
מים;

2.   אדני שמעה בקולי. קשובות. בשקל שכולה שכולות;

3.   אם עונות. מי יעמד. כמעט נהיה כלים ואובדים אם   405
תשמור לנו עונותינו;

4.   כי עמך הסליחה. פירש אדוני אבי ז"ל האל נתן ממשלה
לעליונים לעשות חפצו בארץ אבל הסליחה אינה עמהם כי אם
עמו למה שלא יאמרו בני אדם בלבם אם אנו חוטאים יתפיסו
לנו המלאכים וישאו לפשעינו בא להודיע כי אין בהם הסליחה   410

forth and receives the rays of the sun.[1] However, because of its rapidity
in withering, the psalmist uses this hyperbole, just as (elsewhere) he says
'In the morning it flourishes and is renewed; in the evening it fades and
withers' (Ps. xc 6). *Shalaph* indicates the displacement of an object and its
removal from its original position, as in 'A man drew off (*shalaph*) his
shoe' (Ruth iv 7), except that the one is transitive and the other intransitive.

7. Which does not fill (the reaper's hand): that is to say, it does not
reach the reaping stage. *Ḥiṣno* means his arm, as (in the text) 'And they
will bring your sons in their bosom (*bᵉḥoṣen*)' (Isa. xlix 22), 'I also shook
out my lap (*ḥoṣni*)' (Neh. v 13). *Mᵉᶜammer* (means) he who gathers sheaves.

8. While those who pass by do not say: it is customary for those who
pass by to say to the reapers *the blessing of the Lord be upon you*, just as
Boaz greeted the reapers 'The Lord be with you' (Ruth ii 4). And as for
the expression[2] *we bless you in the name of the Lord*, it is a repetition of the
same thought. Now this (manner of greeting) is not uttered in the case of
grass on the housetops, for it does not flourish[3] or come to the reaping stage.
So shall it be with the gentiles, for all their dogmas and beliefs are without
substance and worthless like *the grass on the housetops* – and so they shall
be consumed like *the grass on the housetops*. But as for Israel's *Torah*, this
he describes as a flourishing seed, as we have expounded the verse (beginning with) 'They who sow in tears' (Ps. cxxvi 5).

PSALM CXXX

1. A Song of Ascents. Out of the depths I cry to thee, O Lord: he compares the exile to the depths of the seas.

2. Lord, hear my cry: *qashshuboth* 'attentive' is of the same paradigm as
shakkulah (singular, Song of Songs iv 2, vi 6), *shakkuloth* (plural, Jer.
xviii 21).

3. If sins . . . who could stand?: we would quickly be destroyed and
perish *if thou shouldst hold* against us our *sins*.

4. But with thee is forgiveness: my revered father, of blessed memory,
has interpreted (this as follows): God has given power to the higher intelligences to perform his will on earth, but forgiveness rests not with them
but with him. Why is this so ? It is in order that men may not say to themselves: If we sin, the angels will be reconciled to us and will forgive our

---

[1] Lit. 'and sees the face of the sun'.   [2] Lit. 'and as for what he says'.
[3] Lit. 'a seed of blessing'.

למען שייראו בני אדם את האל למען כי עמו הסליחה לא עם

אחר זולתו והחכם רבי אברהם בן עזרא פירש שאם לא תסלח

לא ייראוך החוטאים ויעשו חפצם בכל אות נפשם;

‎5. קויתי ה׳. אני קויתי אותו בעולם הזה שיראני הישועה

ורקותה אותו גם כן נפשי במותי לאסוף כבודי אליו. ולדברו   415

הוחלתי. שהבטיחני להוציאני מהגלות;

‎6. נפשי. נפשי הומה לה׳ בלילה להיותה מאותם האנשים

השומרים לבקר כלומר שקמים באשמורת הבקר להתפלל. ואמר.

שמרים לבקר. פעם אחרת כלומר שמנהגם כן להיות שומרים

וערים בכל בקר להתפלל לאל וזה המזמור מאמר כל חסיד   420

בגלות והחכם רבי אברהם בן עזרא פירש נפשי קותה לו יותר

משמקוים שומרי החומות לבקר שערים בלילות ויקוו לבקר

מתי יהיה שיוכלו לישון;

‎7. יחל. צווי מבנין פעל הדגוש אמר ישראל קוה אל ה׳

שיפדך מהגלות כי עמו החסד תמיד עם הנבראים ויעשה עמך   425

חסד כי הרבה עמו פדות. כי כבר פדה אותך פעמים ממצרים

ומבבל וממצרות רבות פעמים רבות כן יפדה אותך מזה הגלות

כי לא יחסר לו פדות כי הרבה עמו;

‎8. והוא יפדה. ואם תאמר איך יפדה אותי ואני מלא עון.

הוא יפדה את ישראל מכל עונותיו. תחלה יפדה אותו מעונותיו   430

כלומר שיסלח לו עונותיו שעברו ויתן בלבו לשוב אליו בכל

לבבו ואחרי כן ישיב שיבתו כמו שכתוב ושב ה׳ אליהך את

שבותך ורחמך ושב וקבצך וגו׳, כי תשוב אל ה׳ אלהיך בכל

לבבך ובכל נפשך;

417 C	להיותי	429 B		ואיך
418 P	שקודמים באשמורת הבקר	431 BS		ויתן בלבם
419 B	שמנהגם גם כן	432 B	שביתך	שבותך R
425 N	ויעשה חסד עמך			

sins. (Therefore Scripture) proceeds to make it known that forgiveness is not with them, in order that men may fear God, for with him there is forgiveness and with none other besides him. And the learned Abraham Ibn Ezra expounds as follows: If thou forgivest not, sinners will not fear thee but will do as they please, according to their heart's desire.

5. I wait for the Lord: I wait for him in this world that he may show me salvation; likewise *my soul will wait* at death for him to gather unto himself my glory. *And in his word I hope:* for he has assured me that he will deliver me from exile.

6. My soul: my soul murmurs to the Lord in the night that I may be[1] one of those *who watch for the morning,* that is, those who get up at the morning watch to pray. He says (the words) *who watch for the morning* a second time, implying thereby that it is customary for them to watch and be awake every morning to pray. And this psalm is an expression of what every pious man in exile would say. The learned Abraham Ibn Ezra, however, interprets: *my soul waits* for him more than they who keep watch over the walls waiting for morning; they are awake during the night and wait for the morning, whenever it comes, so that they may sleep.

7. Yaḥel: imperative of the *piel* conjugation. He says: *O Israel, hope in the Lord* that he may redeem you from exile, for with him there is *steadfast love* at all times towards his creatures, and he will deal mercifully with you, for *with him is unbounded redemption:* he has already redeemed you twice – from Egypt and Babylon – and (also) from many tribulations on numerous occasions. So also will he redeem you from this exile, for there is no lack of redemption with him; (indeed) *it is unbounded with him.*

8. He will redeem: but if you say: How can he redeem me, seeing I am full of sin? yet *he will redeem Israel from all his sins:* first of all he will redeem him from his sins, that is to say, he will forgive his iniquities in which he has sinned and will put into his heart (the desire) to return to him with all his heart. Subsequently he will return his captivity, as it is written 'Then the Lord your God will return your captivity and have compassion upon you, and will gather you, etc.' (Deut. xxx 3); 'If you return to the Lord your God with all your heart and with all your soul' (Deut. xxx 10).

---

[1] Lit. 'that it (my soul) may be'

Psalm CXXXI

435   1.   שיר המעלות לדוד ה׳ לא גבה לבי ולא רמו עיני.   זה אמר
דוד על עצמו ואמר זה הענין באלה המעלות שהם על הגלות כלומר
כי כמו שהתנהג הוא כן יתנהגו ישראל בגלות בשפלות ובזה
ירחם האל עליהם כי רם ה׳ ושפל יראה לפיכך אמר בתכלית המזמור
יחל ישראל אל ה׳ אמר.   לא גבה לבי.   בסתר.   ולא רמו עיני.
440   בגלוי.   ולא הלכתי.   פעל עומד אף על פי שהוא מן הדגוש וכן
קדר הלכתי.   בגדלות ובנפלאות ממני.   בדבר האלהות לא התפארתי
בלבי שאוכל להשיג ואדע הדברים והסודות שהם נפלאות ממני לפי
שכלי אלא הלכתי בהם מעט מעט ביראה פן אפרוץ לראות במה שלא
יגיע שכלי אליו ותשתבש דעתי בו ועל זה נאמר כבד אלהים והסתר
445   דבר ואמר דבש מצאת אכל דיך;

2.   אם לא.   מנהג הלשון לאמר אם לא בענין אלה ושבועה כמו
אם לא בתים רבים, אם לא כאשר דמיתי כלומר אם לא יהיה כך
יהיה כך וכך וכן כה יעשה לי אלהים בזה הענין אמר.   אם לא
שויתי ודוממתי נפשי כגמל.   יבוא לי כך וכך ופירוש.   שויתי
450   ודוממתי.   שמתי אותה כגמול עלי אמו כלומר כמו התינוק שנגמ_
משדי אמו שיתחיל מעט להתבונן בענין גדולו ומהלך מעט מעט
ועדין אינו נסמך על עצמו אלא עלי אמו שתדדהו ותרגילהו מעט
כן שמתי נפשי והשתקתי אותה שלא תסמוך בתבונת עצמה בנסתרות
ובנפלאות אלא תסמוך על המלמדים ועל הקבלה שהיא האם והוסיף
455   עוד לחזק הענין ואמר.   כגמול עלי נפשי.   כמו הגמול כן שמתי
נפשי עלי שלא אסמוך בבינתי, ובדברי רבותינו ז"ל.   לא גבה

435	PMAD	זה המזמור אמר דוד	448	N	כה יעשה לי אלהים וכה יוסיף
438	B	יחוס האל P ירחם ה׳	448	R	ורבים בזה הענין
441	M	בדברי האלהות	449	R	שויתי ודוממתי. נפשי כגמול עלי אמו
442	M	ולידע	450	B	שינמל
446	BS	כמו אם ... כאשר דמיתי ח׳	452	N	ואינו נסמך
447	R	אם לא יהיה כך וכך	456	NRMAC	ובדברי רבותינו ... את הארון ח׳

PSALM CXXXI

1. A Song of Ascents. Of David. O Lord, my heart is not proud, my eyes are not haughty: this psalm was composed by David with reference to himself. And this particular theme is introduced[1] among these (Songs of) Ascents which deal with the exile, and means:[2] just as he himself acted (in all humility), so should Israel demean themselves humbly in exile. And because of this the Lord will have mercy upon them, 'for though the Lord is high, yet he regards the lowly' (Ps. cxxxviii 6). Accordingly, he says at the conclusion of the psalm: *O Israel, hope in the Lord.* He says: *my heart is not proud*: in secret; *and my eyes are not haughty*: in public. *And I do not walk about*: *hillakti*: intransitive, though used here in the *piel* conjugation; cf. 'I go about (*hillakti*) mourning' (Ps. xxxviii 7). *In matters too great and too marvellous for me*: as regards the Godhead, I do not boast that I am able to comprehend and know such matters and mysteries[3] as are too profound[4] for my understanding; but in these matters I proceed very cautiously[5] in reverence, lest I be so rash[6] as to ponder upon that unto which my reason cannot attain, so that my mind becomes perplexed in them. And it is said concerning this: 'It is the glory of God to conceal things' (Prov. xxv 2). And it says (further): 'If you have found honey, eat only what you need' (Prov. xxv 16).

2. *'im lo'*: used idiomatically to introduce an imprecation or oath, as in 'surely many houses . . .' (Isa. v 9) and 'surely as I have planned' (Isa. xiv 24), the meaning being: if such and such a matter does not come to pass, then let such and such a thing happen, as in 'God do so to me (and more also)' (2 Sam. iii 35, xix 14; 1 Kgs. ii 23; 2 Kgs. vi 31). In the same way he means to say: *if I have not calmed and quieted my soul like a weaned child*, then let such and such befall me. And the meaning of *I have calmed and quieted (my soul)* is: I have arranged it *as a weaned child upon its mother*, that is to say, just as the young child, weaned from its mother's breast, begins to observe gradually the course of its growth and to walk a little, yet does not depend upon itself but upon its mother to take it by the hand and guide its steps, so have I arranged my soul and quieted it so that it depends not upon its own understanding in regard to deep[7] and profound matters, but relies upon teachers and tradition which are (so to speak) the mother. And he says further, by way of emphasising the thought: *like a weaned child is my soul*: just like a weaned child, so have I arranged my soul not to depend on my own intellectual faculties. And according to the

---

[1] Lit. 'and he utters this theme with these Ascents'.
[2] Lit. 'as though to say'.   [3] Lit. 'secrets'.
[4] Lit. 'too wonderful'.   [5] Lit. 'little by little'.
[6] Lit. 'lest I break forth'.   [7] Lit. 'hidden things', 'secret things'.

לבי.   בשעה שמשחני שמואל למלך.   ולא רמו עיני.   בשעה שהרגתי
גלית.   ולא הלכתי בגדלות.   בשעה שההזירוני ונכנסתי למלכות.
ובנפלאות ממני.   בשעה שהעליתי את הארון;

3.   יחל.   עם המדות האלה שתתנהג בשפלות בסתר ובגלוי ולא   460
יגבה לבך להרים בנפלאות.   יחל אל ה׳ והוא יתן   תוחלתך
מעתה ועד עולם;

Psalm CXXXII

1.   שיר המעלות זכור ה׳ לדוד.   אמר דוד זה המזמור כשבנה
המזבח בגרן ארונה היבוסי על פי גד הנביא והעלה עליו עולות
ושלמים וקרא אל ה׳ ויענהו באש מן השמים על מזבח העולה ואמר   465
זהו בית האלהים וזה מזבח לעולה לישראל ועד אותו היום לא
נודע מקום בית המקדש וכבר אמר לו נתן הנביא כי הוא לא יבנה
הבית כי אם שלמה בנו ׳ולפי ששם דוד כחו ויכלתו להכין בנין
הבית ונענה במקום הנבחר בקש מה׳ ואמר.   זכור ה׳ לדוד את כל
ענותו.   כיון שלא זכיתי לבנותו תעלה לי המחשבה כמעשה וזכור   470
לי מה שעניתי עצמי בעבורו כי גזלתי שנתי מעיני מרב מחשבתי
עליו ונדרתי ונשבעתי שלא אנוח עד שאבננו ולא הייתי מוצא
קרת רוח בביתי ובמשכני אחר שלא היה בית ה׳ נבנה;

2.   אשר נשבע לה׳ נדר לאביר יעקב.   כפל הענין במלות שונות
ואמר לאביר יעקב.   כלומר למי שקראהו יעקב אביר כמו שאמר   475
מידי אביר יעקב לפי שעזרו בכל צרותיו והיה חזקו ותקפו והראה
לו בדמיון .שלא יכול לו אפילו המלאך כל שכן בני אדם לכך
קראו יעקב אביר ואמר גם כן דוד לאביר יעקב ומה שזכר בזה
הענין יעקב לפי שיעקב ראה בחלום מקום בית המקדש והוא הסלם

words of our teachers, of blessed memory, the interpretation is thus:[1] *my heart was not proud*: when Samuel anointed me king; *my eyes were not haughty*: when I killed Goliath. *I do not walk about in matters too great*: when they restored me and I was initiated into the royal office. *Nor in matters too marvellous for me*: when I brought the Ark (to Jerusalem).

3. O Israel, hope in the Lord: by (following) these rules of conduct, viz. by behaving humbly in private as well as in public and in not letting your heart become so ambitious as to aspire to things too profound. *Hope in the Lord* and he will grant your expectation *from this time forth and for evermore.*

PSALM CXXXII

1. A Song of Ascents. Remember, O Lord, in David's favour: David recited this psalm when he built the altar in the threshing floor of Araunah the Jebusite, according to the word of the prophet Gad. And he sacrificed thereon whole burnt offerings and peace offerings, calling upon the Lord who answered him with fire from heaven upon the altar of burnt offerings (cf. 1 Chron. xxi 26). And he said: 'Here will be the house of the Lord God and here the altar of burnt offering for Israel' (1 Chron. xxii 1), for until that very day the site for the Temple was not known. Now the prophet Nathan had previously told him that he would not build the Temple, but Solomon his son, but since David had directed his energy and ability to the preparation for the building of the Temple and was answered in the chosen place, he besought the Lord, saying: *Remember, O Lord, in David's favour, all his adversity*: seeing that I am not privileged to erect the building, do thou account unto me the intention as the act itself and remember how I have suffered[2] on its account, for I have robbed my eyes of sleep because of much thought over the matter and I vowed and swore that I would not rest until I built it. Nor did I find contentment in my home and dwelling place because the Temple of the Lord is not yet built.

2. How he swore to the Lord and made a vow to the Mighty One of Jacob: he repeats the same thought in different words. And when he says *to the Mighty One of Jacob*, he means to him whom Jacob called *Mighty*, as it says 'by the power of the Mighty One of Jacob' (Gen. xlix 24). For he helped him in all his troubles and was his sustaining power and might, showing him in a vision that not even an angel – how much less a human being – could prevail over him. For this reason Jacob called him *Mighty One*. And thus also does David refer to him as *the Mighty One of Jacob*. Now the reason he mentions Jacob in this context is because Jacob beheld in a dream the site of the Temple, which was the ladder that he saw and of

---

[1] *Bamidbar Rabba* 4: 20.   [2] Lit. 'I afflicted myself'.

שראה ועליו אמר מה נורא המקום הזה אין זה כי אם בית אלהים 480

וזה שער השמים על בית המקדש אמר לא על בית אל שהיה שוכב

שם אבל לפי ששם ראה החלום כבד המקום ושם שם מצבה ועשה שם

מזבח ובית התפלה בשזבו מחרן ועליו אמר יהיה בית אלהים

כלומר בית התפלה לאלהים כיון שראיתי בזה המקום הנבחר שיבנה

בו בית המקדש ועיקר החלום בית המקדש הוא שראה וכן הוא אומר 485

בבראשית רבה אמר רבי יהודה בר' סימון הסלם הזה היה עומד

בבית המקדש ושפועו מגיע בבית אל רצה לומר ושפועו שנמשכה

המראה עד בית אל כי שם ראה המראה ואמר וזה שער השמים על בית

המקדש כי הוא מכון כנגד כסא הכבוד וכן אמר ירמיה הנביא

כסא כבוד מרום מראשון מקום מקדשנו והוא טבור העולם וכן 490

אמרו רבותינו ז"ל בא וראה כשם שהטבור הזה נתון באמצע הגוף

כך ארץ ישראל נתונה באמצע העולם שנאמר ישבי על טבור הארץ,

מציון מכלל יפי ארץ ישראל יושבת ביפיו של עולם וירושלים

באמצעיתה של ארץ ישראל ובית המקדש באמצע ירושלים וההיכל באמצע

בית המקדש והארון באמצע ההיכל פירושו מן הצפון לדרום ואבן 495

שתיה לפני הארון שממנה נשתת העולם וזהו שאמר בספר יצירה שש

צלעות לששה צדדים וההיכל הקדש מכון באמצע והיכל הקדש הוא הנקרא

כסא הכבוד וסודו עמוק ואף על פי שראה יעקב אבינו מקום בית

המקדש בחלום אפשר שלא ידעו בהקיץ ואם ידעו לא גלה אותו כי לא

רצה האל שיהיה נודע המקום עד דוד לפיכך זכר דוד בזה הענין 500

יעקב ואמר נדר לאביר יעקב לפי שאליו הראהו תחלה האל ואף

על פי שרמז בו לאברהם אבינו וצוה להעלות את יצחק בנו עולה

באותו המקום אף על פי כן לא נתבאר אם ידע אברהם אבינו שיהיה

המקום ההוא מקום הנבחר לבית המקדש לדורות ואם ידע כמו שרמז

483	RCDS		בית הפלה	497	R	צדדין
496	P	השתת	נשתית NR	500	B	לפיכך זכר דוד בזה הענין

which he said: 'How awesome is this place! This is none other than the house of God, and this is the gate of heaven' (Gen. xxviii 17). It was in reference to the Temple that he said this and not concerning Bethel where he slept. Since, however, it was there that he saw the vision, he honoured that place and erected there a pillar and made an altar and a house of prayer when he returned from Haran. And concerning it he said: 'It will be God's house' (Gen. xxviii 22), that is to say, a house of prayer to God, for I see that this is the chosen place where the Temple will be built. Thus the essence of the dream is that he saw the Temple. And so in *Bereshith Rabba* it says:[1] 'Rabbi Judah ben Simon said: "This ladder stood upon the Temple (site) and its incline reached as far as Bethel"', meaning that its incline was extended out so that the spectacle could be seen as far as Bethel, for there it was that he saw the spectacle. Thus when Jacob says 'and this is the gate of heaven' (Gen. xxviii 17), it is a reference to the Temple, since its location corresponds with that of the Throne of Glory. Similarly, Jeremiah the prophet said 'a glorious throne set on high from the beginning is the place of our sanctuary' (Jer. xvii 12). It is at the centre of the world. And so our teachers, of blessed memory, have commented:[2] 'Come and see! Just as the navel is located in the middle of the body, so the land of Israel is situated in the centre of the world, as it is said "Who dwell in the centre of the earth" (Ezek. xxxviii 12), "Out of Zion, the perfection of beauty" (Ps. l 2). The land of Israel is situated amid the beauty of the world, Jerusalem is the centre of the land of Israel, the Temple area is in the centre of Jerusalem, the Temple is the centre of the Temple area and the Ark is in the centre of the Temple, that is, facing from north to south, and in front of the Ark is the foundation stone upon which the universe is founded.' And this is what is meant by the statement in the book *Yetzira*:[3] 'Six wings of the building corresponding to the six directions, the *hekal haqqodesh* being situated in the centre.' And the *hekal haqqodesh* is usually referred to as the Throne of Glory. Now in all this there is a deeply profound meaning. Although our father Jacob saw in a dream the site of the Temple, it is possible that he was unaware of it on waking up. But if he did know of it, he certainly did not reveal it (to anyone), for God did not wish it to be known until (the time of) David. For this reason, therefore, David refers to Jacob in this context and says: *made a vow to the Mighty One of Jacob*, since it was to him that God showed it first. For although he had hinted at it to Abraham our father, commanding him to offer his son Isaac as a sacrifice in that place, yet it is not certain that our father Abraham knew that that place was chosen for the Temple for all time. But if he

---

[1] *Bereshith Rabba* 69: 7.
[2] *Tanḥuma, Kedoshim* 10.
[3] *Nezikin* 4: 3. Edited by L. Goldschmidt, *Das Buch der Schöpfung* (Frankfort 1894), p. 60.

505   הר ה׳ יראה לא גלה הדבר לאדם. ובדברי רבותינו ז"ל נדר

אביר יעקב. אמר רבי אבהו לאביר אברהם לאביר יצחק לא נאמר

לא לאביר יעקב תלה את הנדר במי שפתח בו תחלה יעקב היה תחלה

נודרים שנאמר וידר יעקב נדר לאמר מהו לאמר לדורות שיהיו

ודרים בעת צרתם יעקב פתח בנדר תחלה לפיכך כל מי שהוא נודר

510   א יהיה תולה את הנדר אלא בו;

. אם אבא באהל ביתי. כמו שאמר אל נתן הנביא הנה אנכי יושב

בית ארזים וארון האלהים יושב בתוך היריעה. ומה שאמר אם

בא, אם אעלה דרך הפלגה כלומר שלא יערב לו שבתו בביתו

נומו על ערש יצועיו עד שימצא מקום לה׳ ואמר ערש יצועי.

515   רש שיש בו מצעות נכבדות הראויות למלך זהו יצועי;

. אם אתן שנת לעיני. רוצה לומר שנה קבועה הת"ו במקום ה"א

אינה לסמיכות וכן שפת לא ידעתי אשמע, רבת תעשרנה, חכמת ודעת,

הדומים להם כמו שכתבנו בספר מכלול. לעפעפי תנומה. כפל

נין במלות שונות;

520   . עד אמצע מקום לה׳. המקום הנבחר. משכנות. כי היו שלשה

תים ומה שאמר לאביר יעקב בזה הפסוק מוכיח מה שפירשתי כי מה

אמרו רבותינו ז"ל אין לו מקום בזה הפסוק;

. הנה שמענוה באפרתה. פירש רבי משה בן גקטלא שמענוה על ידי

וד שהיה מאפרת ואדוני אבי ז"ל פירש כי באפרת יולד מי שיבנה

507   C   יעקב הוא היה   515   R   ו ערש יצועי

513   RMAC   הוא דרך הפלגה   516   BRMAC   י"ו ... בספר מכלול ח׳

515   B ׳מ יצועי בו שיש ערש after יצועי

knew, as indeed it is hinted in 'On the mount of the Lord it shall be seen' (Gen. xxii 14), he did not reveal it to anyone. In the words of our teachers, of blessed memory:[1] *made a vow to the Mighty One of Jacob*: Rabbi Abuhu said: It does not say 'to the Mighty One of Abraham' or 'to the Mighty One of Isaac', but 'to the Mighty One of Jacob', (that is) he associates the vow with the one who was the first to pronounce it. Jacob was the first to make vows, as it is said 'Then Jacob made a vow, saying' (Gen. xxviii 20). And what is the significance of *le'mor* 'saying'? It is to make known (*le'mor*) to succeeding generations that they should offer vows in the time of their distress. Jacob was the first to make a vow. Accordingly, he who makes a vow should associate it with none but him.

3. I will not enter my house: just as he said to the prophet Nathan: 'See now, I dwell in a house of cedar, but the Ark of God dwells in a tent' (2 Sam. vii 2). And when he says *I will not enter . . . I will not get into*, it is to be understood by way of hyperbole. That is to say, he derives no contentment from dwelling in his home or slumbering on the couch of his bed until he finds a place for the Lord. And when he says '*ereś y^eṣu'ay*, he means a couch with commodious mattresses such as become a king. This is (the correct meaning of) *y^eṣu'ay*.

4. I will not give sleep to my eyes: he means to say 'regular sleep'. The *tau* (in *sh^enath*) is in place of *he* and is not an indication of the construct state, just as (*tau* is used instead of *he* in) 'I hear a language (*s^ephath*) I do not know' (Ps. lxxxi 6), 'thou greatly (*rabbath*) enrichest it' (Ps. lxv 10), 'wisdom (*ḥokmath*) and knowledge' (Isa. xxxiii 6), and many similar instances which we have noted in the book *Miklol*. *Or slumber to my eyelids*: he repeats the same thought in different words.

5. Until I find a place for the Lord: (that is) the chosen place. *Dwelling places*: (plural) because there were three houses.[2] As for the reference in this verse to *the Mighty One of Jacob*, it confirms my explanation (set forth above), for the interpretation offered by our teachers, of blessed memory, does not apply fittingly to this verse.[3]

6. We heard of it in Ephrathah: Rabbi Moses Ibn Giḳatilla interprets *we heard of it in Ephrathah* thus: *we heard of it* through David who was from Ephrathah. My revered father, of blessed memory, explains the passage as meaning that in Ephrath will be born the person who is to build it. And

---

[1] *Bereshith Rabba* 70: 1.
[2] The three major parts of the Temple: the *'ulam*, or porch; the *hekal*, the temple proper; and the *debir*, inner sanctuary.
[3] Lit. 'there is not a place for it in this verse'.

525 אותו. והחכם רבי אברהם בן עזרא פירש כי שמעו מפי הנביאים כי
המקום הנבחר קרוב לבית לחם אפרתה רק לא היה נודע אם למזרח
בית לחם או למערבו או לדרומו או לצפונו וידוע הוא כי אין בין
ירושלים ובין בית לחם כי אם שלש פרסאות ובדברי רבותינו ז"ל
הנה שמעונה באפרתה זה ספר יהושע דקאתי מאפרים דכתיב בחלק
530 יהודה ועלה הגבול גיא בן הנם ובחלק בנימין וירד גיא בן הנם
וביניהם היה בית המקדש. מצאנוה בשדה יער. זה בנימין דכתיב
בית זאב יטרף והנראה בעיני כי פירוש שמעונה באפרתה כן הוא.
אמר דוד זה המקום לא ידענוהו עד היום רק שמענו באפרת עירנו כי
עתיד להיות מקום נבחר לבית המקדש לדורות כי אין שילה ונב
535 וגבעון לדורות רק היינו שומעים מפי זקנים בעירנו כי עוד יגלה
המקום הנבחר והנה עתה מצאנוה בשדה יער בגרן ארונה היבוסי.
וקראו יער כי עצי יער היו שם לפיכך אמר באפרתה כי שם נולד
דוד ושם גדל ושם שמע זה הדבר. ומה שאמר מצאנוה שמעונה לשון
נקבה רוצה לומר שכינת הכבוד כי זכר משכנותיו ושם מצא אותה
540 שנאמר ויענהו באש מן השמים;

7. נבואה למשכנותיו. כיון שמצאנו המקום הנבחר נבואה מהיום
ואילך בזה המקום שהוא משכנותיו והדם רגליו. זהו הדם רגליו
באמת שהוא מכון כנגד כסא הכבוד;

8. קומה ה'. אלה שלשה הפסוקים אמרם גם כן שלמה בבית המקדש
545 בחנכתו כמו שכתוב בדברי הימים אלא שיש בין אותם הפסוקים ובין
אלה שנוי מעט והענין אחד אמר דרך משל קומה למנוחתך. כלומר
מהמקומות האחרים שהיה המשכן לזה המקום שהוא בית מנוחתך

525	BRMCS	נביאים	539	M
528	BNRPCS	רק שלש פרסאות	544	MS
534	C	כי אין זה שילה		ND
537	RPMC	וכן נאמר באילו של יצחק נאחז מ'		
		בסבך בקרניו נראה כי עצי יער היו שם		
		after היו שם		

כלומר שכינת הכבוד	
אלה השלשה הפסוקים	
אלה שלשה הפסוקים	

the learned Abraham Ibn Ezra considers it to mean that they heard from the prophets that the chosen place was in the neighbourhood of Bethlehem Ephrathah but that it was not known whether it would be to the east of Bethlehem, or to the west of it, or to the south or to the north, for it is well known that between Jerusalem and Bethlehem there is a distance of only three miles. According to the words of our teachers, of blessed memory, (the meaning is):[1] *we heard of it in Ephrathah*: this is (a reference to) the book of Joshua who comes from Ephraim, for it is written of the (territory) allocated[2] to Judah 'then the boundary goes up by the valley of the son of Hinnom' (Josh. xv 8), whilst of the (territory) allocated[2] to Benjamin it says 'and it goes down the valley of the son of Hinnom' (Josh. xviii 16). The Temple was therefore situated between these two (territories). *We found it in the region of Jaar*: this is in Benjamin, as it is written of him '(Benjamin) is a ravening wolf' (Gen. xlix 27).[3] But to my mind the (most plausible) interpretation of *we heard of it in Ephrathah* is: David said: As for this place, we had not definitely known it to this day, having only heard in our city Ephrath that some place or other would be duly chosen for the Temple throughout the generations, since neither Shiloh nor Nob nor Gibeon are (to serve as sanctuaries) for all time to come. This much only we used to hear from the elders in our city, that the chosen site would yet be revealed. And lo! now *we have found it in the region of Jaar* in the threshing floor of Araunah the Jebusite. He calls it Jaar because forest trees were to be found there. Accordingly, it says *in Ephrathah*, for there David was born, there he grew up and there he heard of this tradition. And the feminine suffix in m^e*ṣa'nuha* and sh^e*ma'^{a}nuha* is to be understood as referring to the Glorious Presence (sh^e*kinath hakabod*), since he refers to *his dwelling place* (*mishk^{e}nothaw*). And it was there that he found it, as it is said 'and he answered him with fire from heaven' (1 Chron. xxi 26).

7. Let us go to his dwelling place: since we have found the chosen site, let us go from now onwards to this place which is *his dwelling place* and his *footstool*. It is indeed his *footstool*, for it corresponds in its location with the *Throne of Glory*.

8. Arise, O Lord: these three verses were recited by Solomon also in the Temple at the dedication of it, as it is written in the book of Chronicles (2 Chron. vi 41–3) except that there is a slight variation between these verses and the above, the meaning, however, being the same. He says metaphorically *Arise, O Lord, to thy resting place*: meaning: from the other places where the Tabernacle had resided to this place which is *thy resting*

---

[1] *Zebaḥim* 54b.   [2] Lit. 'the portion of. . .'.
[3] Presumably the point of the reference is that a forest (*ya'ar*) was where wolves were to be found.

לעולם. אתה וארון עזך. אתה   רוצה לומר ענן הכבוד שנראה
בחנכת בית המקדש אחר שהכניסו הארון בבית קדשי הקדשים זהו
ארון עזך כמו שכתוב ויהי בצאת הכהנים מן הקדש והענן מלא את   550
בית ה';

9. כהניך. בעבודתם ילבשו צדק כהונה שהם בגדי צדק.
וחסידיך ירננו. הלוים ישירו ויזמרו לפניך בעבור דוד שנגלית
לו בזה המקום באש כבודך וגלית לו זה המקום הנבחר בעבורו תעשה   555
שיהיה זה המקום לנצח לא תבטל ממנו עבודת הכהנים ושירת הלוים;

10. אל תשב פני משיחך.   מה שהתפללתי לך על זה המקום ומה
שיתפלל שלמה בני עליו על תשב פנינו בזה שתהיה תפלתנו מקבלת
לפניך ואלה הפסוקים כמו שאמרם דוד אמרם שלמה בתכלית תפלתו;

11. נשבע ה'.   דברו הוא שבועה והוא אמר לו על ידי נתן הנביא
והקימותי את זרעך אחריך אשר יצא ממעיך.   זהו   מפרי בטנך אשית   560
לכסא לך.   ואמר   אמת לא ישוב ממנה   כמו שאמר שם ונאמן ביתך
וממלכתך עד עולם;

12. אם ישמרו.   עדותי זה אלמדם.   עדותי בחול"ם כמו בשר"ק
ארון העדות זו בחולם כמו זאת ואמר   אלמדם   והברית והעדות כתובות
הם ומלומדות ואין מצוה עתידה ללמדה אחר תורת משה אלא פירוש   565
אלמדם.   אעורר אותם על ידי הנביאים תמיד שלא ישכחו התורה;

13. כי בחר ה' בציון.   אמר דוד עתה ידעתי כי בחר ה' בציון

548 BRAS בחנכת המקדש BPS 549. ענין הכבוד	557 BND	פניו
553 R וחסידיך. הלוים. ירננו. ישירו ויזמרו	558 N	כן אמרם שלמה
555 BPS ושירות	559 RMC	השבועה

place for ever. Thou and the Ark of thy power: thou, etc.: he means to say, the cloud of glory which appeared at the dedication of the Temple after they had brought the Ark into the Holy of Holies. And this is (what is meant by) *the Ark of thy power,* just as it is written 'and when the priests came out of the holy place, a cloud filled the house of the Lord' (1 Kgs. viii 10).

9. Thy priests: in the performance of *Abodah*[1] *will be clothed in righteousness,* (that is) priestly robes, since they are the robes of *righteousness. And thy loyal servants will shout for joy:* the levites will sing and offer praises to thee. *For thy servant David's sake:* because thou didst appear to him in this place and in the fire of thy Glory and didst reveal to him this chosen place. For his sake bring it about that this place continue through all eternity and never abolish from it the service of the priests or the songs of the levites.

10. Do not turn away the face of thine anointed one: as for the prayer which I make for the sake of this place and the prayer which my son Solomon will make on its account, *turn not away* our faces in this regard, so that our prayer may be acceptable to thee. Now these verses, just as they were recited by David were (also) recited by Solomon at the conclusion of his (own) prayer (cf. 1 Chron. vi 41-2).

11. The Lord swore: his word is an oath. (He says *swore* because) he had promised[2] him through the prophet Nathan 'and I will raise up your offspring after you, who will come forth from your body' (2 Sam. vii 12). And this is (the meaning of) *of the fruit of your body I will set on your throne.* And he says *in truth he will turn back from it,* just as it says 'and your house and your kingdom will be made sure for ever' (2 Sam. vii 16).

12. If they keep . . . and my decree which I shall teach them: *'edothi* is written with *ḥolem* but is the same as with *Shureq,* (as in) *'aron ha'eduth* (Exod. xxvi 33; xl 21; Josh. iv 16). *Zo* with *ḥolem* is equivalent to 'this'. And he says: *I shall teach them:* now the covenant and the decree have already been written down and taught and there is no further commandment which is to be taught at any time subsequent to (the revelation of) the Law of Moses. But the meaning of *I shall teach them* is: I shall exhort them from time to time through the prophets that they may not forget the *Torah.*

13. For the Lord has chosen Zion: David said: now I know that *the*

---

[1] *'abodah* = 'service', more particularly the service of the priests in the Temple.
[2] Lit. 'for he told him'.

שלכדתי אני כי בעיר ציון נגלה מקום השכינה ואוה אותה האל למושב
לו ואמר עליה:

14.   זאת מנוחתי עדי עד. שלא ילך הארון ממקום למקום כמו שעשה   570
עד עתה;

15.   צידה.   במפיק הה"א והוא מן ביום מכרם ציד שפירושו מזון
אמר האל ציד ציון אברך כלומר אשלח ברכה בתבואתה ובפירותיה יותר
מכל ארץ ישראל לכבוד ביתי שהיא בתוכה ואולי לכך נקראה ארץ
המוריה שהיתה ארץ רויה אחר ששכן בה הכבוד.   אביוניה.   אפילו   575
העניים שבה ישבעו לחם;

16.   וכהניה.   תחת שהם לובשים בעבורי בגדי כהונה אני אלבישם
בגדי ישע שיהיו נושעים בי.   וחסידיה רנן ירננו. הלוים תחת שהם
מרננים ומזמרים לשמי אני אשפיע להם טובה שירננו מטוב לב וקרא
הלוים חסידים כמו שאמר משה רבנו לאיש חסידך;   580

17.   שם אצמיח קרן לדוד.   קרן חזק ומלכות וכן אצמיח קרן לבית
ישראל וכן וירם קרן משיחו ואמר זה הפסוק על המשיח העתיד לפיכך
אמר אצמיח כלומר אף על פי שייבש זה כמה עוד אצמיחנו וכן נאמר
עליו והקימותי לדוד צמח צדיק ונאמר עליו בימים ההם ובעת ההיא
אצמיח לדוד צמח צדקה ואמר שם כי בציון יהיה כמו שכתוב ועלו   585
מושיעים בהר ציון וכן כתוב בימים ההם תושע יהודה וירושלים
תשכון לבטח וזה אשר יקרא לה ה' צדקנו המשיח יקרא צמח צדקה

570	RPMC	שלא ילך עוד הארון	579	R	אשביע
572	BAD	ה"א	ואמר האל B‏ 573.	580	R	משה רבנו עליו השלום
573	N	משלח ברכה בשדותיה	582	R	המשיח העתיד להגלות
574	NMC	שהוא בה	582	BMCS	משיח העתיד
576	B	אשביע לחם	587	B	המשיח ... צדקנו ח'
577	B	לבושים			

Lord has chosen Zion which I myself have captured, for in the city of Zion the place of the Shekinah was revealed and God *desired it for his habitation*. And concerning it he says:

14. This is my resting place for ever: the Ark will no longer move from place to place as it formerly did.

15. Her provisions: *ṣedah* has *mappiq* in the *he*. Its (meaning may be illustrated) from 'on the day they sold food (*ṣayid*)' (Neh. xiii 15) where the meaning (of *ṣayid*) is 'provisions'. Thus God says: *I will bless the provisions of Zion*, that is to say, I will send a blessing on her produce and her fruits more so than in the rest of the land of Israel, out of regard for[1] my house which is in her midst. It is possibly because of this that (Zion) is called *'ereṣ hammoriyyah* (2 Chron. iii 1), for it was a fertile[2] (area of) land since the Divine Presence dwelt there. *Her needy*: even the *needy* who (dwell) in her shall have bread in plenty.

16. Her priests: since they put on the priestly garments for my sake, so *will I clothe them* with the garment of salvation, that is, they will find salvation in me. *And her loyal servants will shout for joy*: as for the levites, since they shout for joy and sing praises unto my name, I will bestow upon them abundant goodness, that they may shout for joy of heart. And he refers to the levites as *ḥᵃsidim* in the same way as our teacher Moses said *lᵉ'ish ḥᵃsideka* 'thy loyal servant' (of Levi) (Deut. xxxiii 8).

17. There I will make a horn to sprout for David: *horn* (symbolises) power and sovereignty, as in 'I will cause a horn to spring forth for the house of Israel' (Ezek. xxix 21), and 'and exalt the horn of his anointed' (1 Sam. ii 10). He says this verse with reference to the Messiah (who will come) at some future time. Therefore he says *I will cause to sprout*, that is to say, though it be withered for some time (past) yet will I cause it to bud. And it is also said concerning him: 'and I will raise up for David a righteous branch' (Jer. xxiii 5). And it says further of him: 'In those days and at that time I will cause a righteous branch to spring forth for David' (Jer. xxxiii 15). The prophet also declares (in this same passage) that all this will occur in Zion[3] as indeed it states (elsewhere): 'saviours will go up to Mount Zion' (Obad. i 21). And thus it is written: 'In those days Judah will be saved and Jerusalem will dwell securely. And this is the name by which it will be called: "The Lord is our righteousness"' (Jer. xxxiii 16), (that is) the Messiah is referred to as 'a righteous branch' and Jerusalem as 'the Lord

---

[1] Lit. 'in honour of'.

[2] Kimḥi is here interpreting *moriyah* from *rawah* = 'to be moist', 'saturated'.

[3] Lit. 'and he says there that this will come to pass in Zion'.

וירושלים ה׳ צדקנו. ערכתי נר למשיחי. כמו שאמר למען היות ניר
לדוד עבדי כי המלך כמו הנר מאיר לעם;

590 18. אויביו אלביש בשת. הפך מה שאמר אלביש ישע לכהניה המשרתים
את פני ה׳ ומתפללים בעד המלך ואויבי המלך אלביש בשת. ועליו
יציץ נזרו. ועל המלך יפרח ויציץ נזרו שעל ראשו כלומר תרבה
גדולתו והדרתו בכל יום ויש מפרשים יציץ ציץ זהב טהור;

Psalm CXXXIII

1. שיר המעלות לדוד הנה מה טוב ומה נעים. פירש אדוני אבי ז״ל
595 כי על ישראל נאמר שהם כלם אחים אמר שיהיה שבתם בירושלים יחד.
טוב ונעים. כמו השמן הטוב היורד על זקן אהרן ועל בגדיו או כטל
חרמון שיורד עליו וכטל שיורד על הררי ציון שהוא מברך מכל טל
שיהיה יורד בעולם והחכם רבי אברהם בן עזרא פירש כי הענין דבק
למעלה שזכר הכהנים ואמר אחים על חברת הכהנים וטעם גם על הכהן
600 הגדול והזכיר אהרן כי הוא היה ראש המשוחים והנראה בעיני כי על
המלך המשיח ועל הכהן הגדול שיהיה בימיו מדבר כי שניהם גדולים
אשר בישראל ואדונים עליהם כי המלך יושב על כסא המשפט והמלוכה
לצוות את ישראל לאשר יראה והכהן הגדול יורה התורה והמצות וקראם
אחים שהם אחים בגדולה ולא יקנאו זה לזה וכן כשעלו מגלות בבל נבא
605 זכריה על שניהם על זרבבל הנשיא ועל יהושע הכהן הגדול וראה אותם
כשני זיתים וקראם שני בני היצהר לפי ששניהם משוחים בשמן המשחה
זה למלוכה וזה לכהונה ואמר ועשית עטרות ושמת בראש יהושע בן
יהוצדק הכהן הגדול כלומר האחת צוה לשום בראש יהושע והאחת על איש

597 R מכל טל שיורד   מכל טל שהיה יורד B   606 BNRPDS שני זיתים
599 B   חבורה   607 B   זה לכהונה וזה למלוכה
600 B   והזכיר אהרן כהן גדול 608 RMC והאחרת על איש
603 N   לאשר ירצה

is our righteousness'. *I have prepared a lamp for my anointed*: just as it says: 'that David my servant may have a lamp' (1 Kgs. xi 36), for the king, like *a lamp*, gives light to the people.

18. His enemies will I clothe with shame: in contrast to what he says *I will clothe with salvation* the *priests* who minister unto the Lord and pray on behalf of the king. But as for the king's *enemies*, them *will I clothe with shame. But upon himself his crown will flourish*: upon the king *his crown* which is upon his head will prosper and flourish, that is to say, thou shalt increase his grandeur and majesty from day to day.[1] But some commentators interpret *yaṣiṣ* from 'and you will make a diadem (*ṣiṣ*) of pure gold' (Exod. xxviii 36).

PSALM CXXXIII

1. A Song of Ascents. Of David. Behold, how good and pleasant it is: my revered father, of blessed memory, explains that this was recited with reference to Israel because they were all brethren. (The psalmist) says that their dwelling together in Jerusalem will be *good and pleasant*, like *the good oil which runs down upon the beard of Aaron* and upon his robes, or *like the dew of Hermon* which falls upon it, or like the dew *which falls on the hills of Zion*, which is more refreshing[2] than any other dew falling upon the earth. But the learned Abraham Ibn Ezra considers that the meaning (is to be understood) in connection with (the passage in) the preceding (psalm) in which he speaks of the priests (cf. Ps. cxxxii 16). Thus he says *brethren* with reference to the company of priests, whilst the particle *gam* 'also' is intended as an allusion to the high priest.[3] And he mentions Aaron because he was the first to be anointed. But to my mind (the psalmist) is here speaking of the Messianic King and the high priest who will live in his time, since both of them are the leaders in Israel and rulers over them, for the King occupies the seat of justice and authority to give to Israel such commands as seem proper to him, whilst the high priest instructs them in the *Torah* and *Miṣwoth*. He calls them *brethren* since they exercise their power jointly and are not jealous one of the other. And likewise, after the return of the exiles from Babylon, Zechariah prophesied regarding both of them, that is, Zerubbabel the Nasi[4] and Joshua the high priest, for he saw them in a vision as two olives, referring to them as 'the two sons of oil' (Zech. iv 14), since they were both anointed with the anointing oil, the one for the kingship and the other for the priesthood. And it says further: 'and make crowns and set the one upon the head of Joshua son of Jehozadak, the high priest' (Zech. vi 11), that is to say, he commanded the one to be

---

[1] Lit. 'each day'.   [2] Lit. 'more blessed'.
[3] Lit. 'and the sense of *gam* is concerning the high priest'.
[4] Nasi = 'prince, ruler'. Used particularly of the chief of the Great Sanhedrin.

שיהיה צמח שמו וזה יהיה זרבבל כי אמר על העתיד על המלך ועל הכהן
הגדול שבת אחים כי כל אחד מהם ישב על כסא גדולה ומה טוב ומה   610
נעים שבתם ואמר גם יחד כי כמו שיהיו אחים בגדולה כן יהיו אחים
בלבותם ויהיו יחד בהסכמה אחת לא יקנא אחד מהם על חברו וכן אמר
על זרבבל ויהושע ועצת שלום תהיה בין שניהם;

2. כשמן.   בפתח הכ"ף להורות על ה"א הידיעה השמן הידוע והוא
שמן המשחה אמר כן יהיה טוב ונעים שבת אלה האחים כמו שהיה טוב   615
ונעים משיחת אהרן הכהן ביום שנתמנה לכהן גדול וזכר משיחת הכהן
ולא זכר משיחת המלך דוד לשני טעמים האחד לפי שמשיחת אהרן היתה
תחלה והיתה העת שחנה הכבוד בישראל כשהוקם המשכן כן לעתיד
כשיבנה בית המקדש ויעמוד המלך המשיח והכהן הגדול יחנה שם הכבוד
ועוד לטעם אחר כי משיחת אהרן היתה לעיני כל ישראל ומשיחת דוד   620
היתה בסתר לפני ישי ובניו וזקני בית לחם ולעתיד יהיה הדבר
בגלוי לעיני כל ישראל ולעיני העמים. על הראש. שיצק משה אותו
על ראש אהרן ירד לו על זקנו ועל פי בגדיו כי תחלה הלבישו בגדי
כהונה ואחר כך יצק השמן על ראשו ומשח אותו מן השמן בין ריסי
עיניו כמו כ"ף יונית והשמן שיצק על ראשו ירד על זקנו ועל פי   625
מדותיו תחת הזקן ופי הבגד הוא בית הצואר והיה השמן מרקח
מבשם טוב ונעים. מדותיו. בגדיו כמו מדו בד;

3. כטל חרמון.   כטל עומד במקום שנים כאלו אמר כטל חרמון וכטל
שירד על הררי ציון וזכר חרמון שהוא מן ההרים הגדולים אשר בארץ
ישראל כמו שאמר תבור וחרמון בשמך ירננו וזכר הררי ציון כי שם   630
תהיה המלוכה ואמר הררי רבים כמו שאמר ירושלים הרים סביב לה

put upon the head of Joshua and the other upon a man 'whose name is the Branch' (Zech. vi 12), and this can refer only to Zerubbabel, since he speaks of the future with reference to the King and the high priest. *The dwelling of brethren*: for each one of them will occupy a seat of dignity, and *how good and pleasant* will be their *dwelling*! He employs the words[1] 'also together' for the following reason: just as they are equal in power, so will they be alike in their thoughts and of one accord; neither will the one be jealous of his associate. So also it says of Zerubbabel and Joshua: 'and peaceful understanding will be between them' (Zech. vi 13).

2. **Like the oil**: with *pathaḥ* under the *kaph* to indicate the definite article, that is, to indicate the celebrated oil, viz. the anointing oil. He says: so will *the dwelling of* these *brethren be good and pleasant*, just as the anointing of Aaron on the day that he was appointed high priest was *good and pleasant*. He refers to the anointing of the priest but not to the anointing of king David for two reasons. In the first place, the anointing of Aaron came first and took place at the time when the *Shekinah* resided in Israel, (that is) when the Tabernacle was in existence.[2] So also, at some future time, when the Temple will be rebuilt and the Messianic King and the high priest take their stand together, the Divine Presence[3] will once more dwell there. And again, for a further reason, viz. because the anointing of Aaron was performed in the presence of all Israel, whilst that of David took place secretly before Jesse and his sons and the elders of Bethlehem. But in the future to come, the event will be (celebrated) in public before the eyes of all Israel and in the presence of all the peoples. *Upon the head*: when Moses poured the oil upon Aaron's head it flowed down upon his beard and *the collar of his vestments*. For he first invested him with the priestly garments and then proceeded to pour oil upon his head, anointing him with oil between his eyelids in the shape of a Greek *chi* (χ).[4] And the oil which he poured on his head ran down upon his beard and the *collar of his vestments* beneath his beard. The *pi* of the garment is where the neck is.[5] And the oil was spiced and perfumed, being good and pleasant. *Middothaw* (means) 'his robes', as in *middo bad* 'his linen garment' (Lev. vi 3 (EVV 10)).

3. **Like the dew of Hermon**: *keṭal* (*like the dew*) is to be understood again[6] as though he were to say *like the dew of Hermon* and *like the dew which falls upon the hills of Zion*. He mentions Hermon because it was one of the greatest mountains in the land of Israel, as it says: 'Tabor and Hermon joyously praise thy name' (Ps. lxxxix 13), whilst he refers to the hills of Zion because the kingdom will be there. And he says *harre* 'hills', plural,

---

[1] Lit. 'and he says'.
[2] Lit. 'when the Tabernacle was erected'.
[3] Lit. 'the Glory'.
[4] See *Horayoth* 12a.
[5] Lit. 'the house of the neck'.
[6] Lit. 'stands in the place of two'.

וכבר זכר משל השמן שהוא משל לכהן גדול וזכר עתה הטל משל על
המלך כמו שכתוב נהם ככפיר זעף מלך וכטל על עשב רצונו ועוד כי
הגאולה נמשלה לטל כמו שאמר כטל מאת ה׳ וזכר טל ההרים שהוא
בהם לברכה והם צריכים לו יותר מן העמקים וארץ המישור. כי שם.
שם בהררי ציון צוה ה׳ את הברכה צוה ויצוה לעתיד.   יצוה שם
את הברכה ויצום שם חיים עד העולם ופירוש עד העולם זמן רב
כמו שכתוב כי כימי העץ ימי עמי ומעשה ידיהם יבלו בחירי או
יהיה פירוש עד העולם לעולם הבא;

635

Psalm CXXXIV

1. שיר המעלות הנה ברכו את ה׳. הנה כאשר יצוה ה׳ לכם את
הברכה ברכוהו גם אתם בתהלתכם כל אחד לפי שכלו לפיכך זכר
כל עבדי ה׳ והם החכמים והחסידים העומדים ממטתם בלילות
ובאים להתפלל לבית ה׳ ולהודות לשמו;

640

2. שאו ידכם. חסר יו׳ד הרבים. קדש. פירשו במקום הקדש
ופירשו שאו ידכם נשיאות כפים שהיו הכהנים נושאים כפיהם
ומברכים את ישראל ולפי דעתי כי פירושו נשיאות ידים לאל
בתפלה על דרך נשא לבבנו אל כפים שפירושו עם כפים וכן בנשאי
ידי אל דביר קדשך וכן אמר שטחתי אליך כפי ויתכן לפרש קדש
אל מקום הקדש כמו שאמר אל דביר קדשך;

645

3. יברכך ה׳. לדעת המפרשים יהיה פירושו שהכהנים יאמרו
לישראל בברכתם יברכך ה׳ ולפירושנו הם דברי המשורר שאמר
ברכו את ה׳ אמר אם תברכוהו הוא יברך אתכם ופירוש מציון כי
שם הכבוד ומשם תבוא הברכה לכל ישראל ואמר עשה שמים וארץ.

650

632	NPD	וכבר זכר השמן	643	B	פירושו במקום הקדש
632	NPD	הטל שהוא משל		C	ופירוש קדש במקום הקדש
635	B	צוה ויצוה ... הברכה ח׳	652	NRMCDS	לכל הארץ
640	B	כפי			

just as it says 'as the hills are round about Jerusalem' (Ps. cxxv 2). Earlier (in the psalm) he refers figuratively to *the oil* to denote the high priest, and now he speaks of *the dew* which is a figurative expression for the king, even as it is written: 'A king's wrath is like the growling of a lion, but his favour is *like dew* upon the grass' (Prov. xix 12). Moreover, the Redemption has also been compared to dew, as it says: 'as dew from the Lord' (Mic. v 6 (EVV 7)). He refers (particularly) to dew upon the mountains, which is a blessing there because they are more in need of it than the valleys or plains. *For there*: there in the hills of Zion *the Lord has commanded the blessing. He has commanded* and will yet command again in the future. He will command there *the blessing*, even *life for evermore*. The interpretation of *'ad ha'olam* is a long period, just as it is written: 'for like the days of a tree shall the days of my people be, and my chosen will long enjoy the work of their hands' (Isa. lxv 22); or perhaps *'ad ha'olam* means the world to come.

PSALM CXXXIV

1. A Song of Ascents. Behold, bless the Lord: *Behold*: when the Lord commands you the blessing,[1] you should, on your part, bless him by saying the psalms of praise, each one according to his ability. This is why he refers to *all you servants of the Lord*: these are the wise and pious men who get up from their beds *in the night* and come to pray *in the house of the Lord* and to praise his name.

2. Lift up your hands: *y'dekem*: the *yod* of the plural is omitted. Some explain the meaning of *qodesh* as 'in the sanctuary' and the meaning of *s'e'u y'dekem* as the lifting up of the hands, since the priests used to raise their hands as they blessed Israel. But in my opinion its interpretation is (rather) the lifting up of the hands in prayer to God, on the analogy of 'let us lift up our hearts and hands' (Lam. iii 41), taking *'el kappayim* as equivalent to *'im kappayim* – so also 'when I lift up my hands toward thy most holy sanctuary' (Ps. xxviii 2). And also it says: 'I spread out my hands to thee' (Ps. lxxxviii 10). And *qodesh* is best understood as *'el m'qom haqqodesh* 'toward the sanctuary', just as it says: 'toward thy most holy sanctuary' (Ps. xxviii 2).

3. The Lord bless you: in the opinion of the commentators, the meaning is that the priests say to Israel as they bless them: *the Lord bless you*. But according to our interpretation they are the words of the psalmist who says (earlier): *Bless the Lord*. What is meant therefore is:[2] if you bless him, he will bless you. And the interpretation of *from Zion* is: since the Glory is there, the blessing for all Israel will come from there. He says: *who made*

---

[1] Cf. Psalm cxxxiii 3.   [2] Lit. 'he says'.

כלומר כי הוא עושה השמים שנותנים הברכה לעולם והוא עושה
הארץ שתתן יבולה לברכה כאשר יצוה הוא יתברך;

Psalm CXXXV

655

1. הללויה הללו את שם ה׳ הללו עבדי ה׳.   מזמור קי"ג הוא
הללו עבדי ה׳ תחלה ואחריו הללו את שם ה׳ לסמיכות הבא אחריו
יהי   שם ה׳ מברך ובמזמור הזה הללו את שם ה׳ תחלה ואחריו
הללו עבדי ה׳ לסמיכות הבא אחריו שעומדים בבית ה׳.

2. שעמדים.   אתם שעומדים בבית ה׳ והם הכהנים.   בחצרות.

660

ואתם שעומדים בחצרות בית אלהינו והם ישראל שהיו מתפללים
בעזרות שלא היו נכנסים להיכל לכלכם אני אומר;

3. הללויה כי טוב ה׳.   וזה אומר כנגד העתידים לעמוד בבית
ה׳ שיבנה שלמה או לעתיד בבית המקדש שיבנה המלך המשיח.   אמר
כי טוב ה׳ וראוי להללו כי הוא טוב ומטיב וכן שמו נעים וראוי

665

להללו והוא שמו ושמו הוא והפסוק כפול בענין במלות שונות;

4. כי יעקב.   ואתם ראויים להללו על כל עם כי אתכם בחר
מכל העמים;

5. כי אני ידעתי.   אמר המשורר המזהיר לכך אני מזהירכם
שתהללוהו ותשבחוהו כי אני ידעתיו מנפלאותיו וממעשיו.   כי

670

גדול הוא.   ואדננו.   שקבלנו אותו עלינו לאדון ולאלהים כי
שאר העמים קבלו לאדון ולאלהים צבא השמים כל אחד לפי מנהגו
אבל אנחנו לא קבלנו עלינו לאדון אלא השם המיחד שהוא גדול
מכל אלהים.   והם צבא השמים והמלאכים המנהיגים העולם.   לכך
נקראו אלהים ואדננו גדול מכלם כי לא יעשו הם דבר אלא בכחו
ובמצותו;

675

6. כל אשר חפץ ה׳ עשה.   ולא כן המלאכים והכוכבים לא יעשו
כל אשר יחפצו כי לא יעשו דבר אלא בחפץ האל.   בשמים ובארץ.

---

653 BRMCS	עשה	669 NPDS	ידעתי
661 B	ולא היו נכנסים בהיכל	675 R	המלאכים הקדושים והכוכבים
663 RMC	אומר	676 B	כחפץ האל
664 B	להלל בו		

heaven and earth: meaning that it is he who made the heavens which impart blessing upon the world, and who made the earth which yields her fruit for a blessing when he, blessed be he, so commands it.

PSALM CXXXV

1. Praise the Lord: Praise the name of the Lord, give praise, O servants of the Lord: Psalm cxiii is the one which has first 'give praise, O servants of the Lord' and then 'praise the name of the Lord' which is immediately followed by 'blessed be the name of the Lord'. In the present psalm, however, we have first of all *praise the name of the Lord* and then *give praise, O servants of the Lord* followed by *you that stand in the house of the Lord*.

2. That stand: you *that stand in the house of the Lord*, that is, the priests. *In the courts*: and (also) *you that stand in the courts of the house of our God* (which refers to the rest of) Israel who used to pray in the Temple courts, since they did not enter the Inner Sanctuary. To all you I say:

3. Praise the Lord, for the Lord is good: this (exhortation) was intended for those who were destined to stand in the house of the Lord to be built by Solomon, or perhaps (is directed) to those who at some future time will stand in the Temple which the King Messiah will build. He says that *the Lord is good*, and it is proper to praise him, for he is *good* and does good. Similarly his name is *gracious* and it is becoming to praise it, for he is his name and his name is he. And the verse contains a repetition of the same idea in different words.

4. For Jacob: it is proper for you to praise him more so than for any other people, since he did choose you from all the peoples.

5. For I know: the psalmist in his exhortation says: On this account I exhort you to praise and glorify him for *I know* him because of his wonderful deeds and works that he is *great*. *And our Lord*: for we have accepted him as Lord and God over us, whilst the other nations have taken the celestial bodies as lord and god, each one after its own peculiar custom. But we have accepted none as Lord over us except the one God who is greater *than all the gods*, that is, the host of heaven and the angels who regulate the universe, for which reason they are called 'gods'. But our Lord is greater than all of them, for they can accomplish nothing except by his power and command.

6. Whatever the Lord pleases he does: this is not so in the case of the angels and the stars who cannot do whatever they please, since they can

אבל הוא עושה חפצו בהם אין מונע ועושה בשמים כל צבאם

להנהיג בארץ וכן בארץ עושה חפצו בה ובכל צבאה. בימים וכל

תהמות. ובארץ שאמר הוא על היבשה לפיכך אמר בימים וכל

680 תהמות ופירוש בימים. ים אוקינוס ושאר הימים. וכל תהמות.

הנהרות וזכר אחד מן הנפלאות הגדולות אשר הוא עושה בארץ

והוא ענין המטר כמו שאמר אליפז עושה גדולות ואין חקר

ונפלאות עד אין מספר ואמר אחריו הנותן מטר על פני הארץ

וגו׳ לפיכך אמר;

685 7. מעלה נשיאים. והם העננים. נקראו כן לפי שהם עולים

מן הארץ ומתנשאים למעלה כמו שכתוב ואד יעלה מן הארץ ופירוש

מקצה הארץ היבשה שהוא הים כי משם הם עולים כמו שכתוב

הקורא למי הים וישפכם על פני הארץ וכן אמר אליהו לנערו

הבט דרך ים ואמר הנה עב קטנה ככף איש עלה מים ואחר כן אמר

690 ברקים למטר עשה שהוא פלא גדול שעושה ברקים עם המטר והברקים

אש ואין המים מכבין את האש ואמר. מוצא רוח מאוצרותיו.

שהרוח מרחפת ורוחפת את המטר אל הפאה אשר הולכת שם מוצא.

כמו מוציא ואמר מאוצרותיו לפי ששלש היסודות נראים לעין

והרוח אינה נראית כמו הדבר הנתון באוצר ופירוש מוצא כי

695 קודם שמרחפת אין מרגישין בה וכשמרחפת מרגישין בה הרי הוא

כאלו הוציאה עתה בעת הרחיפה והחכם רבי אברהם בן עזרא כתב

כי טעם אוצרות לרוח שהיא בכח כי הכח דבר אצור והנה זכר

ארבע יסודות ואמר עוד כל אשר חפץ ה׳ עשה בנבראים;

8. שהכה. הזכיר מכת בכורות בפרט כי על ידה יצאו ואחר

700 כן אמר;

9. שלח אתות ומופתים. והוא כלל לשאר המכות והנה המכות

הם אות ומופת כי כל אשר חפץ ה׳ עשה כי אלו היו המכות ההם

678 MADS להנהיג השפלים 696 B הדחיפה

682 BNMC עד אין חקר 699 BRS הבכורים. 699 N יצאו ישראל ממצרים

693 NPCD שהשלש יסודות 702 C כי כל אלו המכות אלו היו במקרה

696 NM הוצאה P הוצאה

accomplish nothing except by the will of God. *In heaven and on earth*: but he can do with them as he wills – for no one can restrain him – and so he disposes in the heavens all their host to control the world. So also with regard to the earth, he does what he pleases in it and all its host. *In the seas and all rivers*: when he says *and in the earth*, he means on the dry land. Therefore he (also) says: *in the seas and all rivers*. And *in the seas* means the Mediterranean Sea and all other seas. *T^ehomoth* (means) 'rivers'. Next he refers to one of the great wonders which he performs in the earth, viz. the matter of the rain, just as Eliphaz says: 'who does great and unsearchable things, marvels without number' (Job v 9) and afterwards (*ibid.*, *v*. 10): 'who gives rain to the earth . . .'. Accordingly he says:

7. Who makes clouds rise from the end of the earth: *n^eśi'im* are clouds, and are so called because they rise up from the earth and soar aloft to the heights, as it is written: 'but a mist went up from the earth' (Gen. ii 6). And the meaning of *from the end of the earth* is *from the end* of the dry land, that is, the sea, for it is from there that they rise up, as it is written: 'who summoned the waters of the sea, and poured them over the earth' (Amos v 8). Similarly, Elijah said to his servant: 'Look toward the sea' and (the servant) said: 'a little cloud like a man's hand is rising from the sea' (1 Kgs. xviii 43, 44). And afterwards (the psalmist) says: *who makes lightnings for the rain*, which is a great miracle, since he makes *lightnings* together with *the rain*, for *lightnings* consist of fire but (in this case) the water does not extinguish the fire. And he says: *and brings the wind out of his storehouses*: the wind drives the rain and diverts its course in the direction in which it is to go. *Moṣe'* is the same as *moṣi'*. He says: *from his storehouses* because the other three elements are visible to the eye whilst the wind is not visible, just like something placed in a storehouse. And the meaning of *brings out* is: before it moves we do not feel its effect, but when it has already moved we become aware of it. Thus it is as though he had brought it out at the very instant that it is set in motion. But the learned Rabbi Abraham Ibn Ezra writes that the idea of *'oṣ^eroth* suggests the potential character of the wind, for that which is potential is something stored away (*'oṣar*). We observe that (the psalmist) mentions four elements. And he says further: *whatever the Lord pleases he does* – to include the whole of creation.[1]

8. He struck down: he refers specifically to the striking down of the first-born, since because of this (Israel) went forth (from Egypt). Subsequently he says:

9. Who sent signs and wonders: being a general expression to include all the other plagues. And the plagues stand as a sign and a wonder (to

---

[1] Lit. 'with the created things'.

במקרה לא היו המצרים לוקים בהם וישראל נצלים מהם אלא באמת
היו בחפץ האל. בתוככי מצרים. היו"ד נוספת כיו"ד בתוככי
ירושלים והוא כמו בתוכך לנוכח מצרים ותוספת היו"ד לצחות
הלשון. בפרעה ובכל עבדיו. וכל שכן בעמו אלא אפילו פרעה
ועבדיו לא יכלו בכחם להמלט מחפץ האל ועוד עשה חפץ האל;

705

10. שהכה גוים רבים. וישראל היו מעט יוצאים מפרך ועבדות
ואלה רבים ועצומים בארצם והכום בני ישראל וירשו את ארצם
מי עשה זה אלא חפץ האל;

710

11. לסיחון. וזכר סיחון ועוג בפרט לפי שנלחמו בהם תחלה
ועוד שהיו מלכים עצומים יותר מכלם כמו שכתוב ואנכי השמדתי
את האמרי מפניהם אשר כגבה ארזים גבהו וחסן הוא כאלונים.
ואחר כן זכר ולכל ממלכות כנען בכלל;

12. ונתן. אחר כן פירש למי נתנה נחלה לישראל עמו שהם
נבחרים מכל עם נתן להם ארץ נבחרת מכל הארצות;

715

13. ה' שמך. הפסוק כפול בענין במלות שונות רוצה לומר
באלה הנפלאות שעשית עם ישראל יזכרוך בהם לעולם לדר ודר;

14. כי ידין. ואף על פי שהנחלה שנתן להם היא ביד אחרים
והם בגלות לא יהיה זה לעולם כי יבוא זמן שיקח האל דין
עמו ומשפטם מן הגוים. ועל עבדיו יתנחם. כי כבר קבלו
ענשם בכל חטאתם וישיבם לנחלתם;

720

15. עצבי הגוים. ואז יהיו עצבי הגוים לאין ויכירו
עובדיהם כי אין בהם ממש כי לא יושיעום בעת צרתם כי עצביהם
כסף וזהב;

725

703 BRC	מצרים	715 B	אחרי כן
704 B	היו"ד נוספת כמו בתוככי	715 C	שהיו נבחרים
707 BRP	לא יוכלו	716 NRPMCDS	ארץ הנבחרת
707 RMS	ועוד עשה חפצו האל	724 B	ביום צרתם
712 B	כמו שאומר		

demonstrate) that *whatever the Lord pleases he does*. For if these plagues occurred merely by accident, the Egyptians would not have been stricken by them and Israel delivered from them. But in truth they occurred by the will of God. *In your midst, O Egypt*: *b^ethokeki*: the *yod* is paragogic like the *yod* in 'in your midst (*b^ethokeki*), O Jerusalem' (Ps. cxvi 19). It is the same as *b^ethokek* (second person feminine) with reference to Egypt (feminine). The addition of the *yod* is for poetic effect. *Against Pharaoh and all his servants*: how much more so against his people ? For even *Pharaoh and his servants* with all their power were not able to escape from the will of God. And God still *does whatever he pleases*!

10. He struck down many nations: now the Israelites, when they went forth from bondage and slavery were few in number, whilst these (nations) were numerous and powerful in their own lands. Nevertheless, the Israelites struck them down and took possession of their lands. Who effected this if not the will of God ?

11. Sihon: he makes special mention of Sihon and Og since they were the first to fight with them and also because they were the most powerful kings of all, as it is written: 'Yet it was I who destroyed the Amorite before them, whose height was like the cedars and who was as strong as the oaks' (Amos ii 9). Afterwards he refers generally to *all the kingdoms of Canaan*.

12. And gave: he then explains to whom he gave it *as a heritage – to Israel his people* who are the chosen of all people, to them he gave the chosen land.[1]

13. Thy name, O Lord: this verse repeats the same idea in different words. He means: because of these marvels which thou hast done for the people of Israel, they will remember thee for ever, *throughout all generations.*

14. For he will give justice: though the heritage which he gave them is in the possession of others, whilst they are in exile, this will not always be so, for the time will come when God will take up the cause of his people (and exact) their right from the nations. *And have compassion on his servants*: since they have received their punishment for all their sins, and he will restore them to their heritage.

15. The idols of the nations: at that time the *idols of the nations* will be as nothing and those who serve them shall acknowledge that there is no reality in them. For their idols, being mere silver and gold, cannot save them in the time of their distress.[2]

[1] Lit. 'a land chosen from all the lands'.
[2] Lit. 'for they cannot save them in the time of their distress, since their idols are silver and gold'.

16. פה להם. 17. אזנים. כבר פירשנו ענין אלו הפסוקים
במזמור קט"ו. אף אין יש רוח בפיהם. אין צריך לומר שלא
ידברו אלא אפילו רוח אין בפיהם והוא הבל היוצא מן הלב
דרך הפה;

730
18. כמוהם. דרך תפלה או כן יהיה לעתיד בבוא הגואל שיכלו
ויאבדו עושי העצבים וכל אשר בוטח בהם;

19. בית ישראל. אבל בית ישראל אתם שלא בטחתם בהם ברכו את
ה' שהושיע אתכם מיד עובדי העצבים וכן. בית אהרן. והם
הכהנים המשרתים את פני ה';

735
20. בית הלוי. הם המשוררים לפני ה' בפה ובכלי. יראי ה'.
החכמים שבישראל המתבודדים בבית ה' ללמוד או פירושו יראי ה'
אשר בכל עם אשר יבואו להתפלל בבית ה';

21. ברוך ה' מציון. כי שם ישכון הכבוד בירושלים ומשם
תצא הוראה לכל שייראוהו ויברכוהו;

Psalm CXXXVI

740
1. הודו לה' כי טוב כי לעולם חסדו. זה המזמור יש בו עשרים
וששה פסוקים וכלם חותמים כי לעולם חסדו ואמרו רבותינו ז"ל
כי נאמרו כנגד עשרים וששה דורות מבריאת העולם עד שקבלו
ישראל את התורה וזן אותם הקדוש ברוך הוא בחסדו כי לא היתה
תורה בבני אדם שיזון אותם בעבורה ואף על פי שהתורה ישראל
745
לבדם קבלוה כל העולם עומד בזכות ישראל ולפי הפשט כי כל אחד
יש לו ענין במקומו ונמצאו עשרים וששה לפי הענינים המספרים
במזמור. ואמר תחלה. הודו לה'. כל בני העולם הודו לה'
כי טוב הוא ומטיב לעולם וחסדו אין לו הפסק כי לעולם הוא

728	NPMCS	מהלב		739	MC	היראה		ההוראה והיראה R
730	PMC	או כי כן יהיה לעתיד		739	R			שייראוהו ויכבדוהו
730	RM	שיכלו ויאבדו עובדי העצבים		744	R			אף על פי שהתורה נתן לישראל לבדם
736	BRMS	בישראל						וקבלוה

16, 17. They have mouths … they have ears: we have already explained the meaning of these verses in (the commentary on) Psalm cxv. *Nor is there any breath in their mouths*: there is no need to state that they cannot speak, since *there is no breath in their mouths*. (By *ruah* is meant) the breath which issues from the lungs[1] through the mouth.

18. Like them: (this is said) by way of a prayer, or perhaps (is a prediction) that it will be so at some future time, at the coming of the Redeemer. (That is to say) the makers of idols will be destroyed and will perish, and likewise all who trust in them.

19. O house of Israel: but *O house of Israel*, you who do not trust in them, *bless the Lord* who has delivered you from the hands of those who worship idols. So also: *O house of Aaron*: the priests that minister to the Lord.

20. O house of Levi: these are they who sing before the Lord with voice and musical instrument. *You that fear the Lord*: these are the wise in Israel who come in solitude to the house of the Lord to study. Or it may mean all such as are God-fearing among the nations and come to pray in the house of the Lord.

21. Blessed be the Lord from Zion: for there the Divine Glory will dwell, in Jerusalem, and thence will go forth instruction to all – that they fear him and bless him.

PSALM CXXXVI

1. Give thanks to the Lord, for he is good, for his loving kindness endures for ever: in this psalm there are twenty-six verses each of which concludes (with the words) *for his loving kindness endures for ever*. Our teachers, of blessed memory, have said[2] that these were recited with reference to the twenty-six generations extending from the creation of the universe to the time that Israel received the *Torah*. For (during the entire period) the Holy One, blessed be he, fed them in his mercy, since there was not as yet among mankind a *Torah* on account of which he should provide for them. And though Israel alone received the *Torah*, yet the whole world subsists through the merits of Israel. But according to the simple (literal) interpretation, the expression in each verse has a particular meaning depending upon the context. Thus there are twenty-six verses corresponding to the various matters mentioned in the psalm. Firstly he says: *give thanks to the Lord*: all mankind, *give thanks to the Lord, for he is good* and does good to the universe, and *his loving kindness* is unending.[3]

---

[1] Lit. 'from the heart'.   [2] *Pesahim* 118a.

[3] *Hephseq* = 'interruption, end'.

וכן כלם כי לעולם חסדו זהו פירושו וזכר אותו עם כל אחד
להגדיל השבח;

750

2. הודו לאלהי האלהים. הם המלאכים והם אלהים לאשר למטה
מהם והוא אלהים עליהם;

3. הודו לאדני האדנים. הם הגלגלים שהם אדונים על השפלים
ומנהיגים אותם והוא אדון עליהם;

755

4. לעשה. אחר שהזכיר המלאכים והגלגלים שהוא אדון עליהם
אמר לעשה. להורות כי אינם קדמונים כמו שהוא קדמון אלא
שהם עלולים והוא עלה להם כמו שאומרים הפילוסופים לפיכך
אמר לעשה. ללמד שאינם קדמונים אלא הוא עושה אותם והם
חדשים והזכיר תחלה נפלאות גדולות. ואפשר שהוא כלל לאשר

760

זכר אחריו והחכם רבי אברהם בן עזרא פירש לעשה נפלאות.
שהם נפלאות מעין האדם והם העגולות הכבודות שהם צבא השמים
ופירש לעשה השמים. הרקיע שהוא שמי הארץ והנראה בעיני
כי אמר לעשה נפלאות גדולות לבדו על הצורות שאינם גופות
ולא בגופות והם השכלים הנפרדים והם נפלאות מעין האדם כי

765

לא תשיג עין האדם אלא מה שהוא חמר והגלגלים והכוכבים הם
חמר זך ותשיגם עין האדם אבל הצורות שהם בלא חמר לא תשיגם
עין האדם ואף עין המחשבה תלאה להשיגם לפיכך קראם נפלאות
גדלות ואמר לבדו. כי הוא לבדו נשגב עליהם וכל שאר הנבראים
תחתיהם והם קיום העולם לפיכך אמר כי לעולם חסדו כי הנה הם

770

חסד האל על ברואיו והם לעולם אין להם הפסק ורבותינו ז"ל
אמרו לבדו אפילו בעל הנס אינו מכיר בנסו.

שמי השמים	R 762	והמנהיגים	B 754
והם נפלאים מעין בני אדם	P 764	שאינם	R 756
שאינם חמר בלי חמר	N 766	כמו שאמרו R כמו שאומרים חכמי המחקר N 757	
ברצון האל ששם מ׳ N קיום העולם After 769		ואפשר הוא כלל	BC 759
אותם איש. במקומו הראוי לו		עגולות וכדוריות	P 761
		עגולות כדוריות	A

So too in every instance[1] of the phrase *for his loving kindness endures for ever*, this is the correct interpretation. And he inserts it with each verse to augment the praise (of God).

2. Give thanks to the God of gods: these are the angels being referred to as 'gods' because they rule over such things as are inferior to them.[2] But he is Lord over them.

3. Give thanks to the Lord of lords: these are the celestial spheres, since they are *lords* over the lower creatures and control them. But he is *Lord* over them.

4. To him who makes: having referred to the angels and the spheres over which he is Lord, he says: *to him who makes*, to indicate that they are not eternal as he is eternal, but are caused and he their Prime Cause, as the philosophers state. Therefore he says: *to him who makes*, in order to explain that they are not eternal and that he made them and they were created *ex nihilo*.[3] Firstly he speaks of the *great marvels*, which is probably a general expression for those subsequently specified. But the learned Rabbi Abraham Ibn Ezra interprets *le'oseh niphla'oth* as referring to those beings which are hidden from the human eye, (that is) the exalted, celestial bodies, the host of heaven. As for *le'oseh hashshamayim*, he explains *hashsha-mayim* as meaning the firmament which is the vault of the earth. But in my opinion (the most plausible interpretation is that) he says *to him who alone works great marvels* as a reference to the pure forms which are neither matter nor contained in matter, that is, 'the separate intelligences'. They are not visible to the human eye, since the human eye enables man to perceive only what is material. And the spheres and the stars are pure matter, and therefore the senses can perceive them. But pure forms without matter[4] cannot be perceived by the senses, for even man's mind vainly endeavours to perceive them. For this reason he describes them as *great marvels*. He says *alone*, since he *alone* is exalted above them, whilst all other beings are inferior to them. (It must be noted too that) they are (the cause of the) continued existence of the universe. Therefore he says: *for his loving kindness endures for ever*: for through them is made manifest God's *loving kindness* to his creatures,[5] and they are everlasting, infinite.[6] Our teachers, of blessed memory, comment thus: *alone*: even he to whom a miracle happens does not recognise it.[7]

---

[1] Or 'so also for each *for his loving kindness endures for ever*'.
[2] Lit. 'and they are gods to what is downwards from them'.
[3] Lit. 'and they are new (things)'.   [4] Lit. 'forms without matter'.
[5] Lit. 'for they are God's loving kindness to his creatures'.
[6] Lit. 'without end'.   [7] *Niddah* 31a.

5. לעשה השמים. אחרי כן הזכיר השמים והוא כלל לכל הגלגלים
והכוכבים ואמר שהוא עשה אותם והוא חדשם בתבונתו ועשה בחדושם
חסד לעולם ואין להם הפסק. זהו כי לעולם חסדו;

6. לרקע הארץ. זכר מבריאת הארץ מה שהוא חסד מוחלט מאתו   775
שבטל טבע המים שהיה טבעם להיותם על הארץ כמו שהיה מתחלה
וכמו שהם בחצי הכדור והוא בחסדו הקוה אותם אל מקום אחד
ונראית היבשה להיות החיים והצמחים עליה וזה החסד הוא
לעולם כי אף על פי שבמבול הציף המים על היבשה לא היה אלא
לזמן מועט לנקמת הרשעים ועם כל זה עשה חסד והשאיר בתחבולה   780
מיני החיים וכבר נשבע שלא יהיה עוד כל ימי הארץ המבול
הנה כי לעולם חסדו ופירוש לרקע הארץ. אמר שנתן שטח הארץ
על המים ואף על פי שהמים גבוהים על הארץ נתן הוא שתהיה
הארץ כאלו היא גבוהה על המים שלא יעברו על הארץ כמו שאמר
ומים לא יעברו פיו כי הוא נתן חול גבול לים חק עולם ולא   785
יעברנהו וזהו מנפלאותיו;

7. לעשה אורים גדלים. אחר כן זכר בפרט שני המאורות
הגדולים שהם קיום העולם ואמר לעולם חסדו כי אין להם הפסק
וזכר כל אחד לבדו ואמר;

8. את השמש. ונתן השמש שיהיה מושל ביום לתועלת העולם   790
להאיר ולהחם האויר והוא תועלת החיים והצמחים וזהו חסד
מאתו והוא לעולם אין לו הפסק;

9. את הירח. וכן נתן הירח למשול בלילה עם הכוכבים כי
אור הירח והכוכבים צרך הולכי מדברות ויורדי הים וכחם

מעט	780 NM	והם כלל	772 CS
שלא להביא מבול עוד	781 PD	ובחדושם עשה	773 PD
את השמש	790 BR	שהיה טבעם להיות	776 NC
את הירח	793 BR	שהמבול	779 MC
וכן הירח נתן	793 N	כי אף על פי שהציף המים על היבשה 779 PD	
צרכי	794 B	במבול	

5. To him who made the heavens: afterwards he mentions *the heavens*, which is a general term for all the spheres and constellations. The psalmist says that he made them, created them ex nihilo *in his wisdom*, and wrought (an act of) *everlasting loving kindness* by so creating them, for they are not subject to termination. Thus (do we understand) *for his loving kindness endures for ever*.

6. Who laid the earth: (of the phenomena) of the creation, he cites the (one which constitutes) absolute *loving kindness* on his part, viz. the fact that he reversed the nature of the waters, for their natural location was upon the earth, as was formerly the case and as indeed they still are in the (upper) half of the celestial sphere. But he, in *his loving kindness*, collected them into one place and thus there emerged the dry land for living creatures and plants to be upon it. This (manifestation of) *loving kindness endures for ever*, and though by the flood he caused the waters to inundate the dry land, yet this was so only for a short time as retribution against the wicked. Even in this, however, he showed *loving kindness*, since by design he preserved the different species of life. Moreover, he took an oath that there will not be another flood all the days of the earth. Behold! *His loving kindness endures for ever*. And by (the words) *who laid the earth*, he means that he placed the spread of the earth upon the waters. And though the waters are (by nature) higher than the earth, yet he so placed the earth as though it were higher than the waters, in order that they might not flow over the earth. Thus it says: 'that the waters should not disobey his command' (Prov. viii 29), for he placed the sands for the boundary of the sea by a permanent decree that it cannot pass it (cf. Jer. v 22). And this is indeed one of his marvels!

7. Who made the great lights: later he refers more specifically to the two great lights, since they (constitute the basis for) the continued existence of the universe, likewise saying of them *his loving kindness endures for ever* because they are unending. He then proceeds to mention each one separately, and says:

8. The sun: he placed the sun to rule by day for the benefit of the universe, to give light and heat to the atmosphere – which is indeed a great benefit for animal and plant life – and this (too is an act of) *loving kindness* on his part. And (the sun) also endures for ever without interruption.

9. The moon: in the same way he placed the moon to govern with the stars by night, for the light of the moon and the stars is a necessity for those journeying in the deserts or travelling on the sea. Their energy is also required by plants, just as it is written (of the moon): 'the produce of the

795 לצרך הצמחים כמו שכתוב גרש ירחים ויש לו גם כן כח במים ואמר
התקשר מעדנות כימה ומושכות כסיל תפתח וכן לכל כוכב וכוכב יש
לו כח בצמחים או באבנים ובמתכות ובכלל שני האורים קיום העולם
כי הקר והחם סבת קיום החיים ואין להם הפסק לפיכך אמר כי
לעולם חסדו ואחר שספר חסדו על העולם בכללו זכר בפרט חסדו על
800 ישראל והראה בהם נפלאותיו והודיע שהוא לבדו אדון העולם ומשנה
הטבעים כרצונו;

10.11.12. למכה מצרים. הזכיר מכת בכורים לפי שעל ידה יצאו
וכן אמר אחר כן. ויוצא. ואמר אחר כן. ביד חזקה. והוא
כלל לשאר המכות וכל זה כי לעולם חסדו כי חסד גדול היה שיספר
805 לעולם כי היו ישראל בארצם והם לקו בכמה מכות וישראל ביניהם
נצלו מכלם ואמר אחר כן;

13. לגזר ים סוף לגזרים. וזה החסד יספר לעולם כי בעבור
שלא יראו מלחמה לא נחם דרך ארץ פלשתים ושנה בעבורם טבע
המים כדי שיעברו בתוכו ועשה חסד גדול עמהם בקריעת הים שקרעו
810 שנים עשר קרעים לשנים עשר שבטים כדי שלא יכנסו בערבוביא
אלא כל שבט עבר בדרכו שנגזר לו, על זה ראוי לומר ולספר חסדו
לעולם כן פירשו רבותינו ז"ל כי לשנים עשר גזרים נגזר ים סוף
ויש לפרש כי לפיכך אמר לגזרים לפי שנגזר הים לרחבו עד חציו
או יותר ואחר כך לארכו ואחר כך לרחבו כי באותו הרוח שנכנסו
815 בים לאותו הרוח עצמו יצאו כי ממדבר איתם נכנסו לים סוף ומים
סוף יצאו למדבר איתם עצמו כמו שכתוב ואם תאמר אחרי שלא
הוצרכו לעבור הים לרחבו למה נכנסו בו והם יצאו אל המקום

796	P	או מושכות כסיל		802	P	בכוריהם N בכורות
797	C	שני האורים הם סבת קיום העולם		814	B	ואחר כך לארכו ולרחבו
799	BPCS	ואחרי ... כרצונו ח'				

moons' (Deut. xxxiii 14). It also exerts an influence upon the waters. Likewise it says (of the stars): 'can you bind the cluster of the Pleiades, or loose Orion's belt?' (Job xxxviii 31). Thus each star has its effect upon plants, stones and metals. And these two (great) lights (constitute the basis for) the continued existence of the universe, for cold and heat are the cause of the continued existence of life, since they cannot be terminated. Accordingly he says *for his loving kindness endures for ever*. And having recounted his *loving kindness* over the whole universe generally, he now refers specifically to his *loving kindness* towards Israel in that he revealed through them his marvels, thereby making it known that he alone is Lord of the universe and can change the intrinsic nature of things according to his will.

10, 11, 12. Who struck down Egypt: he mentions the plague of the first-born, because as a consequence of this (Israel) was liberated.[1] Thus he says in the following (verse 11): *and brought Israel out from among them*, after which he says (verse 12): *With a strong hand*: being a general expression to include all the other plagues. And all this took place because *his loving kindness endures for ever*. For it was (an act of) great *loving kindness* which will be recounted for ever, since although the Israelites were in their land (the Egyptians) alone were stricken with many plagues, while the Israelites amongst them were saved from all of them. And he says further:

13. Who divided the Red Sea in sunder: and this (act of) *loving kindness* will be recounted for ever, for in order that they might not see war, he led them not by the way of the land of the Philistines, but on their account suspended the natural course of the waters that they might pass through the midst of them. And he dealt most mercifully with them in dividing the sea, for he divided it into twelve divisions, corresponding to the twelve tribes, that there should be no confusion;[2] and each tribe passed through by the route assigned to it. For this reason it is proper to speak and tell of his *loving kindness* for ever. That he divided the Red Sea into twelve divisions is the interpretation given by our teachers, of blessed memory.[3] But it may be explained that he says *in sunder* for this reason, viz. because the Sea was divided breadthways up to a half or more, then lengthways, and then again breadthways, for by the same wind with which they entered the Sea, by that same wind did they come forth from the Sea. It was from the wilderness of Etham that they entered the Red Sea and, likewise, they finally emerged from the Red Sea into the same wilderness of Etham, as it is written (in Numbers xxxiii). And should it be objected that since there was no necessity for them to pass through the sea breadthways, why did

---

[1] Lit. 'they went forth'.   [2] Lit. 'that they might not enter into confusion'.
[3] *Yalkut Shimeoni* on Habakkuk iii 14.

שהיו בו מתחלה לא עשה כן האל ית׳ אלא כדי שיטבעו מצרים
בים ולהראות עצם גדולתו שיעברו ישראל בתוך הים ביבשה ויטבעו
מצרים בתוכו; 820

‏14. והעביר ישראל בתוכו. בעמקו של ים שהוא חציו והעבירם
ביבשה כמו שכתוב ויש לך חסד גדול מזה כי אפילו רגליהם לא
נטבלו במים;

‏15. ונער. שלא היה להם יכלת לשוב לאחוריהם וזה חסד גדול 825
שראו בשונאיהם נקמה גדולה ולא פחדו עוד מהם;

‏16. למוליך עמו במדבר. ארץ אשר לא עבר בה איש ולא היה שם
דרך והוא בחסדו הוליך אותם בעמוד ענן יומם ובעמוד אש לילה
ומראה להם הדרך ועוד במדבר שהיה ארץ ציה וצלמות והוא ספק
להם בחסדו כל צרכם זה החסד יספר לעולם;

‏17. למכה. מלכים. זכרם בכלל ואחר כן פרט אותם להגדיל 830
השבח וכן אמר למכה ואחר כן ויהרג ואחד הוא אלא כפל הענין
במלות שונות וכל זה להגדיל השבח ולספר החסד פעמים רבות
והנה החסד גדול כי לא היו מניחים ישראל לעבור ויצאו להלחם
עמם והם היו עם רב וגבורים וחזקים ונתנם האל ביד ישראל שהם
חלושים ולא היו מלמדי מלחמה ונתנם האל בידם והכו אותם והרגו 835
אותם עד שלא השאירו שריד זה היה חסד גדול;

‏18. ויהרוג. 19. לסיחון. 20. ולעוג. 21. ונתן ארצם
לנחלה. ועוד חסד גדול מזה כי לא די שהכו אותם אלא שנתן

818	RC	בתחלה	
818	RPC	המצרים	
822	M	שאפילו	
827	BCS	הוליך אותם בענן	
831	C	ואחר כך פירש	

833	M	וזה חסד גדול
	R	הנה החסד הגדול אשר עשה לנו
833	RC	לעבור בארצם
834	BS	ונתנם ... מלחמה ח׳
834	RP	שהיו חלושים

they enter it (at all), since in effect they came forth into the very same region where they had been before ? – (the reply would be that) God, blessed be he, did so only to the end that the Egyptians might drown in the Sea and to demonstrate his great power, in that Israel passed through the Sea on dry land, whilst the Egyptians sank in the middle of it.

14. And made Israel pass through the middle of it: (*b^ethoko* means) in the depths of the sea, that is, the middle of it. He made them pass through on dry land, as it is written (in Exodus xiv 29). And a still greater (act of) *loving kindness* than this is (the fact that) even their feet did not become wet in the water.

15. And swept: so that it was impossible for them to turn backwards. And this was (an act of) great *loving kindness*, for (the Israelites) saw great vengeance upon their enemies and were thus no longer afraid of them.

16. To him who led his people through the wilderness: (that is) a land through which no man had ever passed and where there were no trodden paths. But he in *his loving kindness* guided them by a pillar of cloud by day and a pillar of fire by night, thus showing them the way. And what is more, through a wilderness which was 'a land of drought and deep darkness' (Jer. ii 6). Yet he in his *loving kindness* provided for all their needs. This (act of) *loving kindness* will be spoken of for ever.

17. To him who struck down great kings: (at first) he speaks of them generally, but later on refers specifically to each one of them, so as to augment the praise (of God). Thus he (begins by) saying: *to him who struck down* and then *and slew*, but (the meaning) is one and the same;[1] he merely repeats the same idea in different words. The purpose of all this is to magnify his praise and to recount his *loving kindness* a second time. And behold! his *loving kindness* is great! For (these kings) did not permit the people of Israel to pass through (their territories) but went out to fight with them. But though they were numerous, powerful and strong, yet God delivered them into the hand of the Israelites who were helpless[2] and unprepared for war. God delivered them into their hands so that they struck them down, slew them and left none alive.[3] This was (indeed) great *loving kindness*.

18, 19, 20, 21. And slew . . . Sihon . . . and Og . . . and gave their land as a heritage: he showed them even greater *loving kindness*. Not only were they able to strike them down but he also *gave* them *their land as a*

---

[1] Lit. 'but it is one'.   [2] Lit. 'weak'.
[3] Lit. 'they did not leave' a fugitive.

להם ארצם לנחלה שלא באו שאר הגוים ולא נאספו עליהם להוציאם

840 משם וזה חסד גדול מאתו כי חסד הוא תוספת הטובה ובזו הארץ

שנתן להם הוסיף להם בטובתו כי לא נתנה לאברהם אבינו אלא

מעבר הירדן והלאה שהיא ארץ שבעה גוים ועוד שלשה גוים קיני

וקנזי וקדמני ואותם שלשה לא היתה להם עד לעתיד לבוא שיהיו

מגבול ארץ ישראל ואף על פי כן בעולם הזה היו תחת דוד מלך

845 ישראל כי פירשו אבותינו ז"ל כי קיני מעשו וקנזי וקדמני

עמון ומואב והנה מה שנתן לאברהם אבינו עשרה עממים השלשה

את הקיני ואת הקנזי ואת הקדמני והשבעה עממים את החתי ואת

הפרזי ואת הרפאים ואת האמרי ואת הגרגשי ואת הכנעני ואת

היבוסי והנה לא זכר חוי ואמרו רבותינו ז"ל כי הרפאים שזכר

850 אלו החוי אבל מעבר הירדן מזרחה לא נתן לאברהם אבינו דבר

ונתן לישראל נחלה ארץ סיחון שהיתה ממואב תחלה וכן נתן להם

ארץ עוג מלך הבשן וזה היה חסד מאתו ולפיכך לא זכר בזה המזמור

ממלכות כנען כמו שזכר במזמור שלמעלה ממנו לפי שאומר בזה

המזמור כי לעולם חסדו וממלכות כנען שנתן להם אמת היה לא חסד

855 כי כבר נתנה לאברהם אבינו אבל ארץ סיחון ועוג שלא נתנה

לאברהם ונתנה להם זה היה חסד;

22. נחלה לישראל עבדו. נטל הארץ מהם שהיו עובדי אלילים

ונתנה לישראל שהוא עובד האל לבדו;

23. שבשפלנו. ועוד חסדו גדול עלינו כי כשיצאנו מהארץ

860 בעונינו ובחטאתנו והיינו בגלות בשפל זכר לנו ברית אבות כמו

שאמר ואף גם זאת בהיותם בארץ איביהם לא מאסתים ולא געלתים

843	B	אותם שלשה	854	B	באמת לא היה חסד
851	R	שהיא ארץ מואב תחלה	858	B	שהיו עובדים
852	B	לפיכך	860	BNRM	ובחטאינו C ובחטאתינו
853	MCS	לפי שאמר	860	NP	כמו שכתוב MC כמו שנאמר

heritage, for the rest of the nations did not come together against them to drive them out from there. This was great *loving kindness* on his part, for (the word) *ḥesed* (indicates) exceeding goodness. And so with regard to the land which he gave them, he bestowed his goodness upon them to an increased extent. For to our father Abraham he promised only that part of it extending from the western side of the Jordan[1] – the land of the Seven Nations – and also (the territories) of three other nations, viz. the Kenites, Kenizzites, and Kadmonites (cf. Gen. xv 18–21), though these (latter) three (nations) were not to belong to them until the Messianic era[2] when they are to become a boundary for the land of Israel. Nevertheless, even in this world[3] they came under (the dominion of) David, king of Israel, for, as our teachers, of blessed memory, explain,[4] the Kenites are (descendants) of Esau and the Kenizzites and Kadmonites are (descendants) of Ammon and Moab. [And as to these ten nations which he promised to our father Abraham – the triad of the Kenites, Kenizzites, and Kadmonites, and the seven other nations comprising the Hittites, Perizzites, Rephaim, Amorites, Girgashites, Canaanites, Jebusites – note that he does not mention the Hivites. But our teachers, of blessed memory, state that the Rephaim which he mentions (Gen. xv 21) are the Hivites.[5]] But of the eastern side of the Jordan, he promised nothing to our father Abraham, but to Israel he gave as a heritage the land of Sihon, which originally belonged to Moab. Similarly, he gave them the land of Og king of Bashan, which was indeed *loving kindness* on his part. Thus he does not refer in this psalm, as in the preceding one, to the kingdoms of Canaan, for in this psalm he says *for his loving kindness endures for ever*, whereas giving them the kingdoms of Canaan was simply the fulfilment (of his word) and not an additional bounty,[6] since he had already promised it to Abraham our father. But with regard to the land of Sihon and Og, which was not promised to Abraham, but was given to (Israel), that (gift) was indeed (an act of) *loving kindness*.

22. A heritage to Israel his servant: he took away the land from those who worshipped idols and gave it to Israel who worship God alone.

23. When we were cast down: once more was *his loving kindness* great towards us, for when we had to leave the land (of Israel) because of our sins and iniquities, and were dejected[7] in exile, he remembered on our behalf the covenant of the fathers, just as it says: 'Yet even then, when they are in the land of their enemies, I will not reject them nor spurn them

---

[1] Lit. 'from the western side of the Jordan and further on'.
[2] Lit. 'until the future to come'.   [3] That is, in the course of history.
[4] *Bereshith Rabba* 44: 23.   [5] *Bereshith Rabba* 44: 23.
[6] Lit. 'and not loving kindness'.   [7] Lit. 'cast down'.

לכלתם ואמר זה על גלות בבל או על זה הגלות והוא הנכון ואמר.

זכר. ויפרקנו. עבר במקום עתיד כמנהג הנבואות ובדברי רבותינו
ז"ל לזרעך נתתי את הארץ הזאת אתן אין כתיב כאן אלא נתתי
מכאן שמאמרו של הקדוש ברוך הוא מעשה;

865

24. ויפרקנו מצרינו. הנה חסדו הגדול היה עמנו בגלות
להחיותנו בין הגוים ועוד חסד גדול מזה שיהיה חסד לעולם
שיגאלנו מצרינו ועוד לא ימוש חסדו ממנו עד עולם;

25. נתן לחם. אחר שספר חסדו על ישראל אמר בתכלית המזמור
חסדו על כל החיים כמו שאמר בתחלת המזמור חסדו על כל העולם

870

כן אמר עתה נתן לחם לכל בשר וזה חסד גדול מאתו לנבראים
שמזמן לכל בריאה ובריאה מזון הראוי לה ואמר;

26. הודו לאל השמים. כי מן השמים יבוא המטר שהוא סבת
כל מזון כמו שאמר כי כאשר ירד הגשם והשלג מן השמים רוצה
לומר גבה האויר והוא אל השמים והוא יצוה שירד המטר מן השמים

875

והוא חסד גדול שאין לו הפסק זהו כי לעולם חסדו;

Psalm CXXXVII

1. על נהרות בבל שם ישבנו גם בכינו בזכרנו את ציון; זה
המזמור נאמר על לשון הלוים המשוררים אשר גלו בגלות בבל,
כלומר על נהרות בבל היינו שם מתבודדים יושבים ושוממים, גם

880

היינו בוכים בזכרנו את ציון;

2. על ערבים. ערבי נחל כי הערבים גדלים על שפת הנהרות
וכשהיינו יושבים על שפת הנהר וכנורותינו בידינו לעורר שיר

865	C	שאמירתו	872	RMCDS	שמזמין
868	N	שיגאלנו מצרינו ולא ימוש	873	B	בא המטר
868	C	ימיש	876	BNP	זה הוא
870	C	על העולם כלו	879	NDS	ואמר על נהרות בבל
	MS	על כל העולם			

to destroy them utterly' (Lev. xxvi 44). And he said this with reference either to the Babylonian exile or to the present exile, more likely the latter. He says *he remembered . . . and rescued us*: past tense instead of future, as is the regular usage in the prophetic utterances. And in the words of our teachers, of blessed memory:[1] 'to your descendants I have given this land' (Gen. xv 18) – it is not written *'eten* 'I will give' but *nathati* 'I have given', whence (it is to be inferred) that the promise of the Holy One, blessed be he, is (tantamount to) an (accomplished) fact.

24. And rescued us from our enemies: Behold! His great *loving kindness* was with us in exile, preserving us amongst the nations. And there is yet to be further great *loving kindness, loving kindness which endures for ever* – he will deliver us from our enemies, and his *loving kindness* will no more depart from us for ever.

25. Who gives food: having recounted his *loving kindness* towards Israel, he speaks at the conclusion of the psalm of his *loving kindness* towards all living creatures. Just as he spoke at the beginning of the psalm of his *loving kindness* towards the whole universe, so now he says: *he gives food to all creatures*. It is (an act of) great *loving kindness* from him to (his) creatures, in that he provides for every single creature its appropriate food. And he says:

26. Give thanks to the God of heaven: since from the heavens comes the rain which is the cause of all vegetation, as it says: 'for as the rain and snow come down from the heavens' (Isa. lv 10), meaning, (from) the upper atmosphere. He is the God of heaven and commands the rain to come down from the heavens. It is (an act of) great *loving kindness* which continues for ever. And this is why (he adds) *for his loving kindness endures for ever*.

PSALM CXXXVII

1. By the rivers of Babylon we sat down and wept when we remembered Zion: this psalm represents the utterances of the levites, the (Temple) Singers, who were taken captive in the Babylonian captivity. The meaning is:[2] *by the rivers of Babylon* – there we were forlorn as we sat down desolate, weeping *when we remembered Zion*.

2. Upon the willow-trees: the willows of the brook, for willows grow by the edge of rivers. And as we sat down by the river's edge with our harps in our hands to strike up[3] a song – for such we used to do in Zion –

---

[1] *Bereshith Rabba* 44: 22.   [2] Lit. 'as though to say'.
[3] Lit. 'to stir up song'.

כמנהגנו בציון וכשהיינו מעלים על לבנו ציון היינו נוטשים
כנורותינו מרוב יגון והיינו תולים אותם על ערבים והיינו
885   יושבים ובוכים. ופירוש בתוכה. בתוך בבל;

‎3. כי שם שאלונו. מגזרת פעל כמו ושאלך לאמר. כשהיו מוציאים
אותנו הבבליים השובים אותנו והיו אומרים לנו שנשיר להם משיר
ציון אז היינו בוכים ואומרים להם איך נשיר. ופירוש.
ותוללינו שמחה. היו שואלים אותנו דברי שיר ובכנורותינו
890   שתלינו על הערבים היו שואלים אותנו שנשמח בהם. ויש מפרשים
תוללינו כמו יללתנו ויהיה תוללינו בשקל תושבינו כלומר תחת
יללתנו היו אומרים לנו שנשמח;

‎4. איך נשיר. על אדמת נכר. על אדמה אל נכר הפך שיר ה׳;

‎5. אם אשכחך. תשכח ימיני. פירושו תשכח הנגון כי הימין
תניע מיתרי הכנור;

895   ‎6. תדבק לשוני. שלא תוכל לדבר ולשיר שיר. אם לא אזכרכי.
אם לא אזכור חרבנך ואתאבל עליך ולא אשיר. על ראש שמחתי.
כשאשמח בשום שמחה אזכור אבל ירושלים ואעלהו על ראש השמחה.
עד הנה דברי הלוים והשלשה פסוקים האחרונים הם דברי המשורר.
ובעודו מתנבא על גלות בבל ראה ברוח הקדש גלות בית שני
900   שהיתה על ידי אדום. כי טיטוס החריבה שהיה ממלכות רומי
שהיא מבני אדום. וכן אמר ירמיה הנביא במגלת איכה בעודו
מתנבא על גלות בבל ראה חרבן בית שני ואמר שישי ושמחי בת
אדום על דרך גזום כמו שמח בחור בילדותך וכן אמרו רבותינו
ז״ל בת אדום זו קסרי יושבת בארץ עוז זו רומי וכן אמר זה
905   המשורר בעודו מתנבא על גלות בבל ראה גלות טיטוס ואמר;

883	RCS	היינו נוטשים	898	NRCS	הפסוקים
893	N	כי הימין נוגעת יתרי הכנור	901	BPCD	בני אדום
897	P	אזכיר	901	P	בעודנו מתרעם

and as we recalled Zion to our minds, then did we lay aside our harps because of our great sorrow, hanging them upon the willow-trees, and sat down weeping. And the meaning of *in the midst thereof* is: in the midst of Babylon.

3. For there they required of us: *she'elunu* is in the *pa'el* form (of the *qal*) as in 'and asks you (*she'eleka*) saying' (Gen. xxxii 18). When the Babylonians who led us captive took us forth and asked us to sing to them *of the songs of Zion*, then we wept and said to them *how can we sing?* The meaning of *wetholalenu śimḥah* is: they required of us *words of song* and asked us to make merry with our harps which we hung upon the willow-trees. But some interpret *tholalenu* as 'our wailing', in which case it would be of the same paradigm as *tosh'benu*.[1] That is to say: instead of our wailing they told us to make merry.

4. How can we sing ... in a foreign land?: (that is) in the land of a strange god – (quite) the opposite of a song to the Lord!

5. If I forget you ... let my right hand forget: its meaning is: let it forget its musical art,[2] for it is the right hand which modulates the strings of the harp.

6. Let my tongue cling: so that it is not able to speak or sing a song. *If I do not remember you*: (that is) if I do not remember your destruction. But I will mourn over you and refrain from song. *Above my highest joy*: whenever I rejoice at some happy event, I will remember the desolation of Jerusalem and *set* it *above my highest joy*. Thus far are the words of the levites. But the last three verses are the words of the psalmist who, while still prophesying concerning the Babylonian exile, foresees by divine inspiration the exile following the destruction of the Second Temple which was brought about by Edom, for it was destroyed by Titus who belonged to the Roman empire[3] which was of the Edomites. And the prophet Jeremiah expresses a similar thought in the Scroll of Lamentations, for he too, when he prophesied concerning the Babylonian exile, saw the destruction of the Second Temple and said: 'Rejoice and be glad, O daughter of Edom!' (Lam. iv 21). [This, of course, is to be understood by way of hyperbole, just as it says: 'Rejoice, young man, in your youth' (Eccles. xi 9).] Likewise, our teachers, of blessed memory, have said:[4] the daughter of Edom – this is Caesarea; dweller in the land of Uz – this is Rome. So also the author of the psalm employs (the name Edom in the same sense).

---

[1] That is, a substantive from a *pe-waw* root with first person plural suffix.
[2] *Niggun* from *nagan* (piel) = 'to play on a musical instrument'.
[3] Lit. 'kingdom'.　　　　[4] *Lamentations Rabba* to 4: 21. Cf. *Megilla* 6a.

7. זכר ה׳ לבני אדום את יום ירושלים. יום חרבן ירושלים
שהיו אומרים אלה לאלה ערו ערו עד היסוד בה. כלומר החריבו
והפילו בנין ירושלים עד שתגלו היסוד אשר בה;

8. בת בבל. עתה שב למלכות בבל ואמר שתהיה שדודה. ואמר.
אשרי שישלם לך. והוא דריוש המדי שהחריב בבל;

910

9. אשרי שיאחז. על דרך אכזריות כמו שהיו הם אכזרים על
ישראל. וכן אמר ישעיה הנביא הנני מעיר עליהם את מדי וגו׳.
ואמר וקשתות נערים תרטשנה ופרי בטן לא ירחמו.

Psalm CXXXVIII

1. לדוד אודך בכל לבי. בכל דעתי ושכלי וכן אזמרך בגלוי.
נגד אלהים. והם השופטים והחכמים כמו עד האלהים יבוא דבר

915

שניהם. ההודאה תהיה בלב לבדו או עם הפה והמזמור בפה;

2. אשתחוה אל היכל קדשך. הבית שהיה בו הארון. על חסדך
ועל אמתך. החסד הוא שנתן לו המלוכה והאמת שקים לו דבר
המלוכה כאשר הבטיחהו אחרי שעברו עליו צרות רבות ומכלם

920

הצילהו. כי הגדלת על כל שמך אמרתך. כמו הפוך, כי הגדלת
על כל אמרתך שמך. וכן מקום שם קבר כמו מקום קבר שם. לי
יזעקו אלהי ידענוך ישראל. כמו לי יזעקו ישראל אלהי ידענוך.
אף אש צריך תאכלם כמו אף צריך אש תאכלם וכמוהם רבים כמו

In prophesying concerning the Babylonian exile he beheld the exile brought about by Titus and says:

7. Remember, O Lord, against the people of Edom the day of Jerusalem: (that is) the day of the destruction of Jerusalem when they said to one another: *down with it, down with it, down to its very foundations!*: that is to say, destroy and demolish the structure of Jerusalem until you lay bare *its foundations.*

8. O daughter of Babylon: now he returns (to speak of) the kingdom of Babylon and says that it will be *destroyed.* And he says: *happy the man who repays you*: this refers to Darius the Mede who destroyed Babylon.

9. Happy is he who shall seize: an indication of extreme cruelty, just as they were cruel to Israel. Similarly the prophet Isaiah says: 'I will stir up the Medes against them' (Isa. xiii 17) and (in the next verse) he says: 'their bows will slaughter the young men, and they will have no mercy on the fruit of the womb' (Isa. xiii 18).

PSALM CXXXVIII

1. Of David. I give thee thanks with my whole heart: (that is) with my whole intellect and understanding. And similarly, *I sing thy praises* in public. *Before the gods: 'elohim*: these are the judges and wise men as (in the text) 'each party shall bring his case before the judges (*ha'elohim*)' (Exod. xxii 8). A thanksgiving may be (expressed) either inwardly in one's heart or (recited) orally, but a song of praise (is always expressed) orally.[1]

2. I will bow down towards thy holy temple: (that is) the house where the Ark was. *Because of thy loving kindness and faithfulness*: the *loving kindness* consisted in his having given him the kingdom, whilst by *faithfulness* (is meant) that he fulfilled for him his promise with regard to the kingdom, even as he had promised him. For many tribulations had befallen him and yet he delivered him from all of them. *Ki higdalta 'al kol shim^eka 'imratheka* (is to be explained) as though (the text were) reversed to *ki higdalta 'al kol 'imrath^eka shim^eka* 'for thou hast made great thy name because of thy perfect[2] word' (on the analogy of) *m^eqom sham qeber* which is the same as *m^eqom qeber sham* 'a place for burial there' (Ezek. xxxix 11), *li yiz'aqu 'elohay y^eda'^anuka yiśra'el* equivalent to *li yiz'aqu yiśra'el 'elohay y^eda'^anuka* 'Israel shall cry unto me: My God, we know thee' (Hos. viii 2), *'aph 'esh ṣareka tok^elem* equivalent to *'aph ṣareka 'esh tok^elem* 'even your

---

[1] According to Kimḥi, the root *zamar* differs from *yadah* by implying oral recitation.

[2] That is, *kol* = 'whole, complete', hence 'perfect'.

שכתבנו בספר מכלול בחלק הדקדוק ממנו. ופירוש הפסוק לענין

925   שאמר ועל אמתך כמו שפירשנו שקים לו מה שהבטיחהו אמר על

זה הגדלת שמך על כל אמרתך שאתה אומר ועושה, גוזר ומקים

ועל זה הגדלת שמך שיאמרו הכל גדול ה' שכל מה שאומר עושה

כמו שעשית עמי מה שהבטחתני אחרי אשר אמרו הכל כי לא תהיה

לי המלוכה כי ראו שלטולי גדול. זה הפירוש הוא הנראה בעיני

930   בפסוק הזה. ומפרשים אחרים פירשו כי הגדלת על כל הגדולות

שמך ואמרתך. והחכם רבי אברהם בן עזרא פירש. ואודה את

שמך. שם העצם שנכתב ואינו נקרא והנה הטעם כי הגדלת השם

הנכבד שאמרת למשה על כל שם שיש לך כי הם שמות התאר. ולאלה

הפירושים אינו דבק הטעם למה שאמר על חסדך ועל אמתך;

935   3. ביום קראתי. ביום שהייתי בצרה נע ונד וקראתי אליך

ועניתני והושבתני במרחב מהצרה. תרהבני בנפשי עז. בזה

הדבר תחזקני בנפשי בעז, כלומר נתת חזק גדול בנפשי על

אמונתך כי ידעתי כי אין אל זולתך ואתה רואה ומשגיח בעניני

בני אדם;

940   4. יֵדוך ה'. כל מעשיך בזה הדבר שעניתני וקימת לי דבריך

הטוב בדבר המלוכה. יודוך כל מלכי ארץ היודעים אותי.

כי שמעו אמרי פיך. שאתה הבטחתני המלוכה. וכשראו אותי נע

ונד ושאול רודף אחרי להרגני היו נואשים ממלכותי והיה רחוק

בעיניהם שיוכל לחיות. ועתה שקימת לי דברך הטוב יודוך.

945   וזה הפסוק מוכיח הפירוש שפירשתי על כל שמך אמרתך.

5. וישירו. יאמרו שיר ותהלה לה' וישירו בדרכיו ובמעשיו

924	N	שנתבארו בספר מכלול	929	B	ראו כי שלטולי גדול
925	B	שהבטיחנו	930	B	יש מפרשים פירושו
927	B	שאמרו הכל			

adversaries, the fire will consume them' (Isa. xxvi 11). There are many other examples of this, as we have stated in the book *Miklol*, in the grammar section. And (this part of) the verse is to be interpreted in connection with *because of thy faithfulness* (in the previous part of the verse) which, as we have explained, means that he fulfilled what he had promised him. Because of this he says *thou hast made thy name great by thy perfect word*, for thou dost promise (a thing) and perform it, thou dost make a decree and fulfil it. And on this account *thou hast made thy name great*, for everyone will say 'Great is the Lord, for whatsoever he says he accomplishes!' – just as thou hast performed what thou didst promise me, though they all believed that I would not obtain the kingdom when they saw how great was (the misery of) my homelessness. This, in my opinion, is the (most probable) interpretation of this verse. Other commentators, however, explain it as follows: *for thou hast made greater than all* thy marvellous deeds *thy name and thy word*. And the learned Rabbi Abraham Ibn Ezra interprets (the words) *and give thanks to thy name* (as referring to) the Tetragrammaton which may be written but not pronounced. Hence the meaning is: *thou hast made great* the honoured name, which thou didst reveal to Moses, above all thy names, these being mere attributes. But (in fact) neither of these interpretations explains the significance of what he says in *because of thy loving kindness and thy faithfulness*.

3. When I called: (that is) when I was in distress, a fugitive and a wanderer, then I called to thee and thou didst answer me and set me at large out of my distress. *Thou didst increase strength in my soul*: in this matter thou didst encourage me in my soul with strength; that is to say, thou hast infused great vigour into my soul because of thy faithfulness, for I know that there is no God besides thee and that thou dost behold and watch over the affairs of men.

4. They will praise thee, O Lord: (because of) all thy works. Because of this matter, viz. that thou didst answer me and didst fulfil thy good word in the matter of the kingdom. *All the kings of the earth* who know me *will praise thee, for they have heard the words of thy mouth*, how thou didst assure me of the kingdom. When they saw me, a fugitive and a wanderer with Saul in pursuit of me to kill me, they abandoned the idea of my accession to the throne,[1] for it seemed far-fetched to them that (such an event) could come to pass. But now that thou has fulfilled for me thy good word, *they will praise thee*. (Note further that) this verse supports my interpretation of *'al kol 'imrath^eka shim^eka* (*v.* 2 above).

5. And they will sing: they will sing songs and psalms to the Lord and

---

[1] Lit. 'they despaired of my kingdom'.

הנוראים כי בידו הכל להשפיל ולהגביה. ויאמרו תמיד כי
גדול כבוד ה׳ והוא לבדו האל כי במלוך דוד אומר ויצא שם
דוד בכל הארצות וה׳ נתן פחדו על כל הגוים ובפחדם ממנו פחדו
מהאל, כי הכירו וידעו כי מה׳ היתה לו, ומתוך כך הודו באל
כי הוא אדון על הכל שהמליך את דוד אחר שנואשו ממנו כל בני
אדם. וכן שלח חירם מלך צור לשלמה, ברוך ה׳ אלהי ישראל
אשר עשה את השמים ואת הארץ אשר נתן לדוד המלך בן חכם. הנה
מתוך גדולת דוד ומלכותו הודה באל כי הוא עשה את השמים ואת
הארץ;

6. כי רם ה׳ ושפל יראה. אז יודו כי רם ה׳ ושפל יראה
ומשגיח בתחתונים לא כמו שהיו אומרים עבים סתר לו ולא יראה
וחוג שמים יתהלך. כשראו כי ראה בעניי ובשפלותי הודו כי
שפל יראה אף על פי שהוא רם. וגבוה ממרחק יידע. מבנין
הפעיל בשקל ואלמנה לא ייטיב. פירושו והוא גבוה וממרחק
שהם השמים שהם רחוקים מן הארץ משם יודיע דרכיו לבני אדם
שידעו כי הוא רואה אותם. והמפרשים פירשו יידע ישבר כמו
ויודע בהם אנשי סכות, רוצה לומר הוא רם ויראה השפל וייטיב
לו וישבר הגבוה והגאה ואף על פי שהוא לו למרחוק לפי דעתו.

7. אם אלך. אמר דוד כשהייתי הולך בקרב צרה שהייתי קרוב
למות. זהו בקרב צרה. כשאני בעמק הצרה אתה תחיני. על
אף איבי. על אפם ועל חמתם כלומר על כרחם שלא כטובתם תשלח
ידך בקרב הצרה ותושיעני ימינך.

8. ה׳ יגמר בעדי. כמו שהתחיל להטיב עמי כן יגמר חסדו

950

955

960

965

sing of his ways and his great works, for everyone is in his power either to bring low or to raise on high. And they will say continually *for great is the glory of the Lord* and he alone is God. For of the period in which David reigned it is said: 'And the fame of David spread abroad into all lands, and the Lord brought the fear of him upon all nations' (1 Chron. xiv 17). And since they dreaded him, so too were they in dread of God, for they acknowledged and knew that it was from the Lord. Consequently, they praised God because he is Lord over all and made David king, although everyone had given up hope of this. And so also Hiram, king of Tyre, sent to Solomon saying: 'Blessed be the Lord God of Israel, who made heaven and earth, who has given king David a wise son' (2 Chron. ii 11). Thus, because of the greatness of David and his kingdom, he confessed of God that he made the heavens and the earth!

6. For though the Lord is high, he regards the lowly: then will they confess that *though the Lord is high, he regards the lowly* and that he cares for the lower beings – which is the very opposite of what they used to say:[1] 'Thick clouds enwrap him, so that he does not see, and he walks on the vault of the heaven' (Job xxii 14). For when they saw that he did have regard to my distress and my lowly estate, then they confessed that *he regards the lowly*, although he himself *is high*. *He that is on high makes known from afar*: *yᵉyedaʻ* is *hiphil* conjugation on the analogy of 'he has done no good (*yᵉyetib*) to the widow' (Job xxiv 21). The interpretation is: *he is on high* and *from afar*, that is, the heavens, for they are far from the earth. And thence he makes known his ways to men that they may know that he sees them. But the commentators explain *yᵉyedaʻ* as meaning 'he will break' as in 'and with them he chastised (*wayodaʻ*) the men of Succoth' (Jud. viii 16). Thus he means to say: though he is *high*, yet he regards the lowly to do him good; but as for the man who is arrogant and proud, him he chastises – even though such a person thinks that he is too far from him to be aware of him.[2]

7. Though I walk: David says: when I used to walk *in the midst of trouble* – for I was near to death. And this is (the meaning of) *in the midst (bᵉqereb) of trouble*, viz., when I am in the very midst of trouble, *thou dost preserve my life against the wrath of my enemies*: against their wrath and fierce anger, that is to say, against their will and to their own detriment *thou dost stretch forth thy hand in the midst of trouble and thy right hand delivers me*.

8. The Lord will fulfil his purpose for me: just as he has dealt kindly with me in the beginning, so may he fulfil his kindness towards me. *Lord*

---

[1] Lit. 'not as they used to say'.
[2] Lit. 'although he is to him far to know him'.

970 בעדי . ה׳ ענין קריאה . ה׳ חסדך יהיה עמי לעולם ואני שאני
מכיר בטובך וכי אני מעשה ידיך כי אתה עשיתני ואתה גדלתני
והמלכתני אל תרף חסדך ממני .

Psalm CXXXIX

1. למנצח לדוד מזמור ה׳ חקרתני ותדע;‎ חקרת לבי וידעת
אותו כמו שאמר אני ה׳ חוקר לב ובחן כליות;

975 2. אתה ידעת שבתי וקומי . הזכיר מתנועות האדם הישיבה
והקימה כי בחפץ האדם ישב ויקום כי כשישב וירצה לקום חשב
בלבו הדבר שבעבורו ירצה לקום ואם היה עומד וירצה לשבת חשב
בלבו הדבר שבעבורו ירצה לשבת והנה חפץ האדם ומחשבתו ידעם
האל ויבינם למרחוק כלומר קודם שיחשוב . לרעי . למחשבי מן
980 וברעיון לבו;

3. ארחי . והוא מהלכי ביום . ורבעי . והוא שכבי בלילה
שהוא רובץ במטחו מתרגום ותרבץ ורבעת והנה הזכיר ארבע תנועות
האדם שהם הישיבה והקימה וההליכה והשכיבה כי לעולם ינוע
האדם מזו לזו ופירוש . זרית . סבבת מן זר זהב סביב כלומר
985 כל תנועותי ומחשבותי ידעת כי אתה סביב גופי וסביב מחשבי .
וכל דרכי הסכנת . הרגלת כמו ההסכן הסכנתי אמר ידעת כל דרכי
כמו האדם המורגל בדבר שיודע אותו והחכם הכוזרי כתב כן יחשוב
האדם כי כל אבריו מושמים בחכמה וסדר ושעזר ויראה אותם
נשמעים לחפצו והוא איננו יודע מה שראוי להניע מהם על הדמיון
990 שירצה לקום וימצא כל האברים כעוזרים השומעים כבר הקימו
גופו והוא לא ידע האברים ההם וכן כשירצה ללכת או לשבת ושאר

חשב הדבר בלבו	977 B	שאני ח׳	970 BNM
ומחשבו	978 BMD	לבי	973 PCD
שיחשבם	979 PM	שנאמר	974 NCS
מתרגמינן	982 BM	חושב N חשב הדבר בלבו	976 B
ארבעת	982 B	ורצה לקום	976 B

is in the vocative: *O Lord! Let thy loving kindness be* with me *for ever*. And as for me, seeing I acknowledge thy goodness and I am *the work of thy hands* – for thou has formed me and exalted me and made me king – *do not withdraw* thy loving kindness from me.

PSALM CXXXIX

1. To the conductor. A psalm of David. Lord thou hast examined me and knowest me: thou hast examined my mind and knowest it, just as it says: 'I, the Lord, examine the mind and test the heart' (Jer. xvii 10).

2. Thou knowest when I sit down and when I rise up: of the movements of the human being, he refers (particularly) to sitting down and rising up, since it is by his own freewill that man sits down or rises up. Thus, if he sits down and then wishes to rise up, he must have thought over something in his mind as a result of which he wishes to rise up. And (conversely) if he happens to be standing and wishes to sit down, something must have crossed his mind as a result of which he wishes to sit down. But God knows the desires and plans of man and *discerns* them *from afar*, that is, before (man) conceives them. *L^{e}re^{c}i* (is equivalent) to 'my thought', (its meaning being derived) from 'and of the thought (*b^{e}ra^{c}yon*) of his heart' (Eccles. ii 22).

3. My path: that is, my walking about by day. *W^{e}rib^{c}i*: that is, my lying down by night, which (means) his lying in his bed and (is to be explained) from *ur^{e}ba^{c}ath* (which is equivalent) in the Targum to *watirbaṣ* 'and she lay down' (Num. xxii 27). Hence note that he mentions the four movements of a human being, viz. sitting down, rising up, walking and lying down, for a man is continually in a state of motion from one of them to the other. And the meaning of *zeritha* is 'thou dost encompass', (being derived from the sense) of (*zer* in) 'a circlet (*zer*) of gold round about' (Exod. xxv 24), the idea of the verse being:[1] thou knowest all my movements and thoughts, for thou art round about my body and round about my thoughts. *And thou art familiar with all my paths:* (*hiskantah* means) 'you are accustomed', as in *hahasken hiskanti* 'Was I ever wont?' (Num. xxii 30). He says: *thou are familiar with all my paths* just as one who is accustomed to something knows it. And the learned (author of) The Kuzari states:[2] 'Well may man contemplate upon the fact that all his limbs are arranged with consummate wisdom, in proper order and proportion, for he sees how they obey his will, though he himself know not which of them he should move. If, for example, he wishes to rise, he finds that his limbs, like obedient helpers, have raised his body although he does not even know (the nature

---

[1] Lit. 'that is to say'.   [2] Part 3 : 11.

המצבים ולזה רמז באמרו ארחי ורבעי זרית וכל דרכי הסכנת,

ואדוני אבי ז"ל פירש ארחי ורבעי.   ארחי.   אחור וקדם.   ורבעי.

ארבע רוחות מעלה ומטה ימין ושמאל   וזרית   מן אזרה לכל רוח

אמר כי בזה הסכנת ותקנת והועלת עניני בששת צדדים שזרית לי   995

לכל עבר שלא היו לי מצד אחד והחכם רבי אברהם בן עזרא פירש.

וכל דרכי.   חמש ההרגשות שנתן לכל אבר הרגשתו והרגיל אותו

בה וכן לכל אבר משאר האברים מה שיעשה אבר זה לא יעשנו אבר

אחר;

4. כי אין מלה בלשוני.   עוד המלה איננה עדין בלשוני לא   1000

החלותי לדבר   ואתה ידעת כלה.   כלומר כל המלה שאני רוצה

לדבר או פירושו אני חושב להוציא הדבר מלבי ואתה ידעת מחשבי

והדבר שאני מוציא בפי אין בלשוני להוציאו במחשבי ואתה ידעת

מה שאני אוציא בפי ואני לא ידעתיו אף על פי שחשבתיו כמו

שאמר שלמה לאדם מערכי לב ומה' מענה לשון וזה הפירוש הוא   1005

הנכון אצלי;

5. אחור וקדם צרתני.   פירש אדוני אבי ז"ל ביצירת העובר

בבטן אמו ופירש.   צרתני.   ענין צורה ואמר.   ותשת עלי כפכה.

כמו שעושין לגבינה על דרך וכגבנה תקפיאני ורוצה לומר ותשת

עלי למדת הארך השם לעובר מדה;   1010

6. פלאיה.   כן כתוב וקרי פליאה ואחד הוא אלא שהם שני

משקלים כי הכתוב הוא מן והוא פלאי יאמר פלאי לזכר פלאיה

997 B		ומרגיל	1003 P
998 R	מה שיעשה אבר זה לא יעשה אבר אחר ומה		1004 B
	שיעשה אבר זה לא יעשה אבר אחר		

אין כח בלשוני להוציא
ידעתי

of) these limbs. It is the same if he wishes to walk, sit, or assume any position.' And he makes an allusion thereto when he says: *My path and my lying down thou knowest, and art familiar with all my paths*. My revered father, of blessed memory, interprets as follows: *my path* – behind and before (me); and *weribʿi* (refers to) the four directions,[1] viz. above, below, right and left. And (he understands) *zeritha* from 'I will scatter (*ᵉzareh*) to every wind' (Ezek. xii 14). Thus (the psalmist means to) say: in this respect thou hast arranged, prepared and benefited my affairs in all six directions, in that thou hast spread them abroad for me in every direction so that they are not only on one side.[2] The learned Rabbi Abraham Ibn Ezra explains as follows: *and all my paths*: (refers to) the five senses, for to each of the (principal) organs he assigns its (particular) sensibility, training it to react accordingly. And so with regard to each of the remaining organs, the function performed by one organ is not performed by another.[3]

4. For there is not a word on my tongue: the word is not yet on my tongue – I have not begun to speak – *but thou, Lord, knowest it all*: that is to say, the complete word which I wish to speak. The text may also be interpreted as follows: as I am about to give expression to some idea, thou already knowest my thought. And even though I cannot express in speech the thought (which I wish to express), yet thou knowest what I wish to express, though I do not know – and this, despite the fact that I have been pondering it. It is as Solomon said: 'To man belong the plans of the heart, but the reply of the tongue is from the Lord' (Prov. xvi 1). This interpretation is, in my opinion, the correct one.

5. 'Aḥor waqedem ṣartani: my revered father, of blessed memory, explains this (text) with references to the formation of the embryo in the mother's womb, understanding *ṣartani* from the sense of *ṣurah* 'a form'.[4] And (the psalmist) says: *thou hast spread thy hand over me*: just as is done with cheese, after the analogy of 'and curdle me like cheese' (Job x 10). And by *thou hast spread over me (thy hand)*, he means, (thou hast assigned my) dimension, for he gives each embryo its size.[5]

6. Pᵉli'ayah: so it is written but it is to be read *pᵉli'ah*, the meaning in either case being the same, except that they are separate forms. For the *kethibh*

---

[1] *Ruaḥ* = 'wind', 'direction'. Kimḥi's father understands *ribʿi* to be from the same root as the Hebrew word for 'four' (*'arbaʿ*).

[2] The meaning of the passage is obscure. In *Sefer Ha-Shorashim* the reading appears to be *binyani* = 'my constitution', instead of *'inyanay* 'my affairs'.

[3] Lit. 'that which one organ does the other organ does not do'.

[4] Cf. Jer. i 5: 'Before I formed thee (*'eṣorka*).'

[5] Presumably Kimḥi is referring to the hand as a means of indicating a length (*'orek*).

לנקבה והקרי פליא לזכר בשקל נביא פליאה לנקבה בשקל נביאה
ואמר דוד . פליאה דעת ממני . זאת הדעת פליאה ממני ונשגבה
לא אוכל להשיג לה והדעת היא יצירת גוף האדם בארבעה טבעים 1015
זה הפך זה וזה כנגד זה והם החם והקר והלחות והיבש והאל
בחכמתו יצרם בגוף הנוצר ומזגם כדי שיתקים הגוף בהם והחכם
רבי אברהם בן עזרא פירש אלה שני הפסוקים דבק למה שאמר
למעלה ארחי ורבעי ופירש צרתני מן וצרת עליה אל תצרם אמר
צרתני אחור ופנים ותשת עלי כפכה ואין מצור ומצוק כזה רוצה 1020
לומר שאין לי מעמד ומהלך בלתך ואמר . פליאה דעת ממני .
זאת הדעת והמחשבה היא . אנה אלך . כלומר כי אין יכלת באדם
ללכת אם לא יוליכהו רוח השם על כן אנה אלך מרוחך והטעם
כמו מפניך ;

7 . אנה אלך . מלרע וכן אנחנו עלים והשאר כלם מלעיל . 1025
אמר אנה אלך מרוחך אם אחשוב ללכת ולהסתר מרוחך או לברוח
מפניך והטעם כפול במלות שונות . אם אמר לעשות זה לא אוכל
כי אתה נמצא בכל מקום ומקום לא יכילך ;

8 . אם אסק . אם אעלה כתרגומו אם אחשוב שאוכל לעלות שמים
ושם אעלה ולא אמצאך שם אתה . ואציעה שאול . ואם אמר שארד 1030
שאול והוא עמקי הארץ . הנך . הנך שם ואמר . ואציעה . לפי
שהשאול מצע האדם במותו והנה זכר העגולה והמוצק ובכל נמצא
אם כן לא אוכל ללכת שלא אפגע בך ;

1015	B	גוף באדם
1018	PD	דבקים
1021	R	שאין לו
1021	C	שאין לי מעמד בלתך ולא מהלך
1023	B	רוח ה' ית'

1030 After שאול ואציעה P מ' תחתית שהשאול מפני
והמצע הוא תחתית האדם בשכבו אמר כן או אמר
1031 Before ואציעה RC מ' שהיא מפני אוציעה ואמר
תחתית והמצע תחתית האדם בשכבו, או אמר
ואמר C but for אמר או

is exemplified from 'it is wonderful (*peli'y*)' (Jud. xiii 18), that is, masculine *pel'iy*, feminine *p^eli'yah*, whilst the *qere* has the masculine form *peli'* of the same form as *nabi'*, the feminine being *p^eli'ah* of the form *n^ebi'ah*. And David says: *such knowledge is too wonderful for me*: this knowledge is so *wonderful* and so *high* that *I cannot reach it*. And by *such knowledge* (he means) the creation of the human body (and its preservation in accordance with the principle of the harmonious co-operation of) the four natural qualities, each one being the opposite and contrary of the one corresponding to it, viz. heat and cold, moisture and dryness. For God in his wisdom so fashions them and combines them in the body of the created being to the end that the body may continue to exist as a result of their interactions.[1] The learned Rabbi Abraham Ibn Ezra, however, interprets both these verses in connection with what (the psalmist) says above, viz. *my path and my lying down*. He explains *ṣartani* from 'you shall besiege (*w^eṣarta*) it' (Deut. xx 12), 'do not contend with them (*t^eṣurem*)' (Deut. ii 19). Thus (the psalmist) says: *thou didst beset me behind and before, and hast spread thy hand over me*: no manner of siege or distress is comparable to this state in which I am,[2] for I can find no place to stand or walk where thou art not. And he says: *such knowledge is too wonderful for me*: the knowledge and thought (referred to here consist in knowing) *where can I go*, for man by himself can go nowhere without being moved[3] by the spirit of the Lord. Therefore *where can I go from thy spirit?*, the meaning of *meruḥeka* being the same as *mippaneka* 'from thy presence'.

7. *'anah 'elek*: the accent is *milra'* as in *'anah '^anaḥ^enu 'olim* (Deut. i 28), but in all other instances the accent is *mil'el*. He says: *where can I go from thy spirit*: were I to think of going away to hide from thy spirit or escape from thy presence – a repetition of the same idea in different words – were I to think of doing so, I would not succeed, for thou art to be found in every place and space cannot contain thee.

8. *'im 'essaq* means 'if I ascend', being used in this sense in the Targum. Though I were to imagine that I could ascend to heaven and succeed in ascending there without finding thee – *thou art there*. *If I make my bed in Sheol*: and if I were to say that I shall go down to Sheol – that is the nethermost part of the earth – *behold thou art*: behold thou art there. He says *if I make my bed* because Sheol is (as it were) man's resting place upon death. Thus he includes the upper and the lower regions,[4] for he is to be found

---

[1] Lit. 'so that the body may continue to exist by them'.

[2] Lit. 'there is no siege or distress like this'.

[3] Lit. 'unless the spirit of the Lord move him'.

[4] *Muṣaq*: a peculiar use of the term, occasionally employed in this sense by the Jewish Philosophers of the middle ages. Cf. J. Klatzkin's *Thesauros of Philosophical Terms*, 4 vols. (Berlin 1928–33).

9. אשא כנפי שחר . אם אמרתי אקח כנפי שחר ואעוף בהם ממזרח
למערב אם אמצאנו הנה לא אוכל ללכת בלתו כי בכל מקום הוא .   1035
ואמר . כנפי שחר . כי השחר מתפשט כרגע ממזרח למערב ואחרית
ים הוא המערב ואמר באחרית ים רוצה לומר בסוף העולם כי הים
סובב הארץ ואחרית ים הוא סוף העולם כלומר אם אלך ממזרח
למערב ברגע אחד לא אוכל ללכת בלתך , כל בכל מקום תנחני ידך   1040
ותאחזני ימינך .

10. גם שם . מפרש;

11. ואמר . ישופני . מגזרת נשף שנים שרשים וענין אחד נשף
ושוף כמו נמל ומול נפץ ופוץ . אמר אם אמר ואחשוב כי החשך
יחשיכני ויסתירני שלא תראה אותי ומעשי ומחשבותי . ולילה
אור בעדני . הלילה שהוא חשך האיר בעדני ותראני בלילה כמו   1045
ביום;

12. גם חשך . שנה הענין ושלש ורבע להודיע כי כן הוא כי
אין חשך וצלמות להסתר מלפניו . לא יחשיך . פעל יוצא פירושו
לא יחשיך דבר ממך שלא תראהו כי הכל שוה לנגדך והלילה כמו
היום יאיר לך . כחשיכה כאורה . שני כפ"י הדמיון כמו כי   1050
כמוך כפרעה , כעבד כאדניו , כמלוה כלוה , והדומים להם והוא
דרך קצרה רוצה לומר זה כזה וזה כזה;

13. כי אתה . ואיך יסתרו מחשבותי ממך ואתה קנית כליותי
כי הם תחלת המחשבה כי הכליות יועצות והלב גומר ואם אתה

1036	BM	ח׳	ואמר ... תנחני ידך
1039	NRC		ללכת בלתו
1050	N		אלו שני כפי הדמיון

1053 After כליותי M׳ ואמר קנית כי ענין הקניה
המצא דבר שלא היה או למי שלא היה לו
ואמר כליותי

everywhere. Such being the case, I can go nowhere without meeting thee.

9. If I take up the wings of the dawn: were I to say that I will take up *the wings of the dawn* and fly by means of them from east to west (to see) if I may (not) find him, behold I can go nowhere beyond him, since he is in every place. He says *the wings of the dawn* because the dawn spreads in an instant from east to west, for (the expression) *the limit of the sea* signifies the west. Thus when he says *the limit of the sea* he means in the one extremity of the universe, for the sea encompasses the earth and (in this way) *the limit of the sea* represents the one extremity of the universe. Hence the meaning of the verse will be:[1] though I were to travel in one instant from east to west, I could not go without finding thee,[2] because in every place *thy hand will meet me and thy right hand will hold me fast.*

10. Even there: the meaning is clear.

11. He says *will cover me:* *y^eshupheni* cognate with the root *nashaph*, (that is) two distinct forms of the root – *nashaph* and *shuph* – with the same meaning. So too (we have) *namal* and *mul*; *naphaṣ* and *puṣ*. He means: if I were to think and imagine that the darkness could conceal and hide me so that thou seest neither me nor my works and thoughts, then would *the night about me be light*, (that is) the night which (ordinarily) is dark would throw light about me, and thou wouldst see me by night even as by day.

12. Even the darkness: he reiterates the same idea, (repeating it) a third and a fourth time to make it known that such is the case, viz. that there is no manner of darkness or deep darkness through which one may be concealed from him. *Yaḥ^ashik:* a transitive verb, the meaning being: cannot obscure anything from thee that thou canst not see, for all is alike to thee, for to thee the night gives light as the day. *The darkness is as the light:* *kaḥ^asheka ka'orah* (an example of) the double *kaph* for comparison, as in 'for you are as Pharaoh' (Gen. xliv 18), 'as with the servant, so with his master' (Isa. xxiv 2), 'as with the lender, so with the borrower' (Isa. xxiv 2), and many other instances. It is an abbreviated form of expression, that is, (written fully it would be) the former is like the latter and the latter like the former.

13. For thou: how can my thoughts be hidden from thee seeing that *thou didst form my inward parts*? For the latter are the seat of thought, since the *inward parts* prompt and the mind[3] completes (the thinking). If thou hast

---

[1] Lit. 'as though to say'.   [2] Lit. 'I could not go without thee'.
[3] Lit. 'the heart'.

9

קנית אותם איך יסתר ממך מה שהם יועצות ועוד כי אתה. תסכני   1055
בבטן אמי. שהוא מקום חשך ואין שם אור ואם שם יצרתני ובעצמות
וגידים סוככתני איך לא תדע כל הסתרים ויש אומרים כי זכר כליותי
מפני שהם תחלת היצירה בגוף האדם כי הם כמו שני סדני הגלגל.
ועניין קנית כעניין קנה שמים וארץ;

14. אודך. נוראות. עלילות נוראות יש ביצירתי ואודך עליהם   1060
כי נפלאתי ביצירה רוצה לומר נפליתי שנפלאים מעשיך בי.
ונפשי ידעת מאד. טעם מאד דבק עם נפלאים מעשיך כלומר מעשיך
נפלאים מאד. ונפשי ידעת. כלומר נפשי המשכלת אמר אף על פי
שבשאר החיים נפלאים מעשיך אין בהם מי שיכיר אבל בי נתת הנפש
המשכלת יותר על שאר החיים והיא תדע מעשיך הנפלאים ותודה לך   1065
עליהם ונוראות היצירה הם נגלים לחכמים. כי כל אבר ואבר
נברא בחכמה ועל התכונה שנברא הוא לצרך ולתעלת וכל אדם צריך
להתבונן בהם ומתוך כך יכיר נפלאות היוצר ויודה לו עליהם ואם
באנו לספר בזה החבור תכונת האברים ותעלתם ומזג הכחות ותעלתם
יארך הספור אבל המשתוקק להם ימצאם בספרי החכמים;   1070

15. לא נכחד עצמי. לא נכחד כעניין לא נכחד מאדני. עצמי.
העי"ן נקראת בקמץ חטף ויש מפרשים אותו כמו עצמי בפתח העי"ן
שפירושו גופי אמר לא נכחד גופי ממך כאשר עשיתי בסתר בבטן
אמי וכאשר רקמתי בתחתיות ארץ והוא הרחם שהוא מקום שפל ואפל
כמו תחתיות ארץ וכן אופן אחד בארץ רוצה לומר שפל כנגד האופנים   1075

1056 R	החשך	חשוך C	P	מ׳	לפי שמהם ... הערוה
1057 B		כל הסתום			הם נכרים
1058 After הגלגל M מ׳ אברהם ר׳ החכם פירש כן			1066 N		ואם באתי
והנשיא רב אברהם בר חייא פירש כי הזכיר			1068 N		תחתיות הארץ
תחלה הכליות לפי שהם גומרות יצירת גוף			1075 BRC		
האדם לפי שמהם ירד הזרע לגיד הערוה					

formed them, how can that which they prompt be hidden from thee ?
And besides *thou didst cover me in my mother's womb*: which is a dark place
where there is no light. If thou didst form me there and cover my bones
and sinews, how couldst thou not know all secrets ? But some claim that he
says *my inward parts* because these constitute the nucleus of the embryo
in the human body,[1] being analogous to the two poles of a sphere. The
meaning of *qanitha* is the same as (in the text) 'maker (*qoneh*) of heaven
and earth' (Gen. xiv 19).

14. I will give thanks to thee: *nora'oth*: in the course of my creation are
(to be seen) wonderful works, because of which *I give thee thanks, for I am
marvellously* formed. Thus by *niphlethi* he means: *marvellous are thy works
in my* (creation). *And, my soul knows, exceedingly*: *exceedingly* is to be
understood in connection with *marvellous are thy works*, that is to say, *thy
works are exceedingly marvellous. And my soul knows*: that is, my rational
soul. He says: though thy works in respect of other living things are marvellous, yet not one of them is capable of thought,[2] but in me, (as against
all other forms of life), thou hast implanted in addition a rational soul
which understands thy marvellous works and gives thee thanks because of
them. And these wonderful (works) of creation are well known to the men
of science, for every single organ is created with (consummate) wisdom,
being designed in its creation to serve the purpose and function for which
it is required.[3] It is therefore the duty of every man to observe these things
as a result of which he will discern the marvels of the creator and thank
him accordingly. But if we were to elaborate in this treatise on (such topics
as) the uses and functions of the organs, and the (harmonious) blending of
the natural forces and their uses, then indeed our discourse would be very
lengthy. However, anyone eager (to know) about (such things) can find
them in the writings of the scientists.

15. My frame is not hidden from thee: *is not hidden* is to be understood (from) 'we will not hide (*n^ekahed*) it from my Lord' (Gen. xlvii 18).
'*osmi*: the '*ayin* is read with *qames-hatuph*. But some explain it as equivalent
to '*asmi* with *pathah* under the '*ayin*, the meaning being *my body*. He says:
my body was not hidden from thee when *I was secretly kneaded into shape*:
in my mother's womb, and when *I was patterned in the depths of the earth*,
that is, the womb, which is a hollow and dark place like *the depths of the
earth*; so also (the meaning of *ba'ares* in the text) 'one wheel upon the
earth' (Ezek. i 15), meaning *below* in contradistinction to the wheels above

---

[1] Lit. 'the beginning of creation in the human body'.
[2] Lit. 'not one of them understands'.
[3] Lit. 'and according to the disposition with which it is created, it is for a need
and use'.

שלמעלה ממנו ופירוש עשיתי מעניין עשו דדי בתוליהן שהוא הכתישה
והסחיטה ואמר זה הלשון בעניין היצירה כמו שדמה אותו להתכת
החלב והקפותו כמו שמקפין ומעשין אותה בידים כי הטפה הראשונה
נתכת ונגררת ואחר כן תשוב קפואה כמו הגבינה מן החלב ואמר
בו רקמתי . דמה מעשה היצירה בגידים ובעצמות ובבשר ועור   1080
למעשה הרקמה שהוא על פנים רבים ועל מהלכים מסתבכים והחכם
רבי אברהם בן עזרא פירש עצמי כחי רוצה לומר הכח שהוא טרם
מעשה ביצירה בכח הזקן בנער ובכח הדבור בנולד כן היה הנוצר
בכח טרם שיצא לידי מעשה וזה נסתר ונעלם ממראה העין גם ממראה
עיני הלב ואף על פי כן ממך לא נכחד;   1085

16. גלמי . הוא הטפה הקפואה קודם שיצירו בה האברים כמו שנקרא
העץ גלם בטרם שנעשה כלי ואמר . ראו עיניך . שנתת בה כח
להתיצר בה האברים. ועל ספרך כלם יכתבו. פירושו לפניך הם
ידועים כמו הדבר הכתוב בספר ופירוש כלם כל האברים טרם ציורם
הם ידועים לפניך. ימים יצרו. בימים רבים תהיה יצירת   1090
האברים כי אינם נוצרים בפעם אחת. ולו אחד בהם. הימים
שיוצרו בהם לא להם הם אחד כי כלם ידעם ברגע אחד והכתוב ולא
באל"ף ופירושו. ולא אחד בהם. שלא ידעו טרם היותו והחכם
רבי אברהם בן עזרא פירש הכתוב כן לא היה האחד באברים נכר
ונבדל בגלם בתחלת יצירתו וכלם היו שם בכח התולדות ולא היה   1095
העין והאזן או האחד משאר האברים נכר ונבדל ואף על פי שהוא
באותו הגלם;

1076	BP	הימנו	1086	BRAC	בהם
1077	BR	והסחיטה	1087	NMCD	טרם
1078	C	והקפאתו	1088	RPM	להתציר
1080	M	ובעור	1088	B	לעתיד הם ידועים
1083	MC	וכח הדבור	1094	A	אחד מן האברים
1086	B	קודם שיכירו באברים בה	1096	M	או אחד

it. And '*uṣethi* is to be interpreted on the analogy of '*iṣu* in (the text) 'their virgin breasts were pressed' (Ezek. xxiii 3) which has the sense of crushing and pressing. He uses this imagery in describing the process of creation, just as he (previously) represented it as the curdling of milk and its coagulation, after the manner in which milk is curdled and crushed with the hands. For so too the drop[1] is first of all poured out and spilled and subsequently becomes congealed in the same way as cheese (is produced) from milk. He says: *I was patterned*: he compares the process of creation – sinews, bones, flesh and skin – to embroidery work because it is (wrought) in manifold patterns and interwoven designs. The learned Rabbi Abraham Ibn Ezra interprets '*oṣmi* as *koḥi*, that is, the potentialities inherent in the created being,[2] (as for example) the potentiality of old age in youth, or the potentiality of speech in the child that is born. So the created being existed *in potentia* before the consummation of its creation. Now all this is hidden and obscured from the sight of the eye, as indeed also from the perception of the mind. Nevertheless, *it is not hidden from thee*.

16. My unformed substance (*golmi*): that is, the congealed drop prior to the formation of limbs therein. So too wood, before it is carpentered into some form or other[3] is referred to as *golem* (rough, unfinished).[4] And he says: *thine eyes saw*: inasmuch as thou hast endowed it with the potentiality whereby the organs might be created out of it. *And in thy book they are all recorded*: the meaning being, before they are known to thee, just as that which is recorded in a book. And the significance of *all of them* is that all the members are known to thee even prior to their formation. *Day by day they are formed*: the creation of the limbs extends over many days, for they are not all formed at the same time. *But to him they are as one*: the days during which they are formed are to God as one day, for he conceived them all at the same instant. The written text, however, is *weloʾ* with *aleph*, *and not*, the interpretation being: *and there is not even one of them* which he does not perceive before its coming into existence. But the learned Rabbi Abraham Ibn Ezra expounds the text thus: in the early stages of its creation not one of the organs could be recognised or distinguished from the rest in the unformed substance, though each one of them existed in it as a result of the generating process. Neither eye, ear, nor any one of the other organs could be recognised or distinguished, and this despite the fact that each one of them was in the same unformed substance.

---

[1] That is, the drop of semen. Cf. *Aboth* iii: 1: *miṭipah seruḥah* 'from a fetid drop'.
[2] Lit. 'the potentiality which precedes actuality in the process of creation'. The term *koaḥ* is found in Jewish philosophy with the sense of the Greek δύναμις 'potentiality'.
[3] Lit. 'before it is made into a vessel'.
[4] See, for example, *Sifre Numbers*, section 158: *kelim welo gelumim* '(finished) vessels, but not half-finished'.

‎17. ‏ולי מה יקרו רעיך אל. ‏ ‏ופירוש יקרו שלא אוכל להשיגם‎
‎כמו ודבר ה׳ היה יקר בימים ההם ופירוש רעיך מחשבותיך כלומר‎
‎כונותיך ביצירה. ‏ מה עצמו ראשיהם. ‏ ‏פירוש עצמו רבו במספר‎   1100
‎כמו שאמר אחר כן אספרם כי לשון עצם נמצא בענין החזק ובענין‎
‎הרבוי כמו עצמו לי אלמנותיו מחול ימים ופירוש ראשיהם כלליהם‎
‎כמו כי תשא את ראש בני ישראל כלומר כללי כונותיך ביצירה הם‎
‎רבים כל שכן הפרטים;‎

‎18. ‏ אספרם. ‏ ‏כשאבוא לספור אותם לא אוכל כי. ‏ מחול ירבון.‎   1105
‎הקיצותי ועודי עמך. ‏ ‏מרב מחשבותי בהם אני חולם בהם כשאישן‎
‎וכשאקיץ אני מוצא עצמי שאני עמך כלומר במחשבות נפלאותיך‎
‎ויש מפרשים. ‏ הקיצותי. ‏ ‏אלו הייתי תמיד מקיץ כי חצי חיי‎
‎האדם הוא ישן. ‏ ‏ועודי. ‏ ‏עמך שאהיה עמך תמיד ולא אמות לא‎
‎אוכל לספרם והחכם רבי אברהם בן עזרא פירש כאשר אני חושב‎   1110
‎בלבי לדעת רעיך והנה הוא כמראה אלהים והגוף שוכב בהדבק‎
‎נשמת האדם בנשמה העליונה אז תראה תמונות על כן אמר הקיצותי‎
‎ועודי עמך. ‏ ‏כי אין זה כדרך כל החלומות;‎

‎19. ‏ אם תקטל. ‏ ‏דבק למה שאמר הקיצותי ועוד עמך שאני מתעסק‎
‎תמיד במחשבתי בנפלאותיך ובמעשיך אבל פעמים שמטריד אותי דבר‎   1115
‎הרשעים ואם תהרוג אותם שמטרידים אותי והם הרשעים ואנשי דמים‎
‎שאומר להם. ‏ ‏סורו מני. ‏ ‏ולא אוכל להם ואם תקטול אותם יהיו‎
‎כל מחשבותי וכל עסקי בך;‎

‎20. ‏ אשר ימרוך. ‏ ‏בחסרון אל״ף פ״א הפעל וכן ולעמשא תמרו‎
‎ופירוש למזמה. ‏ ‏למחשבה כלומר ידברו בך לפי מחשבתם שהיא רעה‎   1120

1100	C		כונתך	1112	B	תמונה	תמונתך P
1107	PMACD		וכשאיקץ	1115	M		מטריד
1107	C	שאני ח׳	M ח׳ עצמי				

17. How precious are thy thoughts to me, O God: by *are precious* he means: I cannot reach them,[1] as in: 'and the word of the Lord was precious (*yaqar*) in those days' (1 Sam. iii 1). *Re'eka* is to be interpreted as 'thy thoughts', that is, thy designs in creation. *How great is the sum of them*: the interpretation of *'aṣemu* is: they are great in number, just as he says subsequently: *if I should count them*, for the root *'aṣam* is found either in the sense of strength or dense numbers, as in: 'their widows are increased (*'aṣemu*) to me above the sand of the seas' (Jer. xv 8). The meaning of *ra'shehem* is: the general principles thereof, as in: 'when you take the number (*ro'sh*) of the children of Israel' (Exod. xxx 12). That is to say, the general principles of thy designs in creation are numerous, how much more (numerous) are the details?

18. If I should count them: if I were to proceed to enumerate them, I could not, for *they are more numerous than the sand*. *When I wake up I am still with thee*: as a consequence of my frequent thoughts concerning them, I dream about them when I sleep, and when I wake up I find that I am with thee, that is to say, in contemplating thy marvels. But some interpret *heqiṣothi*: were I to be continually awake – for man spends half of his lifetime in sleep – and *still with thee*, that is, to be continually with thee and never to die, even then I could not count them. The learned Rabbi Abraham Ibn Ezra explains (*re'eka*) thus: when I meditate to understand *thy thoughts* it is as a vision of God! The body is in a state of rest, whilst the soul is in communion with the Supernal Spirit. Then it sees visions.[2] For this reason he says *when I am awake I am still with thee*, because this kind of vision is altogether different from the ordinary course of dreams.[3]

19. If thou wouldst slay: (the meaning is to be explained) in connection with what he says (in the preceding verse) *when I am awake I am still with thee,* (that is) I am continually engaged in reflecting upon thy marvels and works, but occasionally anxiety on account of the wicked troubles me.[4] But if thou wouldst slay them that trouble me – that is, wicked and *men of blood*, about whom I say *depart from me* but am powerless against them – if thou wouldst slay them, then all my thoughts and interests would be (centred completely) in thee.

20. Who speak of thee: *yomeruka* (appears) with the omission of the *aleph* of the first radical, as in: 'and say (*tomeru*) to Amasa' (2 Sam. xix 14). The interpretation of *limezimmah* is 'in (their) thought', that is to say, they speak

---

[1] *Yaqar* = 'precious, scarce', hence, 'unattainable'.

[2] Poc. 213 reads *temunatheka* 'thy likeness'.

[3] Lit. 'for this is not as the manner of every dream'. See Ibn Ezra's comment to Psalm xvii 15.

[4] Lit. 'the matter of the wicked troubles me'.

ויש לפרש למזמה כמו כי זמה עשו ענין תועבה. נשוא לשוא עריך.
אלה שהם עריך ומשנאיך נשאוך בפיהם לשוא ומלת. נשוא. כמו
נשאו כי בא חסר אל"ף למ"ד הפעל כמו ונשו את כלמתם והאל"ף
הכתובה למשך הנ"ח כמו אל"ף ההלכוא אתו ולא אבוא שמוע ינשוא
כי לא יצעדו והדומים להם שכתבנו בספר מכלול ועריך. משנאיך   1125
כמו ויהי ערך ויש מפרשים נשוא פעול רוצה לומר שמך נשוא
בפיהם לשוא ואמר   עריך   במקום שמך לכנוי;

21. הלא משנאיך. הפסוק כפול בענין במלות שונות כמנהג
ופירשו רבותינו ז"ל כי על המינים נאמר הפסוק הזה שמכירין
וכופרין ומלת   ובתקוממיך. תאר בתוספת תי"ו ופירושו משנאיך   1130
כמו ומתקוממי כעול, ממתקוממים בימינך. אתקוטט. ענין קטטה
בדברי רבותינו ז"ל;

22. תכלית. שנאה גדולה שלא אוכל לשנואם יותר וכפל הענין
לחזק;

23. חקרני. לפי שזכר כי מחשבת הרשעים רעה באמונת האל אמר   1135
חקרני אל ודע לבבי תראה כי לבבי ישר באמונתך וכפל הענין
לחזק. שרעפי. מחשבותי כמו שעפים כי שתי הלשונות בענין
מחשבה כמו שהם באילן סרעפותיו סעפותיו כי המחשבות ללב כמו
הבדים לאילן;

of thee according to their thought, which is evil. But it is also possible to interpret *lime zimmah* as in: 'they commit enormity (*zimmah*)' (Hos. vi 9), which means 'abomination'. *Thine enemies take thy name in vain*: they that are *thine enemies* and they that hate thee take thy name in vain. The word *naśu'* is equivalent to *naśe'u*. It is written defectively without the *aleph* of the third radical on the analogy of: 'they shall bear (*wenaśu*) their shame' (Ezek. xxxix 26). As for the *aleph* which is written, it is for the purpose of drawing out the vowel sound, just like the *aleph* (added in the following instances): 'who went (*hehaleku'*) with him' (Josh. x 24); 'but they were not willing ('*abu'*) to listen' (Isa. xxviii 12); 'they must be carried (*yinnaśu'*), for they cannot walk' (Jer. x 5); and (further examples) like them which we have noted in the book *Miklol*. '*areka* (is the same as) 'they that hate thee', as in: 'he has become your adversary ('*areka*)' (1 Sam. xxviii 16). But some commentators consider *naśu'* to be of the form of the passive participle, meaning: thy name *is taken* in vain in their mouth, '*areka* being substituted for 'thy name'.

21. Do I not (hate) them that hate thee: in this verse there is a repetition of the one idea in different words, according to the regularly accepted usage. But our teachers, of blessed memory, explain that this verse was uttered with reference to the heretics,[1] since these understand and yet deny.[2] The word *ubitheqomemeka* is a participial adjective with the addition of *tau*, the meaning being 'they that hate thee', as in: 'and let him who rises up against me (*umithqomemi*) be like the wrongdoer' (Job xxvii 7); 'from those who rise up (*mimithqomemim*) against thee with thy right hand' (Ps. xvii 7). '*ethqotat* 'I contend' has the meaning of *qetatah* ('quarrel', 'dispute') as used in the words of our teachers, of blessed memory.[3]

22. With complete (hatred I hate them): (that is) with hatred so intense that it is not possible for me to increase my hatred of them. He repeats for the sake of emphasis.

23. Examine me: having previously stated that the thought of the wicked is evil with regard to his (lack of) faith in God, he now says: *examine me, O God, and know my heart*: thou wilt see that my heart is upright in my faith in thee. He repeats for the sake of emphasis. *Śar'apay* (means) 'my thoughts', being the same as *śe'ipim*. Both words are used in the sense of 'thought' in the same way as *sar'apothaw* 'its boughs' and *śe'apothaw* 'its boughs' are used of the (branches of) a tree.[4] For 'thoughts' (stand in the same relation to the) heart as branches to a tree.

---

[1] *Minim* is mostly applied to Jew–Christians. Cf. M. Jastrow, *Dictionary*, II, p. 776.
[2] *Sabbath* 116a.
[3] Cf., for example *Koheleth Rabba* IV: 9: *mere qetatah* 'men of quarrel'.
[4] Cf. Ezek. xxxi 5, 8.

1140

24. וראה. דרך עצב. דרך מרי כמו והמה מרו ועצבו את רוח
קדשו. ונחני. אם תראה בי שום דרך מרי המיתני מיד זהו דרך
עולם כמו אנכי הלך בדרך כל הארץ כי הלך האדם אל בית עלמו;

Psalm CXL

1. למנצח מזמור לדוד. זה המזמור חברו דוד על דואג ועל
הזיפים שהיו מלשינים אותו אל שאול;

1145

2. חלצני ה׳. שלא יזיקו לי דבריהם הרעים והפסוק כפול בענין
במלות שונות;

3. אשר חשבו. חושבים הרעות בלב ואומרים אותם בפה זהו. כל
יום יגורו מלחמות. יאספו כמו יגרהו בחרמו יאמרו לשאול בזה
המקום תמצאנו לך והלחם בו וזה היו אומרים לו תמיד;

1150

4. שננו. כמו חץ שנון שפירושו מחדד כן הם חדדו לשונם לדבר
רעות כמו הנחש שמחדד לשונו כשבא לנשוך. חמת עכשוב. חמת הוא
הארס שמטיל הנחש ועכשוב הוא ממין הנחש והוא קשה ורע מאד. תחת
שפתימו. כי בהתקצף האדם הרע ומדבר בחמה תצא לו מפיו לחה תרד
לו תחת שפתיו ודמה אותו לארס שמטיל הנחש;

1155

5. שמרני. ואחר שספר רעותיהם התפלל לאל שישמרהו מהם שהם
חשבו לדחות פעמיו ביד שאול;

6. טמנו. שאמרו ולנו הסגירו ביד המלך. ליד מעגל. למקום
שיהיה מעגלי ואשורי בו כמו שאמר וראו את מקומו אשר תהיה רגלו
מי ראהו שם;

1160

7. אמרתי. כשהייתי שומע שהיו מארבים לי בכל המקומות אמרתי
לה׳. אלי אתה. אתה חזקי ותקפי אין לי חזק להמלט מידם אם
לא תעזרני אתה;

24. And watch: *derek 'oṣeb* (means) 'a rebellious way' as in: 'yet they rebelled and grieved (*'iṣṣ°bu*) his holy spirit' (Isa. lxiii 10). *And guide me:* if thou see in me any way that is rebellious, put me to death immediately. This is (the correct interpretation of) *in the everlasting way*, being the same as in: 'I go the way (*b°derek*) of all the earth' (1 Kgs. ii 2); 'for man goes to his everlasting home (*beth 'olamo*)' (Eccles. xii 5).

PSALM CXL

1. To the conductor. A Psalm of David. This psalm was composed by David concerning Doeg and the Ziphites who slandered him in the presence of Saul (cf. 1 Sam. xxii 9, xxiii 19f.).

2. Deliver me, O Lord: so that their evil words may do me no hurt. The (two halves of the) verse repeat the same thought in different words.

3. Who plan: they devise evil plans in their heart and utter them with their mouths. And this is (what is meant by) *they gather together (yaguru) continually for war*, for *yaguru* means 'they gather together (*ye'as°phu*)' as in: 'he gathers it (*y°gorehu*) in his net' (Hab. i 15). They said to Saul: You will find him in this place; go and fight against him. And this is what they would constantly tell him.

4. *Shan°nu:* as a sharpened arrow – (*shanun*) means 'sharpened' – so have they sharpened their tongues to speak evil things, just as the serpent which sharpens its fangs when it is about to strike. *Snake's venom:* *ḥ°math* is the poison which is ejected by the serpent. And *'akshub* is a species of serpent which is particularly fierce and vicious. *On their lips:* when a wicked man bursts forth in anger and splutters in rage, saliva issues from his mouth and runs down his lips. And he compares this to the poison ejected by a serpent.

5. Guard me: having told of their evil deeds, he now prays to God to guard him from such as contrive *to trip up* his *feet* (so as to deliver him) into the power of Saul.

6. They have hidden: for they said: 'we are able to surrender him into his majesty's hand' (1 Sam. xxiii 20). *Along the path:* (that is) in the place where my path and steps are likely to be, just as it says: 'find the place where his haunt is, and who has seen him there' (1 Sam. xxiii 22).

7. I said: when I heard that they were lying in wait for me in every place, *I said to the Lord, thou art my God,* (that is) thou art my strength and mainstay; I have no power to escape from their hands if thou dost not help me.

8 . סכתה לראשי . ביום נשק . ביום שיבואו עלי בכלי נשק ברמח
ובחצים . תסך לראשי כלומר שתהיה כובע ישועה לראשי . סכותה .
עבר במקום עתיד וכמוהו רבים;

1165

9 . אל תתן . מאויי . היו"ד דגושה על משקל משמני הארץ אמר
אל תתן לו תאותו כי תאותו הוא ללכדני . זממו אל תפק . אל
תוציא לאור מחשבתו . ירומו סלה . שאם תהיה מחשבתם ירומו
וישאו ראשם הוא וחבריו . תפק . תוציא כמו ויפק רצון מה׳ .

10 . ראש מסבי . לפי שזכר רשע יחיד והוא דואג כמו שפירשנו
בפתיחת המזמור אמר . ראש מסיבי . זה הרשע שהוא ראש הסובבים
לי ללכדני . עמל שפתימו יכסמו . השקר שמדבר עלי הוא וחבריו
השקר ההוא יכסה אותם ויפילם;

1170

11 . ימוטו . ינטו גחלים מן השמים עליהם כלומר אף ה׳ וחמתו .
באש יפילם . עמל שפתימו שזכר . במהמרות . בשוחות עמוקות
יפילם שלא יקומו מהם וכן בדברי רבותינו ז"ל בראשונה היו
קוברין אותם במהמרות נתאכל הבשר מלקטין את העצמות וקוברין
אותם בארונים;

1175

12 . איש לשון . זה דואג שהוא בעל הלשון . בל יכון בארץ .
כלומר לא יהיה נכון ונשא בארץ אלא יבוא לידי שפלות . איש
חמס רע יצודנו למדחפות . הרע שהוא עושה יצוד אותו עד שיטילנו
למדחפות שיהיה נדחף מרעה אל רעה;

1180

13 . ידעתי . וכתוב . ידעת . כי הכתוב כנגד האל אתה ידעת
מחשבות הרשע עלי עשה לי דין ממנו והקרי ידעתי פירושו אני

1163	BRMCDS	ביום שבאו	1174	PD	ינטו עליהם גחלים מן השמים
1167	M	הוא ח׳		N	ימיטו עליהם גחלים מן השמים
1168	M	שאם תחקיים מחשבתם	1179	MS	בעל לשון
1169	P	ראשיהם C ראש	1183	PD	ידעתי . קרי וכתוב ידעת
1171	NP	בתחלת המזמור			

8. Thou hast shielded my head in the day of battle: in the day when they come against me with weapons of war, with spears and arrows, thou shalt shield my head, as though to say, thou wilt be a helmet of deliverance round my head. *Sakkothah*: the past tense instead of the future, and there are many instances of this.

9. Do not allow ... the designs: *ma'^awaye*: the *yod* has a *daghesh*, on the analogy of (*daghesh* in *nun* in) *mish^emane ha'areṣ* 'from the richness of the earth' (Gen. xxvii 39). He says: *do not allow* his desire, for his wish is to capture me. *Do not further his evil purpose*: do not bring forth into the light his plans. *Lest they exalt themselves. Selah*: for if their plans are realised, they will exalt themselves and lift up their heads (in pride), both he (Saul) and his associates. *Tapheq* (means) 'bring forth', as in: 'and draw forth (*wayyapheq*) favour from the Lord' (Prov. xviii 22).

10. As for the head of those who surround me: (he says *ro'sh*, singular) since he is referring to one wicked man in particular, viz. Doeg, as we have explained at the beginning of the psalm. He says: *the head of those who surround me*: that is, the wicked man who is head over them who surround me to capture me. *Let the malice of their own lips overrun them*: the false accusations which he and his associates utter against me – let these same false accusations overrun them and be their undoing!

11. Let (burning coals) fall: let *burning coals* from heaven alight upon them – a figurative expression for the Lord and his wrath. *Let it cast them into the fire*: (the subject of this sentence is) the malice of their lips mentioned earlier. *B^emah^amoroth* (means) 'in deep pits'. Let it cast them down that they rise no more from them. So also in the words of our teachers, of blessed memory:[1] First of all they used to bury them in deep pits; when the flesh had been eaten away, the bones were collected and buried in coffins.

12. The slanderer: he (refers to) Doeg who was an evil-tongued man. *He will not be established in the land*: that is to say, he will not be established or venerated in the land, but will be humiliated.[2] *Let evil hunt down the violent man speedily*: the evil which he (himself) does will hunt him down until it drives him out, thrust after thrust. That is, he will be thrust from one calamity to another.

13. *Yada'ti* (is *qere* but) the *kethibh* is *yada'ta*. The *kethibh* (is to be interpreted) as referring to God: thou knowest the plans of the wicked man

---

[1] Cf. *Yerushalmi, Moed Katon* I: 5, *Yerushalmi, Sanhedrin* VI: 10.
[2] Or 'will be reduced to shame'. *Ba' lide* = 'to arrive at, result in, be brought to'.

ידעתי כי יעשה ה׳ דין עני משפט אביונים. כן יעשה דיני   1185

ומשפטי וינקם לי מהרשע;

14. אך צדיקים. בעשותך משפט ברשעים הצדיקים יתנו שבח

והודאה לשמך ואמר אך הם יודו לך לא הרשעים. ישבו ישרים

את פניך. ישבו תמיד. את פניך. לדרוש אותך ולדעת דרכיך;

Psalm CXLI

1. מזמור לדוד ה׳ קראתיך חושה לי. גם זה המזמור מענין   1190

אשר לפניו. חושה לי. מהרה לי לעזרני;

2. תכון...קטרת. כקטרת. משאת כפי. ומה שאני נושא ושוטח

כפי אליך תחשב כמנחת ערב. ואמר. מנחת ערב. והוא הדין

למנחת הבקר ואפשר כי ערב היה בחברו זה המזמור. ואדוני אבי

ז"ל פירש כי לפיכך אמר מנחת ערב כי אם תהיה מנחת הבקר כהגן   1195

היא מקבלת ואם מנחת הערב טהורה הרי שניה ויותר היא מק̇בלת;

3. שיתה...שמרה. שם בשקל חכמה עצמה ופירושו שיתה ה׳ משמר

לפי שלא אכשל בתפלתי אלא כמו שלבי נכון אליך כן תהיה תפלתי

נכונה כמו שכתוב לאדם מערכי לב ומה׳ מענה לשון. נצרה.

דגש הצד"י לתפארת הקריאה והפסוק כפול בענין במלות שונות   1200

ופירוש. דל שפתי. כמו דלת כלומר מפתח שפתי ונקראו השפתים

דלת לפי שהם נפתחות ונסגרות וראוי למי שהוא נבון לעשות

שפתיו כדלת שהוא נפתח ונסגר לצרך כן לא יפתח שפתיו אלא

לצרך. ואדוני אבי ז"ל פירשו מן דלו עיני למרום פירושו

נשיאות שפתי כלומר הדברים שאשא על שפתי;   1205

1185	NC	יעשה משפטי ודיני	1196	B	ואם תהיה מנחת ערב
1191	BP	ח׳ לי	1196	P	הרי היא רצויה
1194	BRDS	ואדוני אבי פירש כי ח׳	1201	NRM	ונקראו ... לצרך ח׳
1195	BN	בקר	1202	B	נכון

against me; do thou exact my right from him. The *qere* is *I know* and its interpretation is: *I know that the Lord will maintain the cause of the oppressed and the needy*. So too will he maintain my cause and my right and avenge me against the wicked man.

14. Surely the righteous: when thou dost execute judgement against the wicked, the righteous will offer up praise and thanksgiving to thy name. And he says: *surely* they will praise thee, (they and) not the wicked. *The upright will dwell in thy presence*: they will dwell (in thy presence) eternally. *In thy presence*: to seek thee and to know thy ways.

PSALM CXLI

1. A Psalm of David. O Lord, I call to thee, make haste to me!: this psalm (deals) with the same theme as the preceding one. *Make haste to me*: come quickly to me to help me.

2. (Let my prayer) be like incense set (before thee): (*qᵉtoreth* means) *as incense*. *The lifting up of my hands*: and when I raise and spread out my hands to thee, may thou account it as *an evening sacrifice*. And although he says *an evening sacrifice*, there would be no difference in meaning[1] if he were to say a morning sacrifice. It is possible, however, that it was evening when he composed this psalm. My revered father, of blessed memory, interpreted (the text as follows): he says *an evening sacrifice* because if the morning sacrifice is accepted as worthy then the evening sacrifice, if it is pure, being the second (such sacrifice), is all the more acceptable.

3. Set a guard: *shomrah* is a substantive of the same form as *ḥokmah* and *'oṣmah*. The meaning (of the verse) is: set a guard over my mouth, O Lord, lest I err in my prayer, and just as my heart is upright before thee, so let my prayer be duly accepted, even as it is written: 'the plans of the mind belong to man, but the utterance of the tongue is from the Lord' (Prov. i 16). *Niṣṣᵉrah, keep watch*: the *daghesh* in the *ṣadhe* is for euphony. The verse repeats the same thought in different words. And the meaning of *dal sᵉphathay* is the door (*deleth*) of my lips, that is, the opening of my lips, the lips being referred to as a door because they too open and close. And it is the duty of an intelligent person to regard his lips as a door which is opened and closed when it is necessary. In the same way he should not open his lips except when occasion requires it. My revered father, of blessed memory, understands (this verse) from: 'my eyes are lifted up (*dallu*) on high' (Isa. xxxviii 14), the meaning being 'the utterances (*nᵉsi'oth*) of my lips', that is, the words which I take up on my lips.

---

[1] *Wᵉhu' haddin*, a Rabbinic idiom meaning 'the same applies', 'it is the same'.

4 . אל תט. הנה התפלל על מוצא שפתיו ועתה מתפלל על הלב

כמו שהוא עתה נכון כן יהיה לעולם ולא יוכלו פועלי און

להטותו ואמר. אל תט. כי אם לא יעזרהו להכין לבו הרי

הוא כאלו מטה לבו. להתעולל עללות ברשע. לעשות מעשה רשע.

ובל אלחם במנעמיהם. ושלא אתאוה לאכול במנעמי מאכלם כלומר   1210

שלא ימשך לבי אל תאות העולם כמו שנמשך לבם;

5 . יהלמני. מנעמיהם לא יערבו לי אבל אם יכני הצדיק

ויוכיחני יערב לי ואחשוב לו לחסד ולשמן ראש. אל יניא

ראשי. אותה המכה לא ישבור ראשי אבל יהיה נחשב כמו שמן

ראש פירושו שמן טוב שמושחין ממנו המכה. שמן ראש. כמו   1215

בשמים ראש. כי עוד ותפלתי ברעותיהם. כי בעודני תפלתי

תהיה ברעות הרשעים שיצילני האל ממעשיהם הרעים ואיך יערבו

לי מנעמיהם. ואדוני אבי ז"ל חלק הפסוק ופירש שמן ראש על

הרשעים. אמר מכת הצדיק ומוסרו טוב לי וחסד עושה עמי אך

הרשע אם ימשח אותי בשמן ראש אצעק ואומר. אל יניא ראשי.   1220

אל ישבור ראשי;

6 . נשמטו. ישמטו בידי סלע שיפילו אותם מן הסלע ואמר זאת

הקללה על שופטיהם שהם המנהיגים אותם ולא ימנעו מהם הדרכים

הרעים אבל יחזיקום בידם ואז ישמעו אמרי כי נעמו אולי באבוד

מנהיגיהם יוסרו וישמעו התוכחות שאני מוכיח אותם ויכירו כי   1225

נעמו אמרי ותוכחתי;

7 . כמו פלח ובקע בארץ. פלח ובקע ענין אחד במלות שונות.

פלח. כמו ויפלח אל סיר הנזיד. יפלח כליותי ופירוש הפסוק

כמו בוקע עצים שמתפזרים הבקעים הנה והנה כן. נפזרו עצמינו

4. Turn not: he has just prayed concerning the utterance of his lips and now prays concerning his heart – even as it is now upright, so may it be forever so that *the evildoers* may not be able to turn it. And he says *turn not* because if he were not to help him to keep his heart upright, behold, it is as though he were actually to turn his heart. *L^ehith'olal 'aliloth b^eresha'* (means) to do wicked deeds. *And let me not eat of their dainties*: let me not desire to eat their dainty food, that is to say, let not my heart be drawn to worldly desires even as their heart is so drawn.

5. Let him strike me: their dainties are not palatable for me, but if a righteous man were to strike or rebuke me, I would be pleased and account it to him as an act of kindness, (indeed) as choicest oil. *It will not break my head*: that blow will not break my head but will be reckoned as *shemen ro'sh* which means 'goodly oil' used for smearing a wound. (The word *ro'sh* in *shemen ro'sh*) is as in 'finest (*ro'sh*) spices' (Exod. xxx 23). *For my prayer is continually against their wicked deeds*: for as long as I live my prayer will be against the evil deeds of the wicked, that God will deliver me from their wicked deeds. (This being so) how then can their dainties be acceptable to me? My revered father, of blessed memory, in his division of the verse considers *shemen ro'sh* to belong to the second half which refers to the wicked man.[1] Thus he says: the blow (administered by) the righteous and the rebuke (given by) him are acceptable to me; indeed (by so doing) he renders me a great kindness. But as for the wicked, though he were to anoint me with choicest oil, I would cry out and say *'al yani ro'shi* (which means) 'let him not break my head'.

6. They are thrown down: they will be *thrown down by the sides of the rock*, (that is) they will be hurled down from the rock. He pronounces this curse upon their judges, since they are the leaders and yet do not refrain from evil ways but indeed hold fast to them. But at that time they will hear *my words that they are acceptable*: (that is) perhaps when their rulers have perished, they will receive instruction and listen to the admonition with which I admonish them and will acknowledge that my words and admonition are acceptable.

7. As when one cuts open and breaks apart on the ground: *poleah* and *boqea'* are two distinct roots with the same meaning. (The meaning of) *poleah* is as in 'and he sliced (*way^ephalah*) them into the pot of stew' (2 Kgs. iv 39); 'he cut deep (*y^ephalah*) into my kidneys' (Job xvi 13). The interpretation of the verse is: just as when a man chops wood, splinters are scattered hither and thither, so *our bones are scattered at the mouth of Sheol*,

---

[1] Lit. 'My revered father, of blessed memory, divides the verse and explains *shemen ro'sh* as referring to the wicked'.

לפי שאול. כלומר עד שהיינו קרוב מן המות ופזור העצמות הוא   1230
על דרך הפלגה מרב הפחד ינוע וירעד הגוף עד שידמה שהעצמות
מתפרדים זה מזה וכן אמר והתפרדו כל עצמותי ואמר. עצמינו.
הוא והאנשים אשר היו עמו כי כבר כתבנו כי זה המזמור חברו
דוד בברחו מפני שאול;

8. כי אליך. בכה. מלא בה"א הנחה. אל תער נפשי. כמו   1235
ותער כדה ענין שפיכה ויציקה וכצאת הנפש מן הגוף כאלו נשפכת
ממנו על דרך ואשפוך את נפשי;

9. שמרני. יקשו לי. הפח ששמו לי למוקש. ומקשות. שמרני
גם כן מידי מקשות פעלי און אחרים שאינם מבני עמי או ענין
הפסוק כפול;   1240

10. יפלו במכמוריו. ברשתות שפרשו לי בם יפלו הרשעים. יחד
אנכי עד אעבור. פירשוהו כמו הפוך עד אעבור אנכי כלומר שאעבור
שלא אלכד ברשתם ויש לפרשו בלי הפוך ועד פירושו כמו עדי עד
ואל לעד תזכר עון שפירושו עולם כלומר הם יפלו ברשתם ואנכי
לעולם אעבור בבטחה שלא אכשל בהם ובזולתם ואמר. במכמוריו.   1245
לשון יחיד על שאול ואמר. יפלו רשעים. לשון רבים עליו ועל
הנסמכים עמו לרדוף אחרי דוד;

Psalm CXLII

1. משכיל לדוד בהיותו במערה תפלה. כשהלך שאול לבקשו על
פני צורי היעלים ונחבא דוד במערה מפניו כמו שכתוב ודוד
ואנשיו בירכתי המערה יושבים ושם במערה חבר זאת התפלה ואמר;   1250

ולא אלכד	1243	B	קרוב למות	1230	N
בלתי הפוך	1243	RM	המזמור הזה	1233	RPMCDS
בהבטחה	1245	M	ובצאת	1236	NRMC

that is, to such an extent that we are on the verge of death. And 'scattering of the bones' is used by way of hyperbole; (that is) as a result of terrible fear the body shakes and trembles (so violently) that our bones would appear to be disjointed one from another. Similarly he says: 'and all my bones are out of joint (*wᵉhithparᵉdu*)' (Ps. xxii 15). He says *our bones* (referring to) him and the men who were with him, for we have already stated that this psalm was composed by David when he fled from Saul.

8. But unto thee ... in thee: *bᵉkah, scriptio plena* with quiescent *he. Do not pour out my soul:* as in: 'and she emptied (*watᵉʿar*) her jar' (Gen. xxiv 20), (where *tᵉʿar*) has the sense of 'spilling', 'pouring out', for when the soul departs from the body it is as though it were poured out from it, after the analogy of: 'and I poured out (*wa'eshpok*) my soul' (1 Sam. i 15).

9. Keep me ... they have set for me: (that is) *the trap* which they have set as a snare for me. *The snares*: *keep me* also from *the snares* of those other *evildoers* who are not of my own people. Or (perhaps) the meaning of (the first half of) the verse is repeated.

10. Let them fall into their own nets: (that is) into the nets which they have spread for me; let the wicked themselves fall into them. *Whilst I at the same time pass on*: (for the purpose of) its interpretation (the text has to be) reversed thus: '*ad 'eᵉbor 'anoki: till I pass through*. That is to say, that I may pass through without being caught in their net. But an explanation is also possible without reversing (the text), '*ad* being interpreted as '*ᵃde 'ad* or as '*ad* (in the phrase): 'and remember not iniquity for ever (*laʿad*)' (Isa. lxiv 8), where the meaning is 'forever' ('*olam*). Thus he says: they will fall into their nets, but I will pass on forever in the (full) confidence that I will not stumble because of them or their like.[1] And he says *in his nets*, (that is) singular in reference to Saul. But (when) he says *let the wicked fall*, it is the plural number to refer both to him and to such as have joined him in the pursuit of David.

PSALM CXLII

1. A Maskil of David, when he was in the cave. A prayer: (uttered) when Saul went in search of him by the Rocks of the Wildgoats (cf. 1 Sam. xxiv 2) and David hid himself from him in the cave, as it is written: 'Now David and his men were sitting in the innermost parts of the cave' (1 Sam. xxiv 3). And there in the cave he composed this prayer and said:

[1] Lit. 'or those beside them'.

2. ‏קולי אל ה׳ אזעק.‏ ‏קולי אל ה׳ אתחנן ואליו אזעק מצרתי
‏וכפל הענין;‏

3. ‏אשפוך...שיחי.‏ ‏תפלתי.‏ ‏צרתי לפניו אגיד.‏ ‏אף על פי
‏שידועה לו אגידנה לפניו בתפלתי;‏

4. ‏בהתעטף עלי רוחי.‏ ‏כמו נפשם בהם תתעטף וזה לרב הצרה   1255
‏ידכה ישוח כאלו מתעטף קצתו בקצתו   והרוח בגוף.‏ ‏ואתה ידעת
‏נתיבתי.‏ ‏כי איננו הולך בדרך רע כמו שהם הולכים כי אני אין
‏בי עון ולא חטאתי להם והם רודפים אחרי.‏ ‏בארח זו אהלך.‏
‏באיזה דרך שאלך הם מרגלים אחרי וטמנו פח לי בכל מקום שאלך;‏

5. ‏הבט ימין וראה.‏ ‏שניהם מקור הבט וראה ואינו צווי רוצה   1260
‏לומר כשאביט ימין ושמאל אין מי שיכירני ויחוש עלי ועל
‏טלטולי.‏ ‏אבד מנוס ממני.‏ ‏כי כשאחשוב בזה המקום אלך ושם
‏לא ידעני שאול ולא ירדוף אחרי אין לי מקום שאנוס שם כי
‏בכל מקום שאלך מבקש אותי וזכר ימין ולא זכר שמאל דרך קצרה
‏כמנהג המקרא כי מהאחד יובן האחר כמו עמו הראובני והגדי   1265
‏לקחו נחלתם פירושו עם חצי שבט המנשה האחד ולפי שזכר לתשעת
‏השבטים וחצי שבט המנשה סמך ולא זכר חצי האחר ואמר עמו כאלו
‏זכרו וכן רבים במקרא על זה הדרך בחסרון המלים במקום שיובן
‏הענין מהנזכר כמו שכתבנו בספר מכלול.‏ ‏אין דורש לנפשי.‏
‏מכל גואלי וקרובי אין מי שידרוש לנפשי שמבקש שאול לקחת   1270
‏כי מיד מלך לא אמצא גואל אם אתה לא תגאלני לפיכך זעקתי
‏אליך ה׳.‏

1259 B	וטמנו לי פח	1266 NM	חצי ח׳
1260 N	ואינם צווי	1268 BNRCS	שיחבונן הענין
1265 R	כמנהג המקומות		

2. I cry aloud to the Lord: I cry aloud to the Lord and appeal to him in my distress. He repeats the same thought (in the second half of the verse).

3. I pour out my complaint: *śiḥi* (means) 'my prayer'. *I tell my trouble before him*: though it be known to him, yet will I declare it before him in my prayer.

4. When my spirit is faint: as in: 'their soul fainted (*tith'aṭaph*) within them' (Ps. cvii 5). This is (a result) of his great distress because of which he crouches and bows down as though he were to shrivel up altogether and the spirit in his body.[1] *But thou knowest my way*: viz. that I do not walk in the way of evil as they do; for, as for me, there is no iniquity in me, nor have I sinned against them; yet they pursue me. *In the path where I walk*: whichever way I go, they spy out after me *and hide a trap for me* in every place where I walk.

5. I look to the right and watch: *habeṭ* and *r'eh* are both infinitives and not imperatives. He means to say: When I look up to the right or to the left, there is no one who takes notice of me to sympathise with me in my wanderings. *No refuge remains to me*: if I say to myself: I will go to such a place where Saul will neither know of me nor pursue me, then (I find that) there is no place to which I might flee, for wherever I go he searches me out. (Notice that) he speaks of (looking to) the right but does not mention (looking to) the left. This is in the interests of brevity,[2] in accordance with Biblical usage, because the one is easily understood from the other, as in: 'with him the Reubenites and the Gadites received their inheritance' (Josh. xiii 8), (where 'with him' is rightly) understood as with the other half of the tribe of Manasseh. Since he has spoken (in the previous verse) of the nine tribes and of the half tribe of Manasseh, he deems it unnecessary[3] to mention the other half. And so he says 'with him' as though he had (actually) mentioned him.[4] And there are in Scripture many instances of the omission of words in such passages where the sense may be deduced from something previously referred to, as we have stated in the book *Miklol*. *No one cares for my soul*: of all my kinsmen and relations there is none who cares for my soul which Saul seeks to take away, for I can find no one to protect me from the power of the king if thou dost not protect me. Therefore *I cry to thee, O Lord*.

---

[1] Lit. 'as though his part was fainting in his part'.
[2] Lit. 'by way of shortening'.
[3] *Samak* = 'to support', and is used in the sense of supporting or deriving an opinion by reference to or from a Biblical text.
[4] In other words, 'with him' is to be taken by inference as a reference to the other half of the tribe of Manasseh, the first half having been mentioned in the previous verse.

6. זעקתי...בארץ החיים.   עוד תהיה חלקי בארץ ישראל שאני
בורח ממנה ופירוש חלקי כמו ה' מנת חלקי וכוסי ובפסוק בארצות
1275   החיים פירשנו הטעם למה נקראת ארץ ישראל ארץ החיים;

7. הקשיבה אל רנתי.   אל זעקתי.   כמו יעבור הרנה במחנה.
כי אמצו ממני.   אינני יכול למלך ולעמו שרודפים אחרי;

8. הוציאה ממסגר.   לפי שהיה נסגר במערה.   להודות את שמך.
כי אתה לבדך הצלתני.   בי יכתרו צדיקים.   כי תגמל עלי
1280   ותצילני יתפארו בי הצדיקים ויעשוני כתר לראשם כי יאמרו
הלא דוד לפי שבטח באל לבדו הצילהו והוא יחיד או במעט עם
ממלך ועמו;

Psalm CXLIII

1. מזמור לדוד.   גם זה המזמור מענין אשר לפניו ואמר.   ה'
שמע תפלתי באמונתך ענני בצדקתך.   פירוש.   באמונתך.   שהבטחתני
1285   ודברך אמת.   בצדקתך.   כי אתה צדיק וישר ותראה כי עמי הצדק
ועם אויבי העול;

2. ואל תבוא.   עתה שאני בצרה גדולה אל תבוא במשפט עמי אם
חטאתי לך אל תענישני עתה כי ידעת כי אני עבדך.   כי לא יצדק
לפניך כל חי.   אם תביט אל כל מעשיו ואיך אצדק אני לפניך;

3. כי רדף.   דכא לארץ חיתי.   כאלו היא לארץ כי קרובה היא   1290
למיתה.   במחשכים.   ירכתי המערה שהיה יושב בה נחבא שאין שם
אורה והנה הוא כמת שהוא בחשך תחת הארץ ואמר.   כמתי עולם.
כלומר שמתו זה זמן רב שנואש אדם מהם מהתקומה ומהאור יותר

1275 C	פירשתי	1288 N	אל עתה תענישני
1280 R	צדיקים	1291 P	בה נחבא ח'
1281 PD	ובמעט עם	1293 M	שנואש אדם מתקומה מהם
1282 RMA	המלך ועמו		

6. I cry . . . in the land of the living: *my portion* will yet be in the land of Israel from which I now flee. The meaning of *ḥelqi* is as in: 'The Lord is my allotted portion (*ḥelqi*) and my cup' (Ps. xvi 5). And in the verse (containing the words) 'the land of the living' (Ps. cxvi 9) we have explained why the land of Israel is called the land of the living.

7. Give heed to my cry: ('*el rinnathi* means) 'to my cry (*za'ªqathi*)', as in: 'a cry (*harinnah*) went through the army' (1 Kgs. xxii 36). *For they are too strong for me*: I cannot prevail against the king and his people who pursue me.

8. Bring me out of prison: for he (David) was shut up in the cave. *That I may give thanks to thy name*: for thou alone deliverest me. *The righteous will be crowned in me*: when *thou wilt deal bountifully with me* and deliver me, the righteous will glorify themselves in me and regard me as a crown (*kether*) round their heads,[1] for they will say: Surely because David trusted in God alone, he delivered him, and this although he was isolated or with few followers as against[2] a king and his people.

PSALM CXLIII

1. A Psalm of David. This psalm deals with the same theme as the preceding one. And he says: *Lord, hear my prayer . . . In thy faithfulness answer me, in thy righteousness*: *in thy faithfulness* means: thou hast given me a promise and thy word is truth. *In thy righteousness*: for thou art righteous and upright and thou seest that right is with me and that my enemies are in the wrong.

2. Enter not: now that I am in great trouble, *enter not into judgement* with me; if I have sinned against thee, do not punish me, for thou knowest that I am *thy servant*. *For no man living is righteous before thee*: if thou dost examine all his deeds. How then can I be justified before thee?

3. For he has pursued . . . he has crushed my life to the ground: (that is) as though it were (thrust) to the earth, for it is near death. *In darkness*: (this means) the innermost parts of the cave where he used to sit in hiding, for no light penetrated there.[3] Indeed, he was like a dead man in as much as he was in darkness below the ground. Thus he says: *like those long dead*: that is to say, those who have been dead for a long time, so that people have given up hope for their resurrection and of their (seeing again) the light, more so than in the case of those who have been

---

[1] In *Sefer Ha-Shorashim* and under the root *kathar* Kimḥi interprets the phrase *bi yaktiru ṣaddiqim* as meaning: 'they will consider me as a crown upon them'.
[2] Or 'from a king and his people'.   [3] Lit. 'for no light was there'.

מאשר מתו מזמן קרוב אף על פי שאלה ואלה אין להם דרך תקומה

מדרך הטבע זכר הרחוקים יותר מדרך התקומה שכבר נשחתה צורת 1295

גופם;

4. ותתעטף. פירשנוהו במזמור שלפני זה. בתוכי ישתומם לבי.

כפל הענין במלות שונות;

5. זכרתי. כשאני בצרה. וישתומם לבי בתוכי. אני זוכר

ימים מקדם שהושעת את אבותינו שהיו בצרה גדולה ואני מתנחם. 1300

הגיתי בכל פעלך. בפעלים ובנפלאות ובמעשי ידיך שעשית עמהם

אהגה ואשוחח ואתנחם בהם ואמר ללבי כי כן תעשה עמי;

6. פרשתי. כארץ עיפה. כמו הארץ הצמאה שהיא מתאוה ומי'חלת

אל המטר כן נפשי צמאה ומיחלת לך;

7. מהר. כי קרוב אני אל המות לפיכך צריך שתמהר שתענני 1305

כי. כלתה רוחי. כמעט אמות. אל תסתר. שאם תסתיר פניך

מעט ממני. ונמשלתי עם ירדי בור;

8. השמיעני בבקר. עת הצרה היא נקראת ערב ועת הישועה בקר.

דרך זו אלך. אנה אלך ואנה אברח מפני הרודפים אחרי. נשאתי

נפשי. כמו ואליו הוא נשא את נפשו ענין התוחלת; 1310

9. הצילני. אליך כסיתי. אמר. הצילני מאיבי ה'. כי לא

גליתי ריבי לבני אדם כי שוא תשועת אדם אלא כסיתי מהם ואליך

לבדך גליתי וזה טעם. אליך כסיתי. אליך צעקתי בסתר ובמכסה

מבני אדם;

10. למדני. בקש על תשועת הגוף ובקש גם כן על תשועת הנפש 1315

ואמר שילמדהו ויעזרהו בלמוד החכמה כדי שידע מהו רצון האל

ויעשהו. כי אתה אלהי. אני מכיר כי לך לבדך הכח והיכלת

1294	RPC	אין להם תקומה	1305	NMC	מן המות
1300	NPMCD ח'	את	1306	R	פניך ממני מעט
1301	MCDS	ובמעשה ידיך	1308	N	ועת הישועה היא נקראת בקר
1302	N	אהגה ואשיחה	1310	N	ענינו ענין התוחלת והתקוה
1304	NPMCD	למטר	1313	RP	ובמכוסה

dead for only a short time. And although there is (in effect) no difference –
since the resurrection will not occur to either of them as a natural phenomenon – yet he refers (especially) to those furthest removed from the
(possibility of a natural) resurrection because the shape of their bodies has
already been destroyed.

4. *Watith'ateph*: we have already commented (on this word) in the
preceding psalm. *My heart within me is appalled*: a repetition of the same
idea in different words.

5. I remember: when I am in trouble and *my heart is appalled within me*,
I remember *the days of old* when thou didst save our fathers when they
were in great distress, and (in this) I find solace. *I meditate on all thy works*:
(that is) on the works and the marvels and deeds of thy hands which thou
hast wrought for them I meditate and muse, and comfort myself in them
and say to myself that thou wilt do likewise for me.

6. I stretch out . . . like a parched land: just as a parched land longs
for the rain and eagerly awaits it, so does my soul thirst and wait for thee.

7. Make haste: for I am near death. Therefore it is necessary that thou
dost make haste to answer me, for *my spirit fails*, (that is) I am about to die.
Hide not: for if thou dost hide thy face from me, (even) for a short time,
then *I will be like those who go down to the pit*.

8. Let me hear in the morning: an occasion of affliction is (sometimes)
referred to as evening, whilst an occasion of salvation is referred to as
morning. *The way I should go*: (that is) where I should go and whither I
should flee from them that persecute me. *I lift up my soul*: as in: 'and sets
his soul upon it (*w^e'elaw hu' nośe' 'eth naphsho*)' (Deut. xxiv 15), (which
expresses) the idea of hope.

9. Deliver me . . . unto thee I have hidden: he says: *deliver me from
my enemies, O Lord*: for I have not disclosed my tribulation to the children
of men, for 'vain is the help of man' (Ps. lx 13), but *I have hidden (kissithi)*
it from them and *to thee* alone I have revealed it. And this is the meaning
of *'eleka kissithi*: *unto thee* do I cry in secret and in concealment from men.

10. Teach me: he requests the salvation of his body, besides making a
request for the salvation of his soul. And he asks to be taught and helped
in the pursuit of knowledge[1] so that he may know the will of God and do
it. *For thou art my God*: I acknowledge that with thee alone is might and

---

[1] Lit. 'that he will teach him and help him in the learning of wisdom'.

ואתה שופט העולם ומנהיגו. רוחך טובה. כח רוח העליוני.

תנחני. ותנהגני בארץ מישור כלומר בדרך ישר לא אכשל בו;

11. למען שמך. בעבור שיגדל שמך בפי האנשים כשתושיעני   1320

ותחיני מהצרה הגדולה שאני בה קרוב למיתה;

12. ובחסדך. כי אני עבדך ולא הם;

Psalm CXLIV

1. לדוד ברוך ה׳ צורי. זה המזמור חברו דוד אחרי מלכו בתחלה

אחר שנצח מלחמת פלשתים ונצל ממלחמת ישראל וממלחמת פלשתים

ואמר. ברוך ה׳ צורי. פירושו חזקי כי הוא הנותן לי כח ומלמד   1325

ידי לקרב וכפל הענין במלות שונות;

2. חסדי. אמר אלהי חסדי ואמר חסדי ואמר אלהי צורי ואמר

צורי ואמר אלהי תהלתי ואמר הוא תהלתך לפי שהשם והתאר ישתוו

בו יתברך. ומפלטי לי. קל הלמ"ד וכמוהו רבים מבנין הדגוש

ומה שאמר לי אחר יו"ד הכנוי הוא תוספת באור כי די באחד מהם   1330

או תהיה יו"ד ומפלטי נוספת ואינה לכנוי כיו"ד המגביהי לשבת,

הישבי. הרודד עמי תחתי. הרודד. פירושו מתרגום וירקעו

ורדידו. עמי. כמו עמים ויתכן לפרשו כמשמעו בלא חסרון מ"ם

אלא שתהיה היו"ד לכנוי המדבר והוא שאול והסומכים אותו;

3. ה׳ מה אדם ותדעהו. אמר זה כנגד שאול שהיה מלך ונפסקה   1335

מלכותו במעט זמן ופירוש. ותדעהו. כמו ותחשבהו כי פירוש

power and that thou art the judge of the universe and its ruler. *Thy good spirit*: (that is) the power of the Supernal Spirit. *Lead me*: and guide me *on a level path*, that is, in the way of equity that I may not err therein.

11. For thy name's sake: that thy name may be magnified in the mouths of men when thou wilt have saved me and preserved me alive from this great trouble as a result of which I am within the grasp of death.

12. And in thy steadfast love: *for I am thy servant*, but they are not.

PSALM CXLIV

1. A Psalm of David. Blessed is the Lord, my rock: this psalm was composed by David soon after becoming king, when he won the battle against the Philistines and was delivered from the war between Israel and the Philistines. And he says: *blessed is the Lord, my rock*: which means 'my strength', for he it is who gives me power and *trains my hands for war*: he repeats the same idea with different words.

2. My steadfast love: it says (in one passage) 'the God of my steadfast love' (Ps. lix 18), and (in another passage) it says 'my steadfast love' (Ps. cxliv 2). So too it says 'God of my rock' (2 Sam. xxii 3) and 'my rock' (Ps. cxliv 1). And we also find[1] 'O God of my praise' (Ps. cix 1) and 'he is your praise' (Deut. x 21). The reason is that the essence and the attributes are united in him, blessed be he. *And my deliverer*: um*ephalṭi*: the *lamedh* is without *daghesh*,[2] there being many instances of this in the *piel* conjugation. And as for the addition[3] of *li* after the pronominal suffix,[4] it is an epexegetical addition, for one of them is sufficient. Or perhaps the *yod* in um*ephalṭi* is paragogic and not a pronominal suffix, like the *yod* in 'who is seated on high (*hammagbihi*)' (Ps. cxiii 5), or 'that sittest (*hayyoshebi*)' (Ps. cxxiii 1). *Who subdues the peoples under me*: *haroded* is to be explained from w*eraddidu* which is the rendering in the Targum for *wayeraqqeʿu* 'and they did beat out' (Exod. xxxix 3). *ʿammi* is the same as *ʿammim* 'peoples'. But it is possible to interpret it just as it is found in the text[5] without assuming the omission of *mem*, in which case the *yod* would indicate the first person pronominal suffix, meaning (*my people*, referring to) Saul and his supporters.

3. O Lord, what is man that thou carest for him: he utters this with regard to Saul who was king but whose kingdom became null and void[6] after a short time. *Watedaʿehu* means: 'that thou dost take account of him',

---

[1] Lit. 'and it says'.   [2] Lit. 'the *lamed* is light'.
[3] Lit. 'and as for what he says'.   [4] Lit. 'after the suffixed *yod*'.
[5] K*emishmaʿo* = 'in its usual sense'. Cf. M. Jastrow, *Dictionary*, II, p. 856.
[6] Lit. 'to be broken', 'split', 'divided', 'cut off'.

הידיעה במקום הזה וכיוצא בו ההכרה וההשגחה לטובה וכן ידעת
בצרות נפשי, אני ידעתיך במדבר, אשר ידעו ה';

4. אדם. מה גדולת אדם נחשבת הרי הוא כמו הבל והוא דבר
שאינו מתקים כמו הבל הפה. כצל עובר. כמו הצל שעובר במהרה 1340
בהתפשט השמש או פירושו כצל העוף העובר בעופפו וכן פירשו
במדרש כצל עובר כהדין עופא דעבר בטוליה וטוליה עבר עמיה;

5. ה' הט שמך. וכן אמר ויט שמים וירד והכל דרך משל כאלו
ירד הוא יתברך לכלות הרשעים במהרה וזאת התפלה אמרה על מלכי
האומות המבקשים להלחם בו. בהרים. הם המלכים שהם חזקים 1345
כהרים על דרך משל. ויעשנו. כשתשלח אש אפך בהם יעלה עשן
מהם כמו שעולה עשן מדבר הכלה באש ורבים רואים עשן האש ואינם
רואים האש כן בכליון רשעים מי שלא יראה בכלותם ישמע וידע;

6. ברוק ברק. בבוא הפעל עם השם הוא לחזק הענין וכן למען
בצוע בצע, כל בוגדי בגד, ומעלה מעל, יבשו בשת, והדומים להם 1350
וכן ברוק ברק. והברקים והחצים הם הגזרות היורדות מן השמים;

7. שלח. ממים רבים. הם האויבים החזקים ואחר כן פירש.
מיד בני נכר. כי עתה שמלך אין לו אויבים אלא בני נכר ופירש.
פצני. כמו הצילני והוא קרוב לענין פציתי פי שהוא ענין פתיחה
כי המציל אדם מיד אדם הרי הוא פותחו ממאסרו; 1355

בכליונם		1348	RPMDS	פירושו במדרש	1341	BM
כי עתה כיון שמלך		1353	MC	והכל הוא דרך משל	1343	R
אחר	ח'	1355	B	כאלו הוא ירד ית'	1343	MC
				מלכי אומות העולם	1344	NPMACDS

for the meaning of 'knowledge' in this context, as in similar passages, is to recognise (a person) and regard him favourably. So also 'thou hast taken heed (*yada'ta*) of the adversities of my soul' (Ps. xxxi 8); 'it was I who knew you (*yᵉda'tika*) in the wilderness' (Hos. xiii 5).

4. Man: how is the greatness of man considered ? Behold, he is as *a breath*, that is, as something which has no permanent existence, just as the *breath* of the mouth. *Like a passing shadow*: like the *shadow* which quickly passes away when the sun spreads out. Or its meaning may be: like the *shadow* of the bird which passes away in its flight. And a similar interpretation is given in the Midrash[1] thus: *like a passing shadow*: like the bird which moves along with its shadow, its shadow moving with it.

5. Bow thy heavens, O Lord: likewise it says: 'he bowed the heavens and came down' (Ps. xviii 10; 2 Sam. xxii 10). It is all (to be understood) figuratively as though the Blessed One were to descend in order to exterminate the wicked. He utters this prayer in reference to the kings of the nations who sought to battle with him. *The mountains*: these are the kings who are (represented) figuratively as being as strong as mountains. *That they smoke*: when thou wilt send against them the fire of thy wrath, smoke will rise up from them, just as smoke rises up from that which is burned up in fire, with many seeing the smoke of the fire and yet not seeing the fire. In the same way he who is not an eye-witness to their destruction will (nevertheless) hear and know of it.

6. Flash forth the lightning: *bᵉroq baraq*: when a verb is followed by a substantive of the same root it is for the purpose of adding emphasis to the context, as in: 'so as to acquire dishonest gain (*bᵉṣo'a baṣa'*)' (Ezek. xxii 27); 'all who deal treacherously (*bogᵉde baged*)' (Jer. xii 1); 'commits a grievous fault (*ma'alah ma'al*)' (Lev. v 21); 'they will utterly be put to shame (*yeboshu bosheth*)' (Isa. xlii 17), and the like. And so too is *bᵉroq baraq* (to be explained). And by lightnings and arrows (he means) the divine decrees which descend from heaven.

7. Stretch forth ... from the many waters: these are the mighty enemies. Subsequently he interprets *miyyad bᵉne nekar* thus: *from the hand of aliens*, for now that he is king he has no enemies other than foreigners. *Pᵉṣeni* means 'deliver me' and is (used here) in a sense very much like that of (*paṣithi* in): 'I have opened (*paṣithi*) my mouth' (Jud. xi 35), that is, the idea of 'opening'. For if one delivers a person from the power of another, behold, it is as though he was freeing him[2] from his chains.

---

[1] *Koheleth Rabba* on *hᵃbel hᵃbalim* (Eccles. i 2).
[2] *Pathaḥ* = 'to open', 'loose', hence 'free'.

8. אשר פיהם. מלכי האומות שהם מתגאים עלי בדבריהם ואומרים
נעשה לו כך וכך שוא והבל דבריהם אחר שתעזרני אתה וכן. ימינם.
כלומר כחם וגבורתם כח שקר והבל הוא;

9. אלהים. בכל עת שתחדש נפלאותיך עמי אחדש לך שיר בפה ובכלי;

10. הנותן תשועה. אף על פי שהם מלכים צריכים הם לתשועתו.   1360
הפוצה. פירשנו ענינו במלת פצני. מחרב רעה. מחרב שאול
וקראה חרב רעה שלא היה לו דרך להשמר ממנה לפי שהיה מלך והיה
מבני עמון;

11. פצני. פירשנוהו כי ⸱⸱העניין כפול במזמור;

12. אשר בנינו. כי כל ענינינו על הנכונה ובלבד שתצילנו   1365
מיד בני נכר כי שלחת ברכה בפרי בטננו ובפרי אדמתנו ובפרי
בהמתנו ושלשתם זכרם במזמור כמו שנזכרו בתורה בברכות ברוך
פרי בטנך ופרי אדמתך ופרי בהמתך ואמר. אשר בנינו כנטיעים.
כמו הנטיעים שהם מגדלים על מים רבים ובמקום דשן ושמן כן
בנינו מגדלים בנעוריהם ברב טובה ובאמונה ישרה ובמעשים טובים   1370
וכן בנותינו מגדלות בטובה והן יפות במראה שוות בקומתן כמו
זויות ההיכל והם פנות הארמון שהם מחטבות אבני גזית נפסלות
היטב במלאכה דקה עד שידמו כל אבני הזויות מרב חטיבתן ביושר
כאלו הם כלם אבן אחת כן הבנות יפות קומה נאות בצורתן כתבנית
ההיכל;   1375

13. מזוינו. פאות הבית כלומר בכל פאה מן הבית מין תבואה
ומרב תבואה מכל מין ומין הם מתערבים זה עם זה ופירוש. מפיקים.
יוצאים כמו ויפק רצון מה׳ שפירושו ויוצא אבל הוא פעל יוצא

יפות מאד במראה N	1371 נאות בקומתן	1371 B	צריכים האל ית׳ לתשועתו	1360 B
אבני	ח׳	1372 N	מבני נכר R	מן בני נכר	1366 NMACDS
מתעכבים המינים		1377 RC	כמו שזכרם		1367 NC

8. Whose mouth: (he refers to) the kings of the people who by their words assume a superior attitude over me saying: 'We will deal with him in such and such a manner.' Vain and empty are their words, seeing that thou wilt help me. So also is *their right hand* (to be understood), that is to say, their strength and might are but a vain and delusive strength.

9. O God: on each occasion that thou dost perform anew thy marvels for me, I will sing to thee a new song with both mouth and (musical) instrument.

10. Who givest salvation: though they are kings, yet are they in need of thy salvation. *Who dost rescue (happoṣeh):* we have explained the meaning of this in connection with the word *pᵉṣeni* above. *From the cruel sword:* (that is) from the sword of Saul. And he refers to it as *the cruel sword* because he had no means of guarding against it, since Saul was king and (also) one of his own people.

11. Deliver me: has already been explained, for (you will have observed) that the one theme is repeated throughout this psalm.

12. We whose sons: all our affairs are in proper order. Only do thou deliver us from *the hand of aliens.* For thou hast bestowed blessing upon the fruit of our wombs, on the fruit of our land and the fruit of our beasts. He refers in the psalm to these three categories in the order in which they are enumerated in the *Torah* among the blessings: 'Blessed will be the fruit of your body, and the fruit of your land, and the fruit of your beasts' (Deut. xxviii 4). And he says: we whose sons are as plants: even as the plants which grow up by many waters and upon a rich and fertile soil, so are our sons nurtured in their youth amid an abundance of perfect and upright faith and good works. And in the same way our daughters are brought up in virtue. And they are beautiful in appearance, being all of them of like stature, just as the corners of a palace, that is, the cornerstones of a palace which are cut out of hewn stones, being elegantly sculptured with refined workmanship with the result that all the cornerstones, because they have been very carefully hewn, appear as though they were but one single stone. So too our daughters[1] are beautiful in stature and comely in form like *the structure of a palace.*

13. Mᵉzawenu (means) the corners of the house. That is to say, in every corner of the house there is (to be found) some manner of produce and because of the abundance of different kinds of produce, they become mixed with each other. (The root idea of) *mᵉphiqim* 'going forth' (may be seen) in *wayyapheq raṣon mehashshem* (Prov. xviii 22) where the meaning (of

[1] Lit. 'the daughters'.

לאחר וזה עומד ואפשר לפרש גם כן זה פעל יוצא ופירושו בני
הבית מוציאים מין זה אל מין זה מרב כל מין ומין לא יכילם   1380
הבית שיהיה זה לבדו וזה לבדו. זן. פירושו מין מתרגום
למינו לזנוהי. מאליפות. מרבבות. יולדות לאלפים ולרבבות
עד שמלאים מהם חוצותינו;

14. אלופינו. שורינו וכן שגר אלפיך ככבש אלוף. מסבלים.
רוצה לומר שורינו חזקים ומלאים ויכולים לסבול משא עבודתם   1385
בחרישה ובמשוך העגלות או פירושו מסבלים בבשר. אין פרץ.
אין בנו ובבהמתנו שכולה כי השכול הוא פרץ כמו פרץ ה' פרץ
בעזא. ואין יוצאת. אין נפש אחת יוצאת לשבי לא מאנשינו
ולא מבהמותינו. ואין צוחה. לא נשמעה צוחה ברחובותינו
שיצוחו ברחובות ויאמרו נגף ישראל במלחמה כי כל ימי מלוך דוד   1390
לא נגפו ישראל לפני אויביהם;

15. אשרי העם שככה לו. שזאת ההצלחה לו ומפני מה היתה לזה
העם זאת ההצלחה לפי. שה' אלהיו. לפיכך אשריו שה' אלהיו
ורבנו סעדיה גאון ז"ל פירש מזמור זה לימות המשיח ומה שאמר
לדוד ברוך ה' צורי דבר על לשון מלך המשיח וכן הפוצה את דוד   1395
עבדו כי המלך המשיח דוד יהיה שמו כמו שאמר ודוד עבדי נשיא
להם לעולם ואז יהיו אלה הענינים הטובים כלם ולא יהיה פרץ
וצוחה;

או פירוש מסבלים מסבלים בבשר	1386	RMC	כן	ח'	1379	MCDS
אין בנו ... פרץ בעזא ח'	1387	B	ופירושו מן הבית מוציאים		1379	C
מבהמתנו	1389	RC	ולא יכילם	1381 N כתרגום	1380	M
זה המזמור	1394	RPCDS	מתרגמינן		1381	B
מלך המשיח	1395	RC	שממלאים		1383	BS

wayyapheq) is 'draws forth', except that (in the latter text) it is a transitive verb governing an accusative, whilst in our text it is an intransitive verb. It is also possible, however, to treat it here as a transitive verb, the meaning (in such case) being that the members of the household bring forth one kind (of produce) to (store it) with another kind; the house will not admit of each being kept separately.[1] *Zan* means 'kind' (just as in) the Targum *l^emino* (is rendered) *l^ez^enohi* 'after its kind' (Gen. i 11). *ma'^aliphoth, m^erubbaboth*: they increase by thousands and tens of thousands until *our fields* become filled with them.

14. *'alluphenu* (means) 'our oxen', as in 'the increase of your cattle (*'^alapheka*)' (Deut. vii 13), and 'like a sheep or an ox (*'alluph*)' (Jer. xi 19). *Laden*: he means that our oxen are strong and huge and able to bear the burden of their work in ploughing and in dragging the carts. Or perhaps the meaning is: *heavily laden* with flesh. *There is no miscarriage*: there is no miscarriage either amongst us or our cattle, for by *pereṣ* (is meant) 'loss of offspring' like *pereṣ* in 'the Lord's (anger) *broke out* upon Uzza (*pereṣ* b^e'*uzza*)' (1 Chron. xiii 11). *None goes forth*: (that is) not one soul[2] (among us), neither from our menfolk nor our cattle, is taken captive.[3] *Cry of distress*: no *cry of distress* is to be heard *in our streets* (meaning that no one) cries aloud in the streets saying: 'Israel has been defeated[4] in battle', for throughout all the days of the reign of David Israel was not once defeated before their enemies.

15. Happy are the people for whom it is so: (that is) who enjoy this good fortune. And why did this good fortune come to this people? Because the Lord is their God! Therefore, happy are those people[5] whose *God is the Lord*. And our teacher the Gaon Saadya, of blessed memory, interprets this psalm as referring to the Messianic era. Thus when it says *A Psalm of David. Blessed is the Lord, my rock*, it is to be taken as an utterance of the Messianic King. This is also what he means when he refers to God as delivering his servant David,[6] since the Messianic King will be named David, even as it says: 'and David my servant will be their prince for ever' (Ezek. xxxvii 25). At that time all these good things will come to pass; there will be neither *miscarriage* nor *cry of distress*.

---

[1] Lit. 'the house will not contain them if each one be by himself'.
[2] Kimḥi thus takes the feminine participle to refer to *nephesh*.
[3] Lit. 'goes forth into captivity'.   [4] Lit. 'smitten'.
[5] Lit. 'happy is he'.
[6] Lit. 'and thus the one who delivers David his servant'.

Psalm CXLV

1. ‏תהלה לדוד ארוממך. אלה הששה מזמורים עד סוף הספר הם
כלם תהלות האל ושבחו לפיכך החל בהם בתהלה ומשלים בהם בתהלה   1400
לגדל התהלה וזה המזמור תחלת הפסוק הראשון תהלה ותחלת הפסוק
האחרון תהלה והחמשה הלליה בראש ובסוף והכל לגדל התהלה ומתי
תהיה תהלת האל גדולה בקבוץ גליות שיראו כל העולם הנפלאות
שיעשה עם ישראל לפיכך הזכיר בהם קבוץ גליות ובנין ירושלים
והמזמור הזה הוא כלו תהלות האל לפיכך חברו באל״ף בי״ת ולא   1405
חבר בו אות הנו״ן ולא ידענו למה ודרשו רבותינו ז״ל, מפני
שיש בה מפלתן של שונאי ישראל דכתיב נפלה ולא תוסיף קום וגו׳
והמתבוננן בזה המזמור יראה בו נפלאות הבורא ומשפטיו על ברואיו
לפיכך אמרו רבותינו ז״ל כל האומר תהלה לדוד בכל יום מובטח
לו שהוא בן העולם הבא לא אמרו על האומרו בפיו בלבד אלא בפיו   1410
ובלבו ואמר. ‏ארוממך אלהי המלך. ‏ארוממך בלבי ובלשוני
שאתה הוא המלך באמת וכל המלכים והמנהיגים תחתונים ועליונים
תחת ממשלתך ואתה רם עליהם והמכיר רוממותו יאמר אלהי
אבל הוא אלהי כל בשר ואלהי האלהים. ‏לעולם ועד. ‏שמך
שהוא קים לעולם ועד או פירושו אני אברכנו לעולם ועד והוא   1415
כל ימי חיי או פירושו. ‏ארוממך. ‏בזה העולם. ‏ואברכה שמך.
לעולם הבא שהוא עולם ועד ואמר תחלה ארוממך ואחר כך אמר שמך

1409	N	בכל יום שלש פעמים מ׳
	C	בכל יום שלשה פעמים
1410	R	ולא האומר בפיו בלבד
	N	ולא אמרו האומרו בפיו בלבד
	P	ולא ׳אמרו זה על האומרו בפיו בלבד

1399	NMC	אלה ששה המזמורים
1402	N	והחמשת מזמורים הלליה
1403	B	שיראו כל עם
1406	N	אמנם רבותינו ז״ל דרשו מפני מה לא נכתבה
		נו״ן מפני שיש בה וגו׳
1408	R	עם ברואיו

PSALM CXLV

1. (A Psalm of) Praise. Of David. I will extol thee: the following six psalms which complete the Book of Psalms[1] are all concerned with the praises of God and his glorification. Thus he commences each one of them with praise and concludes with praise *ad laudem (Dei) majorem*. In this psalm (observe that) the first verse begins with praise and (likewise) the last verse begins with praise. The same is true of the five Hallelujah Psalms, both as regards introduction and conclusion, and all this is done for the purpose of magnifying the praise of (God). And when will the praise of God be magnified? At the ingathering of the exiles, for then all the peoples will see the marvels which he will do for Israel. For this reason he includes a reference to the ingathering of the exiles and the (re)building of Jerusalem. Now, inasmuch as this psalm in its entirety is a praise of God, he composed it in the form of an acrostic[2] but he did not compose (a verse beginning with) the letter *nun*, for some reason or other which we do not know. Our teachers, of blessed memory, explain,[3] however, that the omission is due to the fact that it would, by implication, refer to the downfall of the enemies[4] of Israel, as it is written: 'the virgin of Israel is fallen; she shall no more arise' (Amos v 2).[5] He who reflects on this psalm will observe in it the marvels of the Creator and his judgements upon his creatures. Thus our teachers, of blessed memory, declare:[6] He who recites each day (the psalms beginning with) *t^ehillah l^edawid* may rest assured that he will have a part[7] in the world to come. (However) they do not say this of the person who merely recites it,[8] but only of him who recites it with devotion. He says: *I will extol thee, O God my king*: *I will extol thee* with my heart and my tongue, for thou art in truth the King and all kings and rulers, both in the lower and upper regions, are under thy dominion, since thou art exalted above them. Now he who acknowledges the greatness of God will (naturally) say (on his part) *my God*, but in truth he is the God of all flesh and the God of gods. *For ever and ever*: (that is) *thy name*, which exists *for ever and ever*; or the interpretation may be: I will bless it *l^e'olam wa'ed*, that is, all the days of my life. Or perhaps the verse is to be interpreted: *I will extol thee* – in this world; *I will bless thy name* – in the world to come, which is what is meant by *for ever and ever*. He says in the first place: *I will extol thee*, and subsequently he says: *thy name* – in order to make it known that

---

[1] Lit. 'these six psalms to the end of the book'.
[2] Lit. 'he composed it in the form of an *aleph-beth*'.
[3] *Berakoth* 4b.
[4] 'Enemies of Israel' is used euphemistically for Israel. Cf. *Berakoth* 4b.
[5] The point of the comment is that the letter *nun* would likely be associated with this verse in Amos which begins with *nun* (*naph^elah*). Cf. *Berakoth* 4b.
[6] *Berakoth* 4b.   [7] Lit. 'will be a son of the world to come'.
[8] Lit. 'who simply says it with his mouth'.

להודיע כי הוא שמו ושמו הוא והוא השם הנכתב ולא נקרא כי
האחרים הם שמות התאר וכפל הענין ואמר;

2. בכל יום אברכך. בעולם הזה. ואהללה שמך לעולם ועד.   1420
לעולם הבא ואמרו רבותינו ז"ל בכל יום ויום תן לו מעין
ברכותיו וסמכו זה לפסוק ברוך ה' יום יום וגם זה הפסוק הוא
סמך לזה;

3. גדול ה'. ואם אמר אגדלנו ואהללנו הוא גדול ומהלל על
כל תהלותי עד כי לגדולתו אין חקר ולא ישיגנה האדם ברב החקירה   1425
כי אין לה חקר אלא שיהללנו האדם לפי שכלו;

4. דור לדור. אפילו עם יהיו חיי בני אדם ארכים לא יוכלו
להשיג בכל ימיהם כל שכן שהם קצרים אלא מה יש להם לעשות לפי
קצר ימיהם כי דור הולך ודור בא יספר זה הדור ההולך טרם
לכתו לדור הבא המעשים הנוראים שראו בימיהם והגבורות שראו   1430
בחייהם לפי שישבחוהו הדור הבא על מה שעבר שלא ראו אלא שהגד
להם ועל מה שיראו בימיהם;

5. הדר. כמו שאני עושה שאשיחה לבני העולם. הדר כבוד
הודך. ופירושו יפי כבוד עזך כי בעזו ובנפלאותיו הוא נכבד
כמו שאמר ואכבדה בפרעה. ודברי נפלאתיך. שעשית עמי שיעשו   1435
הם גם כן בכל עת שיקבלו חסד האל יאמרו אותו ויספרוהו לרבים;

6. ועזוז. כמו שאני גדולתך אספרנה כן יאמרו הם גם כן
עזוז נוראותיך וכתוב. גדולתיך. ביו"ד הרבוי שהם רבות

he is identical with his name,[1] the reference being to (the Tetragrammaton, that is) the name which may be written but not pronounced, for all other names are simply attributive descriptions. He repeats the same idea and says:

2. Every day will I bless thee – in this world; *and I will praise thy name for ever and ever* – in the world to come. Our teachers, of blessed memory, have said: day by day give him the appropriate blessing, in support[2] of which they cite the verse 'blessed be the Lord day by day' (Ps. lxviii 20).[3] But this verse (in our text) may likewise be considered as supporting it.

3. Great is the Lord: if I should say that I will magnify and praise him, yet is he exalted above and more highly to be extolled than all my praises to such an extent that *his greatness is unsearchable*. Man cannot comprehend it, even after much study, since *it is unsearchable*, but can only praise him according to his understanding.

4. One generation to another: though men's lives were of long duration, they still would not succeed in the course of their days in forming an (adequate) conception (of God) – how much more so when life's span is so brief![4] What, then, should they do in view of the shortness of their days, for one generation passes away to be succeeded by another? Let the generation which is about to pass away tell, before it passes away, to the succeeding generation the marvellous deeds which they have seen in their lifetime, so that the next generation may praise him, both on account of past events which they have not witnessed but which have been narrated to them, as well as of the things which they experience in their own lifetime.

5. The splendour: even as I do in talking of them to the children of men.[5] *H*^{a}*dar k*^{e}*bod hodeka* means 'the beauteous splendour of thy majesty', for by his might and marvels he is glorified, even as it says: 'I will win glory at the expense of Pharaoh' (Exod. xiv 17). *And thy marvellous works*: which thou hast wrought for me, that they[6] too may do so; on each occasion that they are the recipients of God's grace, let them tell of it and declare it in public.

6. And the might: just as I (on my part) *declare thy greatness*, so let them speak of *thy awful acts*. *G*^{e}*dullotheka* (*kethibh*) is written with *yod* indicating the plural number, since to him who receives they are many. But the *qere*

---

[1] Lit. 'he is his name and his name is he'.
[2] See above, p. 115 n. 3.   [3] *Berakoth* 40a.
[4] Lit. 'how much more when they (their days) are short'.
[5] Lit. 'to the sons of the world'.   [6] Referring to 'the children of men'.

אצל המקבל וקרי גדולתך כי הכל הם כאחת אצל האל ית׳ ואלה
השמות הנזכרים בזה המזמור גבורה, גדולה, מעשה, הוד, כבוד, 1440
טוב, צדקה מלכות נפלאות נוראות והם עשרה לענין ידוע אבל
אינם דוקא כל אחד במקומו הנזכר אלא כל אחד ענינו במקום
חברו גם כן אלא מפני ששנה בהם חלקם בשמות משנים זה מזה;

7. זכר רב טובך. רב הוא שם לא תאר כאלו אמר גדל טובך.
יביעו. ידברו כמו תבענה שפתי. וצדקתך ירננו. יאמרו אותה 1445
בקול רם בפני בני אדם;

8. חנון ורחום. אלה המדות שהם טוב וצדקה מאתו יביעו
וירננו כי הוא חנון שחונן הבריות ונותן להם צרכם ורחום
שמרחם וחומל עליהם ושומר אותם מן הנזקים ומפגעי העולם.
ארך אפים. שמאריך אפו לרשעים ולא יענישם מיד. וגדל חסד. 1450
הדל״ת נקראת בקמץ חטף אמר שהוא גדל חסד שמגדיל חסדו על
בני אדם יותר ויותר ממה שהם ראויים לקבל;

9. טוב ה׳ לכל. אפילו למיני החיות והבהמות והעופות הוא
טוב ומרחם וכן ראוי לאדם ללכת בדרכיו אלה ואין לו לאדם
להשחית החיים כי אם לצרך או להשמר מנזקיהם וכן מצאנו כי 1455
רבנו הקדוש הזהיר שפחתו שלא לאסוף החולדות הקטנות עם רמץ
הבית אלא תניחם להיות דרים בעקרי הבית אמר לה ורחמיו על
כל מעשיו כתיב;

10. יודוך. אף מיני החיים שאין בהם דעת מתקון יצירתך
בהם והכנת מזונותיהם יודוך האדם המבין בהם והרי הם כאלו 1460
יודוך. וחסידיך יברכוכה. בכתיבה חה״א הנחה אמר ומי הם

1439	MDS	כאחד	1460	BNRMACDS	מזונותם
1453	N	הבהמות והחיות	1460	M	כאלו הם יודוך
1456	RPMCS	עם רמן הבית			

is g*dullath*ka (singular) since to God, blessed be he, they are all as one single act. Now the following are the attributes enumerated in this psalm: might, greatness, works, majesty, glory, goodness, righteousness, royalty, marvels, awful acts – ten in number corresponding to something well known.[1] They are not strictly independent the one of the other, for in truth the underlying idea of each one is also to be found in the other. Since, however, he (wishes to) distinguish between them, he discriminates by assigning to them names distinct one from the other.

7. Zeker rab ṭub*ka: rab is a noun and not an adjective; it is as though he were to say 'the greatness of thy goodness'. Yabbi'u (means) 'they will utter', as in: 'let my lips utter (tabba'nah)' (Ps. cxix 171). And sing of thy righteousness: (that is) let them recite it in loud voice in the presence of men.

8. Gracious and compassionate: of these characteristics (of God), since they constitute goodness and righteousness emanating from him, let them speak and sing. He is gracious in that he deals graciously with his creatures, providing for them their necessities; he is compassionate in that he has mercy and pity upon them, keeping them from injury and mishap in the ordinary course of life.[2] Slow to anger: he is long suffering with the wicked in not imposing immediate punishment upon them. And of great mercy: g*dol: the daleth is read with qameṣ-ḥatuph. He says that he is of great mercy in that he bountifully bestows his mercy upon mankind – in greater measure by far than they deserve to receive.

9. The Lord is good to all: even to the various species of beasts, cattle, and birds he is good and merciful. So also man should follow in these ways of his, (that is) he should not destroy living creatures except for the necessities (of life) or to guard against injuries from them. Thus we find that Rabbenu Haqqadosh[3] warned his maid-servant not to remove the little weasels together with the refuse of the house, but to allow them to remain in the corners of the house; he said to her: it is written: and his tender care rests upon all his works.

10. They will give thee thanks: even those animals which are unaware of the process of their creation and of the manner in which their food is prepared will give thee thanks. Of them (thy creatures) man alone understands (all this); but in regard to the others, it is as though they were to give thee thanks. Thy pious ones will bless thee: y*bar*kuka is written with

---

[1] Ten Sefiroth. Cf. J. Abelson, Jewish Mysticism (London, 1913), pp. 110f.
[2] Lit. 'which happens in the world'.
[3] 'Our saintly Rabbi', a title accorded to Rabbi Judah, compiler of the Mishna. Cf. Baba Meẓia 85a.

המודים החסידים שהם מתבוננים תמיד במעשיך והם יברכוך

תמיד כי בכל עת ראותם החדושים המתחדשים תמיד ביצורים

והתקון אשר בהם בחי ובצומח יברכוכה וכן תקנו רבותינו

ז"ל ברכה לכל דבר כפי ענינו כמו שאמרו הרואה כך וכך מברך   1465

כך ואמר. וחסידיך. כי כל לשון חסד הוא יתרון הדבר

והמתבוננים תמיד במעשי האל ויברכוהו תמיד בכל עת התבוננם

הם החסידים ואמרו רבותינו ז"ל האי מאן דבעי למהוי חסידא

לקיים מילי דברכות;

11. כבוד מלכותך. באותם הברכות יזכרו כבוד מלכותך וגבורתך   1470

כי אתה מלך על הכל ובורא הכל ובגבורתך וביכלתך הוית היצורים

כלם;

12. להודיע. וכמו שהם מברכים ומודים בינם לבין עצמם כן

צריכן להודיע לבני האדם שלא ידעו ולא הכירו בגבורותיו

ובכבוד מלכותו;   1475

13. מלכותך. אינה כמלכות בן אדם שיש לו הפסק או בחייו

או במותו אבל מלכות האל אין לה הפסק כי היא. מלכות כל

עולמים. רוצה לומר כל הזמנים וכפל הענין במלות שונות;

14. סומך ה׳. הנופלים. והכפופים. והם העניים המרודים

הוא ברחמיו מרחם עליהם וסומך וזוקף אותם וכן כתוב מאשפות   1480

ירים אביון להושיבי עם נדיבים וגו׳;

15. עיני כל אליך ישברו. וכן אמר כלם אליך ישברון כי כל

נבראי מטה החיים בראת אותם ובראת מאכלם כי יש אוכל עשב ויש

1465 B	הרואה כך מברך כך וכך	1474 BMDS	שלא יכירו M ולא יכירו
1468 BRAS	האי מאן ... דברכות ח׳	1477 B	כי מלכותו מלכות כל עולמים
(M inserts this after החסידים on line 1462)		1480 P	שהוא M והוא

silent *he*. He says: Who are they that give thee thanks? (They are) the pious men who meditate continually upon thy works. They bless thee continually, for on each occasion that they behold the works of creation, constantly manifested in created things and their structure – both in animals and plants – *they will bless thee*. So too our teachers, of blessed memory, have instituted a blessing for each occasion[1] according to the nature thereof, for they say: he who sees such and such is to pronounce such and such a benediction. He purposely uses[2] the word 'and thy pious ones (*waḥᵃsideka*)', for whenever the term *ḥesed* occurs it signifies something in a superlative degree.[3] Thus (only) those who reflect continually upon the works of God, blessed be he, on each occasion that they so reflect are deemed to be 'pious ones'. So our teachers, of blessed memory, state: He who desires to be pious, let him fulfil the precepts in regard to the blessings.[4]

11. The glory of thy kingdom: in those same benedictions let them recite *the glory of thy kingdom and thy might*, for thou art King over all and Creator of all, and by thy might and power thou hast brought into existence all creatures.

12. To make known: just as they pronounce a blessing and thanksgiving privately amongst themselves, so is it incumbent upon them *to make known* (these things) *to the children of men*, that neither know nor acknowledge his mighty deeds and the glory of his kingdom.

13. Thy kingdom: it is not as a kingdom of man, which comes to an end, either in his own lifetime or at his death; but rather the kingdom of God, blessed be he, is interminable, since it is *an everlasting kingdom*, which means a kingdom for all ages. He repeats the same idea in different words (in the second half of the verse).

14. The Lord upholds ... who fall ... those who are bowed down: these are the afflicted that are oppressed. He in his mercy has compassion upon them and *upholds* them and *raises them up*. Similarly it is written: 'who raises the poor from the dunghill, giving them a place among princes' (Ps. cxiii 7, 8).

15. The eyes of all wait upon thee: in like manner he says: 'these all wait upon thee' (Ps. civ 27). For as to all the lower species of beings, thou

---

[1] Lit. 'for each thing'. Cf. *Berakoth* 54a. [2] Lit. 'he says'.
[3] Cf. Maimonides, *Guide for the Perplexed*: 'we have explained *ḥesed* as denoting an excess (in the same moral quality)' (ed. and trans. by M. Friedländer, Part iii, ch. liii, New York 1904). Cf. also Ibn Ezra on Leviticus xx 17.
[4] *Baba Kama* 30a.

אוכל זרע ויש אוכל חי כמותו וכלם עיניהם תלויות אליך ואתה
נותן להם את אכלם והוא על ידי השתלשלות הסבות ואמר. בעתו.
לשון יחיד כי כל מין ומין יש לו עת ידוע יזדמן בו מאכלו
ואמר. אליך ישברו. ואף על פי שאין בהם דעת הם ישברו לפי
טבעם אל חקם הנתון להם ואנחנו היודעים כי אליך הוא התקוה
כי אתה הנותן והמכין;

16. פותח. שאתה נותן להם אכלם בהשפעה עד שישבעו. רצון.
כל אחד לפי רצונו ולפי תאותו.

17. צדיק ה׳. כי בצדק ובישר נותן לכל אחד אכלו ואף על
פי שהחי טורף את החי ואוכלו כמו החתול לעכבר וכן האריה
והדב והנמר ושאר החיות האוכלות חיות אחרות וכן העופות
הדורסים עופות אחרים הכל צדק מאתו כי גם לחיות ולעופות
המטרפים נותן להם גם כן מאכלם בחייהם אלא שבהגיע קצם למות
גזר מקודם שתהיה מיתתם פעמים בהנאת בעלי חיים אחרים ואחד
הוא לנטרף ימות מיתת עצמו או על ידי אחר וזה מבוכה גדולה
בין החכמים כי מהם אומרים כי כשטורף החתול העכבר והאריה
הכבש והדומה להם הוא ענש לנטרף מאת האל וכדומה לזה מצאתי
בדברי רבותינו ז״ל רבי יוחנן כד הוה חזי שלך ששולה דגים
מן הים הוה אומר משפטיך תהום רבה ומהם אומרים כי אין גמול
וענש בכל מיני החיים אלא לאדם בלבד ואנחנו נאמר כי יש

1484	NR	כמוהו
1484	PM	תלויות לך
1487	RD	לפי טבעם וחקם
1490	N	את אכלם
1491	B	ולפי תאותו ח׳
1494	N	וכן במעופפים העופות הדורסים עופות אחרים
1495	M	הדורסות
1496	NRM	בחייהם מאכלם

1496	R	בהגיע
1497	B	פעמים יגזור שימות מיתת עצמו מ׳ ואחד before
1499	MS	או הארריה הכבש
1501	PM	והוא עוף ששולה דגים מן הים
1502	NRPADS	אין גמול ואין ענש
1503	BN	מיני בעלי החיים

didst create them and didst also give them their food. Some of these feed
on herbs, others on plants, and yet others on members of their own species;[1]
and in each and every case their eyes are bent unto thee and *thou givest
them their food*: this occurs through the intermediate links in the chain of
causation. He says: *in its season*, (that is) singular number, for each distinct
species has its particular season when its food is provided for it. And (when)
he says: *wait upon thee* (he means): though they are not endowed with
intellect, yet do they wait upon thee by intuition for the portion assigned to
them. But we (who are rational beings) understand that it is in thee that
we hope,[2] seeing that thou art he that gives and prepares.

16. Thou openest: for thou givest them their food in abundance until
they are satisfied with it. *Desire*: (that is) each one according to its desire
and its appetite.

17. The Lord is righteous: in righteousness and uprightness[3] he gives to
each one its food. (It must be admitted that) one animal preys on the other,
devouring it, as for instance a cat preying upon a mouse, or for that matter
the lion, the bear, leopard, and the rest of the beasts of prey; so also birds
that prey on other birds.[4] Yet in all these instances he deals righteously,[5]
since to those same beasts and birds that fall prey to others, he likewise
gives them their food so long as they live. When, however, the time for
their end is reached, (it may happen) that he has decreed in advance that
it shall take place through the satisfaction of the appetite of some other
animal, for it is one and the same to the victim, if it die a natural death or
at the hand of another creature. This subject is, however, a matter of great
perplexity among philosophers, some of them arguing as follows:[6] when
the cat preys on the mouse or the lion on the lamb, and so forth, it is a
punishment from God upon the victim. And to this effect also we find in
the words of our teachers, of blessed memory, thus: Rabbi Joḥanan, on
observing a cormorant catching a fish from the sea, remarked: 'thy judgements are like the great abyss' (Ps. xxxvi 7).[7] Others, however, state that
the doctrine of reward and punishment does not apply to the diverse species
of animals, but only in the case of the human being.[8] For our part,[9] it is our

---

[1] Lit. 'and one eats a living creature like itself'.

[2] Lit. 'that unto thee is the hoping'.

[3] Or 'with impartial judgement'.

[4] Because of the length of the sentence some freedom has been taken in the re-
arrangement of the clauses.

[5] Lit. 'it is all righteousness from him'.

[6] Lit. 'there are some of them who say'.   [7] *Ḥullin* 63a.

[8] Lit. 'but some of them state that there is no reward or punishment for any species
of animal except for man alone'.

[9] Lit. 'but we'.

גמול ועונש לשאר החיים בעסק האדם כי הנה מצאנו מיד כל חיה

אדרשנו ונאמר ושד בהמות יחיתן ונאמר בגמול ולא שבר החמור 1505

ואמרו רבותינו ז"ל מה נשתנו פטרי המורים מכל בהמות לפדותם

ופירשו לפי שטענו בזתם של ישראל ונאמר לכלב תשליכון אותו

בזכות לא יחרץ כלב לשונו מלמד שאין הקדוש ברוך הוא מקפח

שכר כל בריה ויש דעת אחרת ואין ראוי לכתבה. וחסיד בכל מעשיו.

שנותן להם מה שהוא איננו מחיב לתת והם אינם ראויים לקבל אלא 1510

שחסדו גבר עליהם;

18. קרוב ה' לכל קוראיו. מאיזה עם שיהיה ובלבד שיקראוהו

באמת שיהיו פיו ולבו שוים;

19. רצון יראיו. כי יראיו הם יקראוהו באמת ויעשה רצונם

במה שיבקשו ממנו וישמע שועתם ויושיעם מצרה שתבוא בעולם או 1515

שתבוא להם לכפרת עונם;

20. שומר ה'. אוהביו. טובים מיראיו כי יאהבוהו ללא

תקוה טובה וללא פחד ענש אלא מאהבה זכה וישמרם שלא תבוא

עליהם צרה לעולם וכן יהיו כל ישראל לעתיד לבוא ואז. ואת

כל הרשעים ישמיד. שלא ישאר רשע בעולם כמו שאומר והיו כל 1520

זדים וכל עשי רשעה קש ולהט אתם היום הבא וגו';

21. תהלת ה' ידבר פי. ואז תהלת ה' ידבר פי כי אחיה

המתים שיחיו ואז יברך כל בשר שם קדשו רוצה לומר כל בני

אדם כי כלם יעבדוהו שכם אחד וכן אמר יבואו כל בשר להשתחוות

1505		After החמור Bosniak reads רז"ל ופירשו		עונותם
1506	N	גמול בבהמות כגון החמור והכלב		ולא מפחד עון
		ואמרו רז"ל לכלב תשליכון אותו בשכר		רוצה לומר ... וכל בשר
		לא יחרץ כלב לשונו מלמד שאין הקב"ה		
		מקפח שכר כל בריה. וכן מה נזתנו פטרי		
		חמורים לפי שטענו אותם ישראל מבזת מצרים		

decided opinion[1] that all other species are subject to reward and punishment in regard to their dealings with man. Thus we find: 'from every animal I will require it' (Gen. ix 5); so also it says: 'and the destruction of the beasts which made them afraid' (Hab. ii 17). And as an instance of a reward it says: 'it did not break the back of the ass' (1 Kgs. xiii 28). And our teachers, of blessed memory, have said:[2] For what reason is there discrimination in favour of the firstborn of asses as against other animals in the matter of their redemption? They explain thus: because they carried the spoil of Israel. So it is said: 'you shall throw it to the dogs' (Exod. xxii 30) – as a reward (for what it says in scripture) 'a dog shall not whet its tongue' (Exod. xi 7). Whence we learn that the holy one, blessed be he, does not withhold the reward of any creature. (And concerning this discussion) there is yet another view which, however, is not worth noting.[3] *And gracious in all his works*: inasmuch as he gives them what he is not obligated to give them, and which they do not deserve to receive, only that his mercy is great towards them.

18. The Lord is nigh to those who call on him: irrespective of whatever people they belong to, but above all they must *call upon him in truth*, (that is) their words and thoughts should be alike.[4]

19. The desire of those who fear him: for those *who fear him call upon him in truth*, whatever they ask of him, and *he will hear their cry and save them* from distress which befalls the world or which befalls them as an expiation of their sins.

20. The Lord preserves (all) who love him: (*those who love him*) are more pious than *those who fear him*, since they *love him* not out of hope of reward[5] nor from dread of punishment, but out of pure love; and *he will preserve* them that trouble may never befall them. So too will it be with Israel in the future to come, and then: *all the wicked will be destroyed*: that there remain not a wicked man in the world, even as it says: 'and all the wicked and all evildoers will be as chaff, and that day when it comes will set them ablaze' (Mal. iii 19).

21. My mouth will speak out the praise of the Lord: and then *my mouth will speak out the praise of the Lord*, for I will be revived with those of the dead that are to be resurrected, and then *all flesh will bless his holy name*: he means to say the whole human race, for they will all serve him with one consent. Thus it says: 'all flesh will come to worship before me'

---

[1] Lit. 'we say'. [2] *Bekoroth* 5b.
[3] Lit. 'but it is not worth writing it'.
[4] Lit. 'that his mouth and heart should be alike'. [5] Lit. '(material) good'.

1525   לפני וכל בשר רוצה לומר כל בני אדם לבדם ולא שאר החיים

התחתונים וכן כי היא היתה אם כל חי רוצה לומר כל חי מדבר;

Psalm CXLVI

1. הללויה הללי נפשי את ה׳.   בראותו ברוח הקדש קבוץ גליות אומר כנגד ישראל. הללויה. וכן אמר נפשי הללי את ה׳ עמהם ובלתם;

1530   2. אהללה ה׳.   עתה בעודני בחיים אהללנו ואזמרה לו ואודיענו ברבים ואמר להם;

3. אל תבטחו.   על דרך שאמר ירמיה ומן ה׳ יסור לבו אלא אם יבטח באדם ישים העיקר האל שיתן בלב האדם הנדיב לעזרו וכפל הענין במלות שונות.   שאין לו תשועה.   שאם לא ברצון
1535   האל אין ביד אדם להושיע חברו מצרתו כי לה׳ לבדו התשועה והוא יסובבנה על יד בני אדם כמו שסבב תשועת גלות בבל על ידי כורש וכן לעתיד יסבב גאולת ישראל על ידי מלכי הגוים שיעיר את רוחם לשלחם כמו שכתוב והביאו את כל אחיכם מכל הגוים מנחה לה׳ וזה יהיה לפי שבטחו ישראל בגלותם באל לבדו;

1540   4. תצא רוחו.   ואיך תהיה לאדם תשועה והנה איננו שליט ברוחו לכלוא את רוחו כי תצא רוחו פתע וישוב לאדמתו ומה שחשב לעשות לא יוכל כי הנה יצאה רוחו המעמידה אותו והנה ביום מותו אבדו עשתנותיו רוצה לומר מחשבותיו וכן בארמית ומלכא עשית חושב ואיך יושיע אחרים ואין בידו להושיע את
1545   עצמו.   עשתנותיו.   העי״ן בסג״ול;

5. אשרי שאל יעקב בעזרו.   יעקב אבינו כי הוא בטח באל׳כי אחיו היה מתנכל להמיתו וברח מפניו ולא בטח בלבן שיתן לו

1525	P		בעלי חיים התחתונים
1526	NPCDS	מ׳ מה	מדבר after
1533	NRPC		באל
1534	R		כי אם לא ברצון האל

1537	N	וכן לעתיד יסבב האל יתעלה
1540	N	שולט
1541	P	פתע פתאם

(Isa. lxvi 23). (The expression) *all flesh* denotes all mankind, to the exclusion of the rest of the lower orders of creation; so too we find: 'she was the mother of all living' (Gen. iii 20) (where *all living*) means 'all rational beings'.

PSALM CXLVI

1. O praise the Lord. Praise the Lord, my soul: as he beholds by divine inspiration the ingathering of the exiles, he addresses Israel thus: *praise the Lord.* And so also he says: *praise the Lord, my soul:* (both in unison) with them and alone without them.

2. I will praise the Lord: now while I am alive I will praise him, *make melody* to him and make him known among the multitudes. And he says to them:

3. Put not your trust: just as Jeremiah says: 'and whose heart turns away from the Lord' (Jer. xvii 5). But if he puts his trust in man, let him regard God as the source (of his confidence) seeing it is he who puts it in the heart of a princely man to help him. And he repeats the same idea in different words. *In whom there is no help:* unless it be by the will of God, it is not within the power of a man to save his fellow man from trouble, since to the Lord alone belongs salvation and he brings it about through the agency of human beings, just as he effected the redemption from the Babylonian exile by the hand of Cyrus. In the same manner, at some future time he will bring about the redemption of Israel at the hands of the kings of the nations, for he will stir up their spirit that they set them free, even as it is written: 'and they will bring all your brethren from all the nations as an offering to the Lord' (Isa. lxvi 20). And this will come to pass because Israel in exile puts trust in God alone.

4. His breath departs: how can there be help in man when in truth he has no control over his own breath to retain it? For *his breath departs* suddenly and *he returns to his dust* so that it is impossible for him to accomplish that which he intended to do because the spirit which sustains him has departed. And behold, on the day of his death *his plans cease to be.* (By '*eshtonothaw*) he means to say 'his plans' just as in Aramaic (we have) *umalka*' '*a*shith 'and the king planned' (Dan. vi 4) (where the meaning of '*a*shith is) 'planned'. How then can he save others, seeing he has not the power to save himself? '*eshtonothaw*: (note that) '*ayin* is pointed with *seghol*.

5. Happy is he whose helper is the God of Jacob: (he refers to) our father Jacob, for he had faith in God. For when his brother was planning

צרכי מחיתו ואף על פי שהיה הולך אליו אלא באל באל שאמר ונתן

לי לחם לאכל ובגד ללבש וכן ישראל בניו שבטחו בו הוציאם

מן הגלות וכפל הענין במלות שונות;   1550

6. עשה שמים. בו ראוי לבטוח כי הוא עושה הכל ובידו להרים

ולהשפיל ולעשות בנבראיו כרצונו. וארץ. היא היבשה לפיכך

זכר. את הים. וטעם ואת כל אשר בם. לשלשה הנזכרים בשמים

המלאכים והצבא הגדול ושבעה משרתים בארץ חיה ועוף ואדם ובים

התנינים הגדולים וכל נפש חיה הרומשת והוא יעשה בכלם חפצו   1555

והוא. השומר אמת לעולם. שומר הבטחתו לזמן רב כמו שעשה

לישראל שהבטיחם להוציאם מהגלות ואחר שהיו שם זמן רב עד

שנואשו כל הגוים מגאולתם הוציאם הנה תראו כי בו לבדו ראוי

לבטוח;

7. עושה משפט לעשוקים. בכל דור ודור עושה משפט בעבורם   1560

בעושקיהם וכן יעשה בעבור ישראל שהם עשוקים בגלות כמו שאמר

עשוקים בני ישראל ובני יהודה יחדו וכל שביהם החזיקו בם

מאנו שלחם. נתן לחם לרעבים. בכל דור וכן עשה לישראל

בגלות ובצאתם מן הגלות דרך מדברות אומר לא ירעבו ולא יצמאו

ולא יכם שרב ושמש. ה' מתיר אסורים. בכל דור ודור וכן   1565

עשה לישראל שהתירם ממאסר גלותם;

8. ה' פקח עורים. שהם עורים מחלי העין הוא ירפאם ואמר

זה החלי כי העור כמו האסור לא ימוש ממקומו או פירוש עורים

מרב צרה כי הצרה דומה לחשך והישועה לאור ובמקרא פסוקים

to kill him and he fled from him, he did not put his trust in Laban to provide him with the necessities for his existence – though it was to him that he went (for protection) – but in God. For thus he said: 'and he will give me bread to eat and clothing to wear' (Gen. xxviii 20). And it was the same with Israel (in exile): because his children put their trust in him, he brought them forth from exile. He repeats the same idea in different words.

6. Maker of heaven: in him it is proper to put one's trust, seeing that he is the maker of all and has the power to exalt or to abase and to deal with his creatures according to his wish. *And earth*: this is the dry land. Hence he speaks (next) of *the sea*. And the expression *and all that is in them* qualifies each of the three things already mentioned.[1] Thus, in the heavens are the angels and the great host and the seven subsidiary spheres; in the earth are beast, bird, and man; and in the sea, the great sea monsters and every living thing that creeps. With all of them he does as he wishes. And he it is *who keeps faith for ever*: he keeps his promise over a long period of time just as he did to Israel whom he promised to take forth from exile. After having been there for so long a time that the nations dismissed as absurd the possibility of their redemption,[2] he did (in fact) bring them forth. Therefore, you see that in him alone it is proper to trust.

7. Who executes justice for the oppressed: throughout every generation, he *executes justice* on their behalf against their oppressors. So also will he do for Israel who are oppressed in exile, just as it says: 'the people of Israel are oppressed, and the people of Judah with them; all who took them captive have held them fast, they refuse to let them go' (Jer. l 33). *Who gives food to the hungry*: in every generation. Likewise also did he unto Israel in exile, for of their exodus from exile through the ways of the wilderness it says: 'they will not hunger or thirst, neither scorching wind nor sun will smite them' (Isa. xlix 10). *The Lord sets the prisoners free*: in every generation. So did he deal with Israel in freeing them from the bonds of exile.

8. The Lord opens the eyes of the blind: (that is) the blind as the result of some disease of the eye, but he heals them. And he cites (in particular) this infirmity because a blind man, like a prisoner, cannot move (freely) from his place. Or possibly we should interpret *blind* as (though it meant blind) from great trouble, for trouble is compared with darkness and the deliverance therefrom with light. And (it is to be noted that) Scripture

---

[1] Lit. 'and the sense of *and all that is in them* is for the three which have been mentioned'.
[2] Lit. 'after having been there for so long a time that the nations had given up hope for their redemption'.

רבים מעידים בזה וכן עשה לישראל שהיו כעורים בגלותם כמו 1570
שאמר נגששה כעורים קיר וכאין עינים נגששה כשלנו בצהרים
כנשף. ה׳ זקף כפופים. והם העניים כמו שפירשנו. ה׳ אהב
צדיקים. ·וכן אוהב ישראל שהם צדיקים בין האומות;

9. ה׳ שומר את גרים. הגר והיתום והאלמנה הם חלושים כי
אין להם עוזר ושומר ולפיכך הזהירה התורה בכמה מקומות 1575
עליהם וה׳ שומר אותם וכן שומר ישראל שהיו גרים בין האומות
וחלושים כיתום ואלמנה. יעודד. פירושו ינשא. ודרך
הרשעים יעות. החלושים ינשא והרשעים יעות דרכם ידחו ונפלו
בה;

10. ימלך. ומתי יהיה זה כשימלך ה׳ לעולם אלהיך ציון כמו 1580
שאמר והיה ה׳ למלך על כל הארץ שכל העולם יכירו במלכותו
וזכר ציון כי משם תצא היראה ממנו לכל העולם ויאמרו כי הוא
מלך על הכל אחר שיעשה משפט ברשעים בעמק יהושפט;

Psalm CXLVII

1. הללויה כי טוב זמרה אלהינו. אז כשימלוך ה׳ הללו יה כל
בני העולם שתכירו אז מלכותו ואז יהיה זמר שלכם טוב ונעים 1585
ותהלתכם תהיה נאוה. נאוה. האל"ף נחה ועניו כמו נאה;

2. בונה ירושלים ה׳. ואז יבנה ה׳ ירושלים ויכנס נדחי
ישראל אל אדמתם;

3. הרופא לשבורי לב. כמו ישראל שהם שבורי לב ועצבים בגלות.
לעצבותם. בדגש הצד"י לתפארת הקריאה; 1590

4. מונה. הנה הסכימו חכמי התכונה כלם כי מספר הכוכבים
אלף וצ"ח אם כן מה הוא מונה מספר לכוכבים. ואמר ישעיה

1570	BM	עורים	1585	NR	במלכותו
1573	M	לישראל	1585	M	זמרכם
	NR	בישראל	1590	C	הדגש בצרי
1582	B	הוראה			

contains many verses bearing testimony to this (metaphorical usage). So also did he unto the people of Israel who were blind, so to speak, in exile, even as it says: 'we grope for the wall like the blind, we grope like those who have no eyes' (Isa. lix 10). *The Lord lifts up those who are bowed down*: that is, the afflicted, as we have explained. *The Lord loves the righteous*: thus he loves Israel, since they are the righteous among the nations.

9. The Lord watches over the strangers: the stranger, the orphan and the widow – these are the forlorn (of humanity), since they have none to help and preserve them. For this reason the Torah strictly admonishes us in many passages concerning their treatment. But the Lord watches over them. In the same way he watches over Israel who are strangers among the nations and helpless as the orphan and widow. The meaning of *ye'oded* is 'uphold'. *But the way of the wicked he makes crooked*: he lifts up the weak; but as for *the wicked*, he makes their way *crooked* so that they are thrust aside and fall therein.

10. He will be king: when will all this come to pass? When *the Lord thy God will be king for ever, O Zion*, just as it says: 'And the Lord will become king over all the earth' (Zech. xiv 9), for the whole world will acknowledge his dominion. And he mentions Zion because thence shall go forth the fear of him to the whole world so that men will say that he is king over all, after he executes justice against the wicked in the valley of Jehoshaphat.[1]

PSALM CXLVII

1. Praise the Lord! For it is good to sing praises to our God: at the time when the Lord will be king, *praise the Lord*, all you children of mankind, that you acknowledge then his kingdom. Thus will your hymn be *good* and pleasant and your praise *seemly*. *Na'wah*: the *aleph* is quiescent and the meaning is the same as *na'ah* 'seemly'.

2. The Lord builds up Jerusalem: then will the Lord *build up Jerusalem* and gather together the outcasts of Israel into their land.

3. He heals the brokenhearted: that is Israel, inasmuch as they are *brokenhearted* and grieved in exile. *Le'asse'botham* has euphonic *daghesh* in the *sade*.

4. He counts: now all astronomers are agreed that the number of the stars is one thousand and ninety-eight. If this is so, what is the meaning of *he counts the number of the stars*? And (similarly) Isaiah says: 'who brings

---

[1] Cf. Joel iv 2, 12.

המוציא במספר צבאם ואמר האל ית׳ לאברהם אבינו הבט נא

השמימה וספר הכוכבים אם תוכל לספר אותם ואמר בלדד השחי

1595 היש מספר לגדודיו ופירש החכם הנשיא רב אברהם בר חייא כי

הכוכבים הגדולים המאירים על הארץ יש להם מספר כדברי חכמי

התכונה והכוכבים הקטנים שאינם מאירים על הארץ רבים אין

יכולים בני אדם לראותם כל שכן למנותם ולדעת מספרם ואותם

שאינם מאירים על הארץ נבראו למשול על הארץ לא להאיר כמו

1600 שאמר ולמשול ביום ובלילה גם מהכוכבים הנראים יש כוכב שיראה

שהוא אחד והם רבים ומפני הגבה הגדול והמרחק הגדול אשר

בינינו ובינו יראה שהוא אחד אבל כל הכוכבים הנבראים אין

יכולת באדם לדעת מספרם אבל הקדוש ברוך הוא היודע הנסתרות

הוא יודע מספרם כי הוא בראם. לכלם שמות יקרא. וכן אמר

1605 ישעיה לכלם בשם יקרא ופירושו כי האל בראם כלם במספר ידוע

אצלו ולכל אחד מהם קרא שם הנאות לו לפי הדבר אשר בעבורו

נברא לסבת אותו הדבר אחר סבת עצמו כי כל הכוכבים יש להם

כח וממשלה על יצורי מטה כל אחד על מין ידוע שנותן בו הכח

לעשות מלאכתו כמו שאמרו רבותינו ז"ל אין לך כל עשב ועשב

1610 מלמטה שאין לו מזל מלמעלה מכה אותו ואומר לו גדל;

5. גדול אדונינו. כי מלך בשר ודם שיש עליו להנהיג מדינות

רבות ילאה להנהיגם כלם כאחת הקרובות אליו והרחוקות ממנו

ואם ינהיג הקרובות על הסדר הנכון לא יעשה כן ברחוקות כי

ילאה כחו בזה ואם יהיה בו הכח לא תהיה בו התבונה אבל

1615 אדונינו הוא מנהיג העולם כלו הנהגה ישרה כי הכח והתבונה

בו כי הוא גדול ורב כח. לתבונתו אין מספר. פירושו לדברים

שיש לו תבונה בהם אין מספר כי אין נשוא התבונה מספר כי

תבונה ממין האיכות ומספר ממין הכמות לפיכך צריך לפרשו כך.

אבל נשוא תבונה חקר וכן הוא אומר ואין חקר לתבונתו;

1595 B	כי הכוכבים ... חכמי התכונה ח׳	1612 NS	כלם כאחד
1598 BPCS	ולאותם	1615 B	הוא מנהיג את כל העולם
1602 BS	ידמה שהוא אחד	1615 R	כי הכח והתבונה לו
1606 C	ולכל אחד מהם קרא שמו	1616 B	שהוא גדול
1610 P	מזל ברקיע		

out their host by number' (Isa. xl 26), whereas God, blessed be he, said to our father Abraham: 'Look toward the heaven, and number the stars, if you are able to number them' (Gen. xv 5). (Likewise) Bildad the Shuhite said: 'is there any number to his armies?' (Job xxv 3). The learned Nasi, Abraham ben Ḥiyya, explains that the greater stars which illumine the earth have a (fixed) number, just as the astronomers maintain. But the lesser stars which do not illumine the earth are so many that man cannot even see them, how much the less count them and determine their number. And these stars which do not shed light upon the earth were created to rule over the earth and not to illumine it, as it says: 'to rule over the day and over the night' (Gen. i 18). Besides, even of the stars which are visible there is (here and there) one which appears to be a single star, whilst (in fact consisting of) many, for because of the great height and distance separating us from it, it appears to be a single (star). Hence it is impossible for man to know the number of all stars which have been created. But the Holy One, blessed be he, who knows all secrets, he knows their number, since he created them. *He gives to all of them their names*: in like manner Isaiah says: 'he calls them all by name' (Isa. xl 26), the meaning being that God created them all according to a number determined[1] by him, giving each one its appropriate name according to the purpose for which it was created, (that is) in consideration of the effect produced as a result of its natural properties. For all the stars have power and dominion over the lower created beings, each one over a determinate species, to which it gives the power to perform its function. Thus our teachers, of blessed memory, have said:[2] You cannot find a single plant on earth[3] which has not a (corresponding) planet in heaven[4] which strikes it and says to it 'Grow!'

5. Great is our Lord: an earthly king[5] who has to rule over many provinces vainly endeavours to rule all at once, both those that are near and those which are remote from him. If he governs the more proximate ones with just rule, he will not do so in the case of the more remote, for his energy will have been exhausted. And even if he has the strength, he will not (in all likelihood) have the understanding (to do so). But *our Lord*, he directs the entire universe with just rule, for his is the strength and the understanding, since he is *great and abundant in power. His understanding is beyond measure*: this means: the things which he conceives are innumerable, for number cannot be predicated of understanding, since understanding is a qualitative and number a quantitative concept. Hence we must interpret the passage as above, since *understanding* can only be qualified by some

---

[1] Lit. 'known'.   [2] *Bereshith Rabba* 10: 6.
[3] Lit. 'below'.   [4] Lit. 'above'.
[5] Lit. 'a king of flesh and blood'.

6. מעודד. ואף על פי שהוא גדול ורב כח הוא משגיח על 1620
העניים והשפלים והחלושים ומנשא אותם ומשפיל הרשעים המתגאים
עדי ארץ ואף על פי שזה הוא עושה בזמן הזה אינו עושה זה
תמיד כי פעמים רבות יצליחו הרשעים אבל לעתיד יעשה זה על
דרך השלמות כמו שאמר ואת כל הרשעים ישמיד;

7. ענו. אמר כנגד ישראל שירו לה׳ בפה. זמרו. לו בכלי 1625
והשיר יהיה שיר תודה שתודו לאל על כל הטובה הגדולה שעשה
עמכם בהוציאו אתכם מן הגלות ברוב טובה ובכבוד גדול וזהו
גבורה גדולה מאתו להוציא עם מעט מעמים רבים ובספור גבורותיו
ספרו הגבורות שעושה בעולם תמיד והוא המטר כי כן אמר אליפז
עושה גדולות ואין חקר נפלאות עד אין מספר ואמר אחריו הנותן 1630
מטר על פני ארץ וגו׳ וכן אמר איוב בזה הלשון ואמר גם כן
ורעם גברותיו מי יתבונן ואמר ירעם אל בקולו נפלאות עשה
גדלות ולא נדע ואמר אחריו כי לשלג יאמר הוא ארץ וגשם מטר
וגו׳ ושיבת הגלות תדמה למטר שאין מיחלים בעבורו אלא לאל 1635
ית׳ וכן אמר מיכה הנביא והיה שארית יעקב בקרב עמים רבים
כטל מאת ה׳ כרביבים עלי עשב אשר לא יקוה לאיש ולא ייחל
לבני אדם לפיכך אמר;

8. המכסה שמים בעבים. ואמר. המכסה. כי שמים בהירים
וטהורים ומזהירים ובהיות העבים באויר השמים מכסים מעין האדם.
המצמיח הרים חציר. אפילו ההרים שהם יבשים וקשים כל שכן ארץ 1640
המישור או זכר הרים לפי שאין דרך ותחבולה להשקותם מן הנהרות.

9. נותן לבהמה לחמה. שאין לה תחבולה להכין מאכלה והוא
מצמיח לה החציר בהרים למאכלה. לבני עורב. לפי שהם לבנים

גדולה גבורה		רבות ח׳ B	1628 B		
ספרו הגבורה RPM ספרו גבורותיו	CS 1628	זמרו לה׳	1625 NRPM		תמיד ח׳ 1623 B
הוה ארץ	1633 BRC	בכלי שיר והשיר יהיה	1625 NPC		
ומזהירים וטובים	1639 N	כל ח׳	1626 NM		
מנהרות	1641 NM	מהגלות	1627 R		

such predicate as 'searching',[1] just as it says: 'his understanding is unsearchable' (Isa. xl 28).

6. He lifts up: for though *he is great and abundant in power*, yet he watches over the downtrodden, the lowly and the weak. He raises them up but *casts the wicked*, who vaunt themselves, *to the ground*. And although he does so at present, he does not always do so, since the wicked very often prosper. But in the future he will accomplish this by way of final compensation, even as it says: 'but all the wicked he will destroy' (Ps. cxlv 20).

7. Sing: he says this to the people of Israel: sing to the Lord with the mouth, *make melody* to him with instruments, and let the song be a song of *thanksgiving* in which you offer thanks to God for all the abundant goodness which he has wrought for you in taking you forth from exile with an abundance of material blessings[2] and great honour. This is (a manifestation) of greatness and might on his part, viz. to bring forth a people few in number from the midst of a numerous people. And in the recital of his mighty deeds, recount also the great deeds which he performs continually, (as for example) the rain. Thus Eliphaz says: 'who does great things and unsearchable, marvels without number' (Job v 9), adding immediately: 'who gives rain upon the earth' (Job v 10). Job gives expression to a similar thought when he also says: 'but the thunder of his power who can understand' (Job xxvi 14). So also he says: 'God thunders wondrously with his voice; he does great things which we cannot comprehend' (Job xxxvii 5), and (immediately) after this: 'for to the snow he says, "Fall on the earth"; and to the shower, etc.' (Job xxxvii 6). And (note that) the return of the exile is compared to rain for which we look in hope to none but God alone, blessed be he. And thus also the prophet Micah says: 'then the remnant of Jacob will be in the midst of many peoples, like dew from the Lord, like showers upon the grass which tarry not for men nor wait for the sons of men' (Mic. v 6). Therefore (the psalmist) says:

8. He covers the heavens with clouds: he says *he covers* since (ordinarily) the heavens are clear, bright and shining. But while the clouds are in the air the heavens are hidden from the sight of men. *He makes grass grow upon the hills*: even upon hills which are dry and hard (land) – how much more so in the case of level countryside? Or perhaps he cites (in particular) the hills because there is no way or means of irrigating them from the rivers.

9. He gives to the beast its food: because it has not the ability to prepare its own food; but he causes the grass to grow upon the hills for its food.

[1] Lit. 'but the predicate of *understanding* is "searching"'.
[2] Lit. 'with abundant good'.

בהולדם ואמותיהם מניחות אותם ולא יביאו להם טרפם כי יחשבו

כי אינם בניהם לפי שהם לבנים והם צווחים כאלו יקראו לאל בעד 1645

טרפם והקדוש ברוך הוא מזמין להם יתושים ואוכלים אותם והנה

הוא עוזר החלושים שאין בהם יכלת מעצמם וכן עשה לישראל שהיו

נטושים בגלות מאין כח כי האל ית׳ רוצה בחלושים ובשפלים לא

במתגברים ומתגאים בכחם וביכלתם לפיכך;

10. לא בגבורת הסוס יחפץ. אינו אומר כי אין האל חפץ בגבורת 1650

הסוס כי הוא שנתן לסוס גבורה וכן אמר הוא ית׳ לאיוב התתן

לסוס גבורה, כלומר כמו שנתתי אני אלא פירושו שאינו חפץ באדם

שבוטח בגבורת הסוס וכן במי שבוטח בשקיו לברוח מן המלחמה

כמו שאמר הנביא וקל ברגליו לא ימלט ורוכב הסוס לא ימלט נפשו;

11. רוצה ה׳. אלא מי הוא רוצה את יראיו שהם מיחלים לחסדו 1655

ואינם בוטחים בגבורת הסוס ולא בגבורתם;

12. שבחי. כי בך רוצה לפי שבטחה בו ומדבר כנגד העיר דרך

משל רוצה לומר יושבי ירושלים והפסוק כפול בענין במלות שונות

כמנהג;

13. כי חזק. שלא תפחד לעולם שיבוא עליה אויב כי האל ישמרנה 1660

כאלו בריחיה חזקים כמו שאמר על חומתיך ירושלים הפקדתי שומרים

כלומר יהיו בלי פחד כאלו שומרים על החומות ומרב בטחון השלום

יהיו השערים פתוחים תמיד כמו שאמר ופתחו שעריך תמיד יומם

ולילה לא יסגרו. ברך בניך בקרבך. שיהיו ברוכים בפרי בטנם

ובמעשי ידיהם בעיר ובחוץ; 1665

14. השם גבולך שלום. וכן יהיו ברוכים בחוץ בשלום ובפרי

אדמתם. הלב חטים. הטוב שבחטים והנבחר כמו חלב תירוש ויצהר;

To the young ravens: since these are white at birth and their mothers desert them and do not bring them their prey, for they imagine that they are not their offspring because they are white. (The young ravens) cry as though invoking God for their prey, and the Holy One, blessed be he, provides for them mosquitoes which they devour. Behold! He helps the weak who cannot fend for themselves. So also did he to Israel who were forsaken in exile, powerless. For God, blessed be he, delights in the weak and lowly but not in them who behave arrogantly and are puffed up in their own strength and power. Accordingly:

10. **He delights not in the strength of the horse:** (the psalmist) does not mean to say that God has no delight in the strength of the horse, since (after all) he himself gives the horse its strength. For thus did he, blessed be he, say to Job: 'Do you give the horse its might?' (Job xxxix 19), that is to say, even as I have given it? But the correct interpretation is: he delights not in the man who puts his trust in the strength of the horse. The same applies also in the case of a man who is confident in the (nimbleness of) his feet to escape from battle, even as the prophet says: 'and he who is swift of foot will not save himself, nor will he who rides the horse save his life' (Amos ii 14).

11. **The Lord takes pleasure:** but in whom then does he delight? *In those who fear* him, for *they hope in his steadfast love* and trust neither in the strength of the horse nor in their own strength.

12. **Praise:** for in you he delights because you trusted in him. He addresses the city metaphorically, meaning (of course) the inhabitants of Jerusalem. And in this verse the same theme is repeated in different words, as is frequently the case.

13. **For he strengthens:** she shall no more be in dread of the enemy coming upon her, since God will watch over her as though her *bars* were impregnable,[1] even as it says: 'upon your walls, O Jerusalem, I have set watchmen' (Isa. lxii 6), which means that the people therein will be without fear as though there were watchmen round about the walls. And because of the great security of peace the gates will be open continually, just as it says: 'Your gates will be open continually; day and night they will not be shut' (Isa. lx 11). *He blesses your sons within you*: they will be blessed in the fruit of their wombs and in the works of their hands, both within the city and outside it.

14. **He makes peace in your borders:** they will be blessed with peace

---

[1] Lit. 'strong'.

‫15. השלח אמרתו ארץ. והוא המטר שבא באמרתו ובדברו מהרה‬
‫כעבד הרץ מהרה לעשות רצון אדוניו. ואמרתו ודברו. הוא רצונו‬
‫וזכר ענין המטר והשלג הנה לפי שהם סבת ברכת פרי האדמה והשבע;‬   1670

‫16. הנתן שלג כצמר. השלג שהוא לבן כצמר הלבן וכן כצמר‬
‫יהיו כצמר הלבן והוצֵדך לזכור לבנותו לפי שברב תראה לבנותו‬
‫ודמה אותו לצמר על אף פי שהוא פחות ממנו בלבן מפני שלא‬
‫יכול לדמותו בלבן ממנו מדברים אשר בארץ. כפור כאפר יפזר.‬
‫הוא שיורד בשחר בימי הקר ודמה אותו לאפר לפי שהוא מפזר ומעט‬   1675
‫לא תראה לבנותו כמו השלג לפיכך דמה אותו לאפר שאינו לבן‬
‫כמו השלג;‬

‫17. משליך קרחו כפתים. הקרח כמו הכפור אלא שהוא חזק ממנו‬
‫ומוליד קר רב לפיכך זכר עם הקרח קרתו ופירוש. כפתים. במו‬
‫הדבר הנבצע לבצעים כי כן הוא יורד לבצעים וחתיכות אסופות‬   1680
‫מדקי הקרח. לפני קרתו מי יעמד. אמר. קרחו. וקרתו. בכנוי‬
‫ומיחסו אל האל ית׳ כי הכל הוא דברו ומצותו אין דבר במקרה‬
‫וכן אמר אליהו מנשמת אל יתן קרח וכמו שהמטר הוא הוריד ברחמיו‬
‫לצרך ברואיו ומורידו לפעמים למשפט ולענש העונות והוא המטר‬
‫השוטף כן השלג והכפור הוא צרך הזרעים והאילנות אבל בהיותו‬   1685
‫חזק הרבה והוא הקרח ותולד ממנו קרה רבה הוא למשפט שהוא‬
‫ממית ומיבש הזרעים ופרחי האילנות וכן הברד ואף על פי שלא‬
‫נזכר וצריך להזכיר בהודאת האל אלה הדברים שהם תמידים לבני‬
‫העולם והם גבורות ונפלאות מהבין כמו שאמר באחד מהם ורעם‬
‫גברותיו מי יתבונן ואמר האל לאיוב היש למטר אב וגו׳ ואמר‬   1690
‫מבטן מי יצא הקרח וכפר שמים מי ילדו לפיכך כשאמר. ענו לה׳.‬

מיחסו	RMCDS 1682	והוא רצונו	R 1669
הוא מוריד	PM 1683	לפי שברבו	NC 1672
אלה הדברים שהם תדירים לבני אדם	P 1688	מן הדברים שבארץ P בדברים	R 1674
או מי הוליד אגלי טל מ׳ R אב After 1690	מדק הקרח	P 1681
		מן הקרח	B

round about and with the fruit of their soil. *Ḥeleb ḥittim* (means) the best and choicest wheat, as in: 'the best' of the oil and the wine (Num. xviii 12).

15. He sends forth his command to the earth: this (refers to) the rain which comes speedily at his command and his word just like the slave who runs promptly to perform his master's wish. *His command . . . his word*: (signify) his will. He makes special mention here of the rain and the snow since the blessings of the yield of the soil and the abundance thereof are dependent upon them.

16. He gives snow like wool: (that is) snow which is as white as wool, as: 'they will become as wool (*kaṣṣemer*)' (Isa. i 18) (where the meaning is) 'like white wool'. He considers it necessary to mention its white colour because its whiteness is very pronounced. And he compares it to wool – despite the fact that the latter is not as white as it – because he cannot find anything in existence whiter than it with which it may be compared. *He scatters hoar-frost like ashes*: this is the substance which falls in the early morning in the cold season. And he compares it to ashes because it is scattered and minute and its whiteness is not as visible as that of snow. For this reason he represents it as dust which is not as white as snow.

17. He casts forth his ice like morsels: ice is (something very much) like hoar-frost except that it is firmer and causes severe cold. For this reason he couples *ice* with *his cold*. *Like morsels*: like something which is broken into morsels, for so it falls in morsels and pieces collected from atoms of ice. *Who can stand before his cold?*: he says *his ice* and *his cold* with (third person singular) pronominal suffix referring to God, for everything is according to his word and command. Nothing happens by mere chance. Thus Elihu said: 'by the breath of God ice is given' (Job xxxvii 10). And just as he in his mercy sends down rain for the needs of his creatures – though sometimes causing it to fall as an act of judgement and retribution for iniquitous deeds as in the case of a torrential downpour – so also the snow and hoar-frost are for the needs of plants and trees; but when it is very much hardened and becomes ice from which severe cold comes, it is for the purpose of exacting judgement since the cold destroys and dries up the seeds and tree blossoms. It is the same with hail, though no mention is made of it here. And in praising God it is necessary to mention those phenomena which constantly occur in the world. They are too formidable and wonderful to be understood, even as it says of one of them: 'but the thunder of his power, who can understand?' (Job xxvi 14). Similarly, God said to Job: 'has rain a father?' (Job xxxviii 28). And he says (further): 'from whose womb did the ice come forth, and who has given birth to the hoar-frost from heaven?' (Job xxxviii 29). Therefore he says: *sing to the*

זמרו לאלהינו. אמר שיזכרו בשירם ובזמרם מגבורותיו אלה

התמידים ואמר. מי יעמוד. כלומר מי יוכל לעמוד בפני הקרה

החזקה כי מפני הקרה נמנעים בני אדם לצאת מבתיהם ולעשות מלאכתם

כמו שאמר ביד כל אדם יחתום וגו׳ וכן החיות כמו שאמר ותבוא חיה 1695

במו ארב ובמעונותיה תשכן;

18. ישלח דברו. חם השמש או המטר שממסה אותם הנזכרים השלג

והכפור והקרח ואמר. ישב רוחו יזלו מים. כי בנשיבת הרוח

מפאת ים יבוא המטר שימסה אלה או פירושו ישב רוחו עליהם ויזלו

מים כי בפזר אותם הרוח ולא יהיו מאוספים כאחד ימסו ויהיו 1700

למים;

19. מגיד. ובספרכם גבורות האל ספרו שנגלה אליכם בכבודו

והגיד לכם דבריו וחקיו ומשפטיו כי המעמד ההוא היה דבר גדול

שלא היה כמוהו כמו שכתוב הנהיה כדבר הגדול הזה או הנשמע כמהו;

20. לא עשה. כמו שכתוב השמע עם קול אלהים וגו׳. ומשפטים 1705

בל ידעום. והמשפטים שנתן להם לא ידעום שאר הגוים כמו שכתוב

ומי גוי גדול אשר לו הקים ומשפטים צדיקים ככל התורה הזאת;

Psalm CXLVIII

1. הללויה הללו את ה׳ מן השמים. בזה המזמור זכר כל הנבראים

בעולם הגדול החל ובעולם הקטן כלה ואמר בתחלה בכלל. מן השמים.

כלומר כל הנהוים מן השמים רוצה לומר מיסוד השמים שהוא יסוד 1710

חמישי ואמר אחר כן הללוהו במרומים. אתם שאתם במרומים ונכלל

בו צורות אמת שאינם גופות ולא בגופות וענין הללו אינו מצוה

אלא כאלו אמר להם נאה להלל;

1692	M		שיזכירו
1693	RM		הקרח
1694	RM		הקרח
1697	N		הנזכרים למעלה
1700	R		כי כשיפזר
1701	RPMCDS		מים
1702	B		גבורת
1703	NMCS		חקיו
1705	After מ׳ N אליהם	כאשר	מדבר מתוך האש
			שמעת אתה ויחי

1706	After הגוים	Bosniak reads ולא גלה להם
1706	N	כמו שאמר הכתוב	כמו שאמר M
1709	R		בגדול החל ובקטן כלה
1710	N		ובקטן כלה
1711	R		ונכלל בו
1712	NRM	ח׳	וענין ... נאה להלל
1713	PA		לכם נאה להלל

Lord, make melody to our God: he bids them record in their song and melody these permanent manifestations of his power. *Who can stand?*: that is to say, who can withstand the severe cold? For because of the cold men are prevented from going forth from their homes to do their work, just as it says: 'he seals up the hand of every man' (Job xxxvii 7). This is so also with the animals, as it says: 'then the beasts go into their lairs, and remain in their dens' (Job xxxvii 8).

18. He sends forth his word: (this represents symbolically) the heat of the sun or the rain which dissolves (the substances) mentioned (above) viz. snow, hoar-frost, ice. And he says: *he makes his wind to blow and the waters flow*: as the wind blows from the extremity of the sea, the rain comes and melts all these things. Or perhaps its interpretation is that he causes his wind to blow upon them so that water flows therefrom, for when they are scattered by the wind and no longer remain in a compact state, they melt and become water.

19. He declares: when you narrate the mighty deeds of God, recount also that he revealed himself to you in his glory and declared to you his words, his statutes and his precepts; for that revelation (at Sinai) was a great event such as has never been equalled, just as it is written: 'whether such a great thing as this has ever happened or was ever heard of' (Deut. iv 32).

20. He has not dealt: even as it is written: 'did any people ever hear the voice of a god, etc.' (Deut. iv 33). *They do not know his precepts*: as for the precepts which he gave them, the other nations do not know them, as it is written: 'and what great nation is there that has statutes and precepts so righteous as all this law?' (Deut. iv 8).

PSALM CXLVIII

1. O praise the Lord. Praise the Lord from the heavens: in this psalm he refers to the whole creation, beginning with the supernal world and concluding with the lower world. Thus he begins by using the general expression *from the heavens*, that is to say, all beings that have their origin in the heavens, meaning such as are composed of the ethereal element, that is, the fifth element. Subsequently he says: *praise him in the heights*: (that is) you that are *in the heights*; (and this expression) includes the transcendental forms which are neither bodies nor connected with bodies. In regard to these, his words are not to be construed as implying a direct demand, but it is as though he were to say to them 'it is meet to praise him'.[1]

---

[1] Lit. 'and the sense of *praise* is not a command but as though . . .'.

2. הללוהו כל מלאכיו . הם השכלים חשוקי הגלגלים גם הם אינם
גופות לא בגופות . הללוהו כל צבאיו . הם הגופות הזכים   1715
והבהירים והם הגלגלים והכוכבים שהם בגלגל השמיני לפיכך אמר
כל צבאיו לפי שהם צבא גדול ואמר בלשון רבים לפי שהם כדורים
חלוקים ;

3. הללוהו שמש וירח . הזכיר תחלה שני המאורות הגדולים ואחר
כן הזכיר החמשה הכוכבים והם כוכבי אור כי הם מאירים על הארץ   1720
יותר מאשר הם בגלגלים החמשה מפני שהם קרובים לארץ מהם ;

4. שמי השמים . יש מחכמינו שפירשו שמי השמים עליוני השמים
כמו מלך מלכים ולדבריהם יהיה זה מה שאינו גוף ומה שאמרו
עליוני במדרגה לא במקום והוא עולם הנשמות ויהיה פירוש . והמים
אשר מעל השמים . גם כן בלתי גוף והוא צורת הצורות שממנה   1725
יוצאות הצורות ועליה נאמר גם כן ובין המים אשר מעל לרקיע
ויש מהם שאומר כי שמי השמים הם אשר מתחת השמים והוא כדור
האש שהוא סמוך אל כדור הלבנה והשמים הוא האויר שנקרא שמים
כמו על פני רקיע השמים ויהיה פירוש . והמים אשר מעל השמים .
כדור הקרח ויש קוראים שמו כדור הסגריר והוא בין כדור האש   1730
והאויר הקרוב לנו והוא מקום תכלית הגעת הגעת העבים ואין חכמי
הפילוסופיא מודים בזה כי אומרים אין כי בינינו ובין גלגל הלבנה
אלא האויר והאש הטבעית אלא אם כן נאמר כי המים פירושו צורת
המים והוא מקום תכלית הגעת העבים באויר ובמקום ההוא מן
האויר ישובו העבים מים ויפלו לארץ בטבעם לא שיש שם גוף אחר   1735

1716	N	בגלגל השמים	1727	CS	ויש מהם שאומרים
1721	RMACDS	בגלגל השמיני			אומרים
1721	B	ח׳ החמשה	1731	P	מקום העבים
1722	BNM	שפירש	1731	PD	חכמי המחקר
1723	NMCS	שאמרנו	1734	C	מרום תכלית
1723	P	ומה שאמר הוא במדרגה לא במקום			

וים מהם R

2. **Praise him, all his angels:** these are the ideals comprehended by the spheres to which they have a desire to attain.[1] These also are incorporeal. *Praise him, all his host:* these are the pellucid and transparent bodies which consist of the constellations and the stars in the eighth sphere. Accordingly, he says *all his host*, since these constitute the Great Host. And he uses the plural number since they are distinct and separate globes.

3. **Praise him, sun and moon:** in the first place he mentions the two great lights and then he mentions the sphere of the five planets, (referred to as) *stars of light* because the former give more light to the earth than those in the five spheres, being nearer to the earth than the latter.

4. **Praise him, you heaven of heavens:** some of our philosophers take (the phrase) *heaven of heavens* to signify the highest of the celestial beings, on the analogy of 'king of kings' and thus meaning the incorporeal forms. For when they use the term *highest* (they intend it to be understood) qualitatively and not as a spatial concept; (in other words) the interpretation is the world of pure spirit.[2] So too the expression *and you waters above the heavens* is (explained as something which is) incorporeal, that is (as referring to) the *forma formarum* from which the pure forms derive. And an allusion to this[3] is to be found in the verse 'from the waters which are above the firmament' (Gen. i 7). Others consider *the heaven of heavens* to mean the sphere which is immediately below the heavens, that is, the fire sphere adjacent to the moon sphere; and *hashshamayim* is explained as meaning the atmosphere which is here termed 'heaven', as also in the text: 'across the firmament of the heavens' (Gen. i 20). The words *and you waters above the heavens* must then be interpreted as meaning the sphere of ice which is also designated by the term sphere of Sagrir. It is situated between the sphere of fire and the atmosphere which is near us and represents the lower limit set to the clouds.[4] But the philosophers will not accept[5] this, for they say that there is nothing between us and the sphere of the moon except the atmosphere and the natural fire. If so, we may say that *the waters* is to be interpreted as meaning (the place) where the water is formed, being the extreme limit of the extent of the clouds in the atmosphere; and in that place, as a result of the action of the air, the clouds become converted into water and return to fall in their natural course upon the earth. We are not to suppose[6] that there is some other corporeal thing

---

[1] Lit. 'these are they that comprehend the desires of the spheres'. Cf. Maimonides, *Guide for the Perplexed*, Part II, ch. 10. Ḥasuq = 'the thing desired', hence, 'object', 'ideal'.

[2] Lit. 'the world of souls'.   [3] Lit. 'and in regard to it, it is said'.

[4] Or 'the ultimate place reached by the clouds'.

[5] Lit. 'will not admit this'.   [6] Lit. 'not that there is there'.

אלא האויר אבל הוא חלוק באיכותו ועל המקום ההוא נאמר והמים
אשר מעל השמים;

5. יהללו את שם ה'. אמר כל אלה העליונים הנזכרים יהללו
את שם ה' ויודו לו כי הוא אדון עליהם כי אף על פי שהם נשגבים
הוא נשגב עליהם והוא. צוה ונבראו. והוא לבדו הקדמון והם
חדשים נבראים. (6) ויעמידם לעד לעולם. כי אינם כמו
הנבראים שאישיהם נפסדים והמין עומד לא כן העליונים אלא
לעולם כל אישיהם עומדים כמו המין והחק שנתן להם בתחלת בריאתם
לעולם לא יעבור כי כן יהיה לעולם לא ישתנה סדרם;

1745 7. הללו את ה' מן הארץ. אחר כן אמר לנבראי מטה שיהללו את
ה' ואמר תחלה. תנינים וכל תהומות. אמר. וכל תהומות. על
המים אשר מתחת לארץ ועל המים אשר מעל לארץ וזכר המים קודם
היבשה כמו שהיתה בבריאה וגם התנינים אשר בהם והם שאמר עליהם
הכתוב ויברא אלהים את התנינים הגדלים כי הם גדולים מחיות
1750 היבשה ומה שאמר. הללו את ה'. והם אינם בני דעה רוצה לומר
שבני אדם יהללוהו מנפלאות האל שרואים בהם ומשכילים בהם;

8. אש וברד. הזכיר הדברים הנהוים באויר שגם הם מן הארץ
והם אש וברד שלג וקיטור כי בריאתם מן הארץ וחכמי התולדות
יקימו זה בראיות גמורות וגם בדברי רבותינו ז"ל מצאנו כן
1755 רבי אליעזר אומר כל מה שבארץ בריתו מן הארץ ומיתי לה מהכא
הללו את ה' מן הארץ וגו' אש וברד וגו' רבי הונא בשם רב יוסף
אומר כל מה שיש בשמים ובארץ אין ברייתו אלא מן הארץ רוצה
לומר בשמים באויר כלומר שהוא באויר והוא בארץ כלומר שיורד

1737	מ' PD מעל השמים After	1743 B	כל ח' כי החק N
	ומה שאמר עזרא ע"ה אתה עשית את	1750 PC	בני דעת
	השמים שמי השמים הוא הרקיע ושמי השמים	1751 P	ומשכילים ויודעים ומכירים
	הם הגלגלים שבם הכוכבים	1752 B	הדברים ח'
1738 R	ואמר כל אלה הנבראים הנזכרים	1754 NRC	בראיות ברורות PD 1754יקימו זאת
1740 R	נשגב יותר מהם	1754 N	ובדברי רבותינו
1742 NM	הנבראים התחתונ'ם		

there beside the air, only that it is a composite body in its constitution. With reference to that place, it is said: *and you waters above the heavens.*

5. Let them praise the name of the Lord: let all these supernal beings which have been mentioned *praise the name of the Lord* and confess to him that he is Lord over them. For though they are exalted, yet he is exalted above them and he it was who *commanded and they were created*: he alone is eternal but they are created *ex nihilo.*[1]

6. And he established them for ever and ever: for they are unlike the lower orders of creation since these as individuals perish, whilst (only) the species persist. It is not so with the supernal beings; on the contrary, they, as individuals, just like the species itself, exist permanently because the law which he imposed upon them at the beginning of their creation will not pass away. So it will remain forever, for their substance[2] is not subject to change.

7. Praise the Lord from the earth: next he commands the inferior creatures to praise the Lord. In the first place he says: *you sea monsters and all deeps*: he says *and all deeps* with reference both to the waters below the earth and to *the waters above the earth.* He gives precedence to the waters above the dry land, as was the case in the primaeval creation. So too he mentions *the sea monsters* concerning which Scripture says: 'and God created the great sea monsters' (Gen. i 21), since they are greater than the beasts of the dry land. And when he says *praise the Lord,* he means that since these are not intelligent beings the children of mankind should praise him because of the marvels which they see manifested in them.

8. Fire and hail: he refers here to those things which, though they have their existence in the air, are originally derived from the earth, as for instance fire, hail, snow, vapour, for all of them are created from the earth and the natural philosophers can substantiate this by decisive proofs. Similarly, in the words of our teachers, of blessed memory, we find: Rabbi Eliezer says: Whatsoever is in the earth can only have its origin in the earth.[3] And he deduces this from the text *praise the Lord from the earth,* etc., *fire and hail,* etc. Rabbi Huna in the name of Rabbi Joseph says: Whatsoever has its existence both in the heavens and the earth has its origin only in the earth. And by 'in the heavens' he means (of course) 'in the air', that is to say, (if a thing exists) both in the air and in the earth, for the air moves in a downward direction towards the earth, in such a case its origin

---

[1] Lit. 'which are created afresh'.
[2] *Seder* = 'order', 'arrangement', 'internal constitution'.
[3] *Bereshith Rabba* 12: 11.

האויר לארץ אין ברייתו אלא מן הארץ שנאמר כי כאשר ירד הגשם
והשלג מן השמים מה הגשם והשלג אף על פי שירידתן מן השמים
אינן אלא מן הארץ כך כל מה שיש בשמים ובארץ אין ברייתו אלא
מן הארץ. אש. הוא אש הברק ששורף הדבר שנופל בו. ברד.
ידוע והוא הפכו שהוא קר וכן שלג קר ותמורתו קיטור שהוא חם
והוא האד העולה מן הארץ דומה לעשן רוח סערה עשה דבו־ו.
והוא האויר המתנועע בסבת האד העולה מן הארץ וכשהוא מתנועע
בחזקה יפיל הארזים הגבוהים והבנינים והאניות שבים ואמר.
עושה דברו. להודיע כי איננה במקרה אלא הוא מצוה אותה
להתנועע ובדברו ובמצותו היא מתנועעת לענש המקבלים וכן אמר
נעמד רוח סערה ואמר ובקעתי רוח סערות בחמתי;

9. ההרים. ואחר אשר זכר הדברים הנהוים באויר וזכרם סמוך
למים לפי שבסבתם יעלו האדים באויר שמהם המטר והשלג והברד
ואחר כן זכר היבשה ואת אשר בה ואמר. ההרים וכל גבעות.
כי הם הדברים העומדים והקימים מנבראי הארץ ואחר שהזכיר
הדומם כלו כי בכלל ההרים המתכות וכן כתוב אשר אבניה ברזל
ומהרריה תחצב נחשת וכיון שהזכיר הדומם הזכיר אחר כן הצומח
ואמר. עץ פרי וכל ארזים. והם כלל לעצים שאינם עושים פרי
והזכיר ארזים כי הם הגדולים שבעצים;

10. החיה. ואחר הצומח הזכיר החי שאינו דברי והחיה היא
המדברית וכל בהמה וכל בהמה היא אשר בישוב והרמש קטני החיות. וצפור
כנף. הוא עליון ממין החי שאינו דברי;

1761	R	אף כל מה		1772	R	ואת כל אשר
1764	PCD after	מ' לעשן והוא חם ויבש		1774	R	כי בכל ההרים והמתכות
1766	BMC	הפיל והאניות בם PMC		1774	M	ארץ מ' אשר before
1768	M	ונאמר		1780	BMCS	והוא עליון
1769	P	ואמר הכתוב		1780	P	מדבר
1769	M	ואומר				

can only be from the earth, as it is written: 'for as the rain and the snow come down from heaven' (Isa. lv 10). Now just as the rain or snow, though they fall from heaven yet have their origin in the earth, so also whatever it be that exists both in the heavens and the earth is derived solely from the earth. *Fire*: (that is) the fire of lightning which kindles the object upon which it alights. *Hail*: (the meaning) is evident. It is the opposite and reverse of the former, being cold.[1] So also the snow which is cold, its contrary or opposite[2] is the vapour which is hot, that is, the mist which rises up from the earth, and bears a close resemblance to smoke.[3] *Stormy wind fulfilling his word*: that is, the mobile air which moves as a result of the rising mist. When it moves about with force it pulls down tall cedars, buildings, and ships on the sea. And he (expressly) says: *fulfilling his word*, to make it known that it does not function by mere accident, but that he commands it so to move about; for by his word and his command it moves about as a punishment for such as sustain injuries therefrom. So also it says: 'and raises the stormy wind' (Ps. cvii 25); and it says also: 'I will even rend it with a stormy wind' (Ezek. xiii 13).

9. You mountains and all hills: now that he has made mention of such things as have their existence in the earth, having spoken of them in connection with the waters – since from the latter[4] arise the mists from which in turn are derived the rain, snow and hail – so now he refers to the dry land and all that is contained therein. He says *mountains and all hills*: because these are the durable and permanent things of the terrestrial creation.[5] He speaks here, in effect, of the whole of the inanimate world, because (the term) *mountains* includes the metals, as it is written: 'a land whose stones are iron and from whose hills you will dig copper' (Deut. viii 9). And so, having already referred to the inanimate world he now proceeds to speak of the plant kingdom. And he says: *fruit-trees and all cedars*: (*cedars* is a general term) to include all such trees as yield no fruit. And (in addition) he singles out the cedars for special mention because they are the tallest of all trees.

10. Beasts: after the plants he refers to dumb animals. Thus *haḥayyah* (denotes) the wild animals and *wᵉkol bᵉhemah* (denotes) the domesticated animals, and by *creeping thing* he means the lowest orders of the animal kingdom. *And winged bird*: (represents) the highest species of dumb animals.

---

[1] Lit. 'it is its reverse and is cold'.
[2] Lit. 'and thus snow is cold and its opposite is vapour which is hot'.
[3] For an exposition of the current views on the matters discussed by Kimḥi here, see Maimonides, *Guide for the Perplexed*, Part i, ch. lxxii, Part ii, ch. xxx.
[4] Lit. 'since through their causation'.
[5] Lit. 'of the creation of the earth'.

11. מלכי ארץ. ואחר שהזכיר החי שאינו מדבר הזכיר החי שהוא
מדבר שהוא סגולת העולם השפל וכן ביצירה הזכירו באחרונה כמו
שנברא באחרונה לומר שהוא מושל על כולם והוא המורכב האחרון
לפי הטבע והזכיר בבני אדם מעלת הכבוד ומעלת הימים ואמר כי
כלם יהללו את שם ה׳, כנכבד כנקלה כקטון כגדול אנשים ונשים   1785
ואמר. וכל לאמים. כי כלם יודו את שם ה׳ בבוא הגואל לישראל;

12. בחורים וגם בתולות. אמר. וגם. לפי שאין דרך הבתולות
להתעסק אלא בקשוט גופן אמר שגם הן יתנו לבן להלל לה׳. זקנים
עם נערים. שהזקנים ילמדום היאך יהללו את ה׳ זהו שאמר. עם.
כי אין בנערים לבדם דעת להלל לפיכך אמר שהזקנים יהיו עם   1790
הנערים וילמדום;

13. יהללו את שם ה׳. אמר כל אלה הנבראים שהם בעולם השפל
יהללו את שם ה׳ כלומר אותם שהם בני דעה יהללו עליהם ועל שאר
הנבראים ואמר. כי נשגב שמו לבדו. ולא אמר כן בעליונים
לפי שהעליונים נשגבים אף על פי כן אמר שיודו לו כי הוא   1795
נשגב עליהם כי הוא בראם אבל התחתונים אין בהם נשגב כי אין
לגדולתם עמידה וקיום לפיכך לא יתגאו מלכי ארץ שרים ושופטי
ארץ בגדולתם כי במעט זמן תסוף ותכלה גדולתם ויודו כי אין
המשגב והגדולה כי אם לה׳ לבדו ועוד לטעם אחר אמר. כי נשגב
שמו לבדו. בעבור כי זאת התהלה תהיה לעתיד לבא בבוא הגואל   1800
ואז יודו כלם כי נשגב שמו לבדו וגדולתם וגבהותם הבל כמו
שכתוב עיני גבהות אדם שפל ושח רום אנשים ונשגב ה׳ לבדו
ביום ההוא. הודו על ארץ ושמים. כי כל הנבראים העליונים
והתחתונים כלם עומדים בכחו והודו עליהם בהשתלשלות הסבות;

1781 NRM	החי הדברי	1788 P	להלל את ה׳
1784	מ׳ P הימים After	1790 PCS	נערים
	מעלת הכבוד מלכי ארץ וכל לאמים	1793 PCS	יהללוהו RM בני דעה
	והימים בחורים וגם בתולות זקנים וגו׳	1798 B	חשוב ותכלה
1785 B	יהללו את ה׳	1800 BS	כי זאת התפלה
	לפי שאין דרך הבתולות אלא לקשט עצמן PD 1787	1803 B	עליונים ותחתונים

11. Kings of the earth: after having made reference to the dumb animals, he now refers to the rational being, since he is the speciality of creation in the lower world. So also in (the account of) creation he is the last to be mentioned, as well as being the last to be created – as an indication that he is to rule over all, since he is the highest complex in creation. And though he mentions in particular the special distinctions of honour and old age, he says that all of them should praise the Lord, both he that is highly respected and he that is lightly esteemed, both the great and the small, both man and woman. He says: *all the people*: for all of them will acknowledge the Lord, at the time that the Redeemer will come to Israel.

12. Both young men and also maidens: he employs the particle *w^egam* 'and also' because it is not usual for maidens to occupy themselves with anything other than the ornamentation of their bodies. He says that even they will be disposed in their hearts to praise the Lord. *Old men together with children*: the old men will instruct them in the manner in which they are to praise the Lord, and this is what he means when he says 'together with'; for young people of their own accord have not the (necessary) knowledge to understand how to give praise. Therefore he says that the old men will be together with the children and will instruct them therein.

13. Let them praise the name of the Lord: he says: all these creatures that are in the lower world – *let them praise the name of the Lord*; that is to say, let such as are endowed with intellect praise him on their own behalf and on behalf of the other creatures. He says: *for his name alone is exalted*, etc.: he does not say this to the higher intelligences, because they too (in a sense) are of the exalted beings. Nevertheless, he bids them offer thanks to him because he is exalted above them, inasmuch as he has created them. As for the lower beings, there is none exalted among them, because their greatness is transient and ephemeral.[1] Therefore let neither kings of the earth nor princes nor judges of the earth pride themselves on their greatness, for in a short time their greatness will have ceased, vanished, and been completely lost, so that they will confess that exaltation and greatness pertain to God alone. Furthermore, for another reason he says: for his name is exalted, viz. because this prayer has a bearing upon the Messianic future on the coming of the Redeemer; for then will all acknowledge that his name alone is exalted, and that their pride and pomp are but vain things, even as it is written: 'the lofty looks of man shall be brought low, and the arrogance of men shall be bowed down, and the Lord alone shall be exalted in that day' (Isa. ii 11). *His glory is above the earth and heaven*: (that is) all created things, both upper and lower, exist in virtue of his power and his glory, which is diffused over them, as a result of the concatenation of causes.

---

[1] Lit. 'because their greatness has neither stability nor permanence'.

14. וירם. והראה זה לכל העולם כי הכל בכחו כשהרים קרן
לעמו שהוציאם מן הגלות ויקבצם מן העמים והרים קרנם על כל
העמים זהו. תהלה לכל חסידיו. שיהללוהו על זה ומי הם כל
חסידיו הם בני ישראל שהם עם קרובו וכלכם הלליה;

Psalm CXLIX

1. הללו יה שירו לה׳ שיר חדש. אמר כנגד ישראל. שירו לה׳
שיר חדש. כלומר שלא יהיה לכם די בשירים האלה הכתובים אלא
אתם תחדשו לו שיר על הנפלאות שעשה עמכם. תהלתו בקהל
חסידים. תהלתו תהיה נאמרת בקהל חסידים והם ישראל;

2. ישמח. בעשיו. בלשון תפארת וכן איה אלוה עשי כי בעליך
עשיך;

3. יהללו שמו. בפה ובכלי שיר יהללו שמו;

4. כי רוצה. להם נאה להלל יותר מכל עם כי בהם רצה מכל
עם והם שהם ענוים מכל עם פארם מכל עם בישועה שהושיעם;

5. יעלזו חסידים. ישראל שהם חסידים יעלזו בכבוד שיעמוד
לעולם. ירננו על משכבותם. ירננו לאל על מנוחתם שתהיה
קימת. משכבותם. מנוחתם כמו ושכבת ואין מחריד, גם בלילה
לא שכב לבו, ועורקי לא ישכבון, והמפרשים פירשו על משכבותם
על מטתם בהתבודדם בלילה;

6. רוממות אל. כשיצאו למלחמה עם גוג ומגוג יתפללו לאל
וירוממוהו שהוציאם מן הגלות כן יתן להם כח על האויבים לכלותם

1806 B	וירם קרנם	ולכם נאה להלל P כי רצה בהם 1816 C
1810 R	באלה השירים 1818 BD	שיעמדו

14. And he has exalted: and this he demonstrated to the whole world, viz. that everything is in his power, when he raised up the horn of his people in taking them forth from exile, and gathered them together from the peoples and exalted their horn above all the peoples. This is *praise of all his saints*: that they praise him on this account. And who are meant by *all his saints*? These are the children of Israel, being *a people near to him*. Therefore, all of you – *praise the Lord!*

PSALM CXLIX

1. Praise the Lord. Sing to the Lord a new song: (the psalmist) says to Israel: *sing to the Lord a new song*: that is to say, these written songs in themselves are not sufficient (in number) for you but you should each one of you compose a new song to him concerning the wondrous deeds which he has performed for you. *His praise in the assembly of the faithful*: his praise will be recited in the assembly of the faithful. And these are the people of Israel.

2. Let Israel be glad in his maker: $b^{e\prime}o\dot{s}aw$ (plural used) as an expression of majesty, as in: 'where is God, my maker (*'o\dot{s}ay*)' (Job xxxv 10): 'for thy maker (*'o\dot{s}ayik*) is your husband' (Isa. liv 5).

3. Let them praise his name: with voice and musical instrument *let them praise his name*.

4. For (the Lord) delights: it is especially appropriate for them – more so than for any other people – to praise him, because in them *he delights*, more than in the other peoples; and being as they are the most afflicted of peoples, yet has he glorified them above all by the salvation with which he saves them.

5. Let the faithful exult: the people of Israel, since they are *the faithful*, *will exult* in their glory, which abides forever. *Let them sing for joy on their rest*: let them sing for joy to God because of their rest which is to endure forever. *Mishk^ebotham* means 'their rest', as in: 'and you will rest (*ush^ekabtem*) and none will make you afraid' (Lev. xxvi 6): 'even in the night his mind does not rest (*shakab*)' (Eccles. ii 23); 'and the pain that gnaws me takes no rest (*yishkabun*)' (Job xxx 17). The commentators, however, explain *mishk^ebotham* as 'upon their couches', that is, in their (private) meditations by night.

6. Let the high praises of God: when they go forth to fight against Gog and Magog, let them pray to God and exalt him who brought them forth from the exile. In this way he will give them strength to contend with their

התפלה תהיה בפיהם והחרב בידם ופירוש. פיפיות. חרב בעלת   1825
שתי פיות שתמ,תת משני צדדים ואמר. בגרונם. כי תחלה יוצא
הקול מהגרון ויגמר הדבור בפה או אמר בגרונם לפי שיצעקו
בתפלתם כמו קרא בגרון;

7. לעשות נקמה. שהם באו עליהם להלחם והם יעשו נקמתם
בהם. תוכחות. שיתוכחו עם מלכיהם למה באו עליהם והם לא   1830
ימנעו מלהלחם עליהם לפיכך יעשו בהם נקמה ויהרגו כל העמים
הבאים עליהם למלחמה;

8. לאסר. ויתפשו מלכיהם ונכבדיהם חיים ויאסרום בזקים
ובכבלי ברזל להנקם בהם בחיים;

9. לעשות בהם משפט כתוב. המשפט הנגזר עליהם או הכתוב   1835
בתורה אם שנותי ברק חרבי ותאחז במשפט ידי והוא הכתוב הנה
וביחזקאל ובנבואת זכריה. הדר הוא. ואותו היום יהיה הדר
לכל חסידיו והם ישראל ועל היום ההוא הללויה;

Psalm CL

1. הללויה הללו אל בקדשו. זה המזמור שהוא חותם הספר יש בו
שלשה עשר הלולים רמז לשלש עשרה מדות שבהם מנהיג האל ית' את   1840
העולם אמר תחלה. הללו אל בקדשו. והוא עולם המלאכים ואמר
אחר כן. הללוהו ברקיע עזו. והוא הגלגל העליון התשיעי
ובכללו כל העולם כי הוא מקיף הכל לפיכך אמר עזו כי בו נראה
עז האל;

2. הללוהו. אחר כן אמר לישראל. הללוהו בגבורתיו. שהראה   1845
להם מכל עם. הללוהו. כרב גדלו. שהתגדל והתקדש בעמים על
גאולתם;

1826 NRPMC	פיות שכורתת	1836 BR	ח' בתורה ... הכתוב
1828 R	כמו שנאמר	1840 B	רמז כנגד
1831 After R עליהם מ' כשבאים למלחמה		PDS	כנגד
1834 C	וכבלי	1843 B	שבו ראה
		1845 RMCD	שהראה לכם

enemies so as to exterminate them. And so a prayer will be on their lips and a sword in their hands. *Ḥereb piphiyyoth* means a sword with two edges capable of inflicting death with either edge. And he says: *in their throat*: for sound proceeds in the first instance from the throat and the speech is then completed in the mouth. Or possibly he says *in their throat* because they recite their prayers aloud, as (in the text): 'cry aloud' (Isa. lviii 1).

7. To execute vengeance: since they come to fight against them; but Israel will execute vengeance upon them. *Reproofs*: they will plead with their kings in argument as to why they have come against them. But these people, for their part, will not (be induced to) refrain from fighting against them; therefore will Israel be avenged against them and put to death all the peoples who come to contend with them in battle.

8. To bind: they will seize their kings and nobles alive, and *bind* them in *chains* and *fetters of iron*, so as to take vengeance upon them while they are still alive.[1]

9. To execute upon them the judgement decreed: this may be explained as meaning either the judgement decreed upon them, or that written in the Torah, viz. 'when I whet my shining sword, and my hand will hold it in judgement' (Deut. xxxii 41). And this is (probably) what is meant by what is written in our text, as also in Ezekiel and in the prophecy of Zechariah.[2] *It is glory*: that day will be *a glory*. *For all his faithful ones*: that is, Israel. And out of regard for that day *praise the Lord!*

PSALM CL

1. O praise the Lord. Praise God in his sanctuary: this psalm with which the book concludes contains thirteen recitations of praise corresponding[3] to the thirteen principles whereby God, blessed be he, rules the universe.[4] At first he says: *praise God in his sanctuary*: (meaning the supernatural world of) angels. And subsequently he says: *praise him in the firmament of his power*: this is the ninth upper sphere which may be regarded as including the entire universe, since it encompasses all the worlds. For this reason he says *his power*, since in it the *power* of God is manifested.

2. Praise him: afterwards he says to Israel: *praise him for his mighty deeds* which he has shown you above all other peoples. *Praise him according to his immeasurable greatness*: for he was magnified and sanctified by the peoples as a result of Israel's redemption.

---

[1] Or 'in their lifetime'.
[2] E.g. Ezek. xxxviii, xxxix; Zech. viii–xiv.
[3] Lit. 'an allusion to'.
[4] *Rosh Ha-Shana* 17b.

‎3.‏ ‎הללוהו בתקע שופר. ובכללו תקע החצוצרות.‏

‎4.‏ ‎הללוהו במנים. שם כלי הנגון לא נודע אצלנו והגאון רב‏
‎סעדיה ז"ל פירש כמו מינים כלומר במינים רבים מכלי הנגון לא‏   1850
‎נזכרו הנה;‏

‎5.‏ ‎הללוהו בצלצלי שמע. צלצלים המשמיעים קול גדול וכן אמר‏
‎בדברי הימים במצלתים להשמיע. בצלצלי תרועה. המשמיעים קול‏
‎תרועה;‏

‎6.‏ ‎כל הנשמה תהלל יה הללויה. ועל כל ההלולים הוא הלול‏   1855
‎הנשמה והוא התבונן במעשי האל ובידיעתו כפי כח הנשמה בעודה‏
‎בגוף ואמר כנגד הנשמות הללויה;‏

1852   RD

בצלצלים

3. Praise him with trumpet sound: this includes also the blast of the cornet.[1]

4. Praise him with strings: ($b^e minnim$) is the name of a musical instrument which is not known to us. But the Gaon Saadya, of blessed memory, explains the word as being the same as $b^e minim$,[2] that is to say, with many 'kinds' of musical instruments not mentioned here.

5. Praise him with loud sounding cymbals: (that is) with cymbals which make a loud sound. So also it says in Chronicles: 'and with cymbals sounding aloud' (1 Chron. xv 19). *With triumphant cymbals*: (that is) which make a sound of a shout of triumph.

6. Let every soul praise the Lord. Praise the Lord: greater than all these recitations of praise is the praise given by the (rational) soul, which consists in understanding the works of God and in the knowledge of him, in so far as the soul is capable of doing so while it is still (lodged) in the body. And it is to the souls (of men) that he addresses the words *praise the Lord*.

---

[1] Kimḥi evidently has in mind Psalm xcvi 6: 'with trumpets and sound of cornet, make a joyful noise before the King, the Lord'.

[2] *Min* = 'kind', 'type'.

GLOSSARY

The following glossary is by no means exhaustive but is intended to be a convenient aid to the less advanced student. Beyond this, reference should be made to M. Jastrow's *Dictionary*, whilst the glossary provided in M. Friedländer's edition of Ibn Ezra's commentary on Isaiah (London 1877) is also helpful.

אבל	but, however
אבר	limb, part
אדום	Edom, Christianity
אויר	air, atmosphere, climate
אולי	perhaps, perchance
אוקינוס	ocean, Mediterranean Sea
אורך	length, lengthiness
אות	sign, letter
אות הגרון	guttural letter
אילך	hither, thither
אילך ואילך	hither and thither
אכזריות	cruelty, severity
אלהות	deity, divinity
אליף	the letter <u>aleph</u>
אמה	cubit
אמצע	centre
אמצעית	central, middle
אפילו	(<u>abbrev.</u> אפי׳) even, even if, although
אף על פי	(<u>abbrev.</u> אע״פ) although
אפשר	a division, space between; <u>hence</u> possibility, it is possible
ארוך	long, tall, lasting

ארס   drop, fluid

באר   break forth, come to light; <u>piel</u>: explain;
<u>nithpael</u>: to be explained

בדד   <u>hithpolel</u>: to be homeless, solitary; <u>hence</u>
forlorn

בזיון   contempt, disgrace

בטח   to be at ease; <u>hence</u> to trust; <u>hiphil</u>:
to assure, promise

בטחון   trust, faith, hope

הבטחה   assurance, promise

בטל   to be void, to cease to be; <u>piel</u>: abolish,
suspend, undo, reverse

בנין   building; constitution; conjugation

בקשה   desire, prayer

ברא, בר   outside of, except, without

בסם <u>or</u> בשם   to be sweet, pleasing, pleasant

גאולה   redemption, delivery

גאון   majesty; <u>hence</u> a title given to heads
of the Colleges in Sura and Pumbaditha
between the sixth and eleventh centuries
C.E., known as the Period of the Gaonim

הגאון   used as a general title for learned men
but especially for Saadya and Rabbi Hai
who was the last of the Gaonim

גבינה   curdled milk, cheese

גדולה   greatness, distinction, dignity, wealth,
high position or office, power

גואל	redeemer, vindicator
גומר (abbrev. ׳וגו)	one finishes or completes (the sentence or quotation), i.e. 'etc.'
גוף	body, person, self
גורל	lot
גזל	to tear away, to rob
גזם	to speak hyberbolically; hence
על דרך גזום	by way of hyperbole, hyperbolically
גזר	to cut, to decree; niphal: to be decreed
גזרה	the root from which a word is derived; category, form, type
גיד	thread, cord; hence sinew
גלוי	appearance, outside; hence
בגלוי	in public
גלות	exile; hence
בני הגלות	exiles, diaspora
גליות	exiles
גמר	to polish, finish, complete
גרה	to be rough, hot; piel: to incite, stir up; hithpael and nithpael: to be inflamed, jealous; to rival; to engage in battle
גרון	throat; hence
אות הגרון	guttural letter
דבק	to adhere to, be connected to, be in accordance with
זה הפסוק דבק ל/עם	'this verse is closely connected with . . .'
דגוש	doubled; hence

פעל הדגוש	the <u>piel</u> conjugation
דחף	to push, thrust, impel
די	sufficiency, plenty, enough
דין	to rule, give equity; <u>hence</u> make equal or the same; <u>hence</u>
והוא הדין	it is the same
דמה	to resemble, be like, to imitate, compare
דעת	knowledge, mind, opinion
דקדוק	grammar
דרום	south
דרס	to tread, stamp; to attack with paws or claws; <u>hence</u> to prey upon
דרש	search; explain
דרש	homiletical exposition or Haggadic exegesis (<u>opp</u>. of פשט . <u>See</u> Introduction)
ה׳	(<u>abbrev</u>.) The Lord
ה׳א	the letter <u>he</u>
ה׳א הידיעה	the definite article
הבטחה	<u>see under</u> בטח
הגבהה	a raising, lifting up
הגן = הוגן	befitting, worthy
הוראה	decision, instruction
הלאה <u>or</u> הלא	further on
הנה	<u>niphal</u>: to be pleased, enjoy, profit
הסכמה	agreement, accord
הפוך	reversed, changed
הפך	the opposite, reverse

הפלגה	separation, singling out
דרך הפלגה	hyperbole, hyperbolically
הרגשה	feeling, sensation, perception
ו׳ו	the letter <u>waw</u>
זהר	(1) to look at, beware; <u>niphal</u>: to be careful, strict, take heed; (2) to be bright, shine
זו = זה <u>or</u> זאת	this, that
זול	<u>polel</u>: to be low, mean, to be a spendthrift, glutton
זון	to provide, sustain
זך	clear, transparent, pure
זכה	to be found worthy of, to succeed, be privileged
זכר <u>or</u> זכרון	memory, memorial, remembrance; <u>hence</u>
זכרו לברכה <u>or</u> זכרונו	may his memory be for a blessing, i.e. of blessed memory (<u>usually abbrev.</u> (ז״ל
ז״ל	<u>see under</u> זכר
זמן	appointed time, term
כל זמן ש׳	all the time that, provided that, as long as
זקוף	erect, upright
זקק	<u>niphal</u>: to join, meet, be engaged in, be coupled with, cohabit
חבר	to join, befriend; <u>piel</u>: compose
חבר	associate, friend, colleague
חברת	company, association
חדד	<u>piel</u>: to sharpen, whet, point
מחודד	<u>pual part.</u> sharpened

חדוש   restoration, renewal

חוץ   outside

מבחוץ   outside

חור   hole, cavity

חורבן   destruction, desolation

חוש   to be anxious for, care for, have sympathy for

חזר   to turn around, return, retreat, repeat;

     <u>hiphil</u>: to bring back, return

חי׳ת   the letter <u>h</u>eth

חליצה   taking out, release, putting off, displacement

חם   warm, hot

חמר = חומר   matter

חנות <u>pl.</u> חניות tent, <u>esp.</u> tradesman's shop

חסר   (<u>abbrev.</u> ח׳) lacking, missing

חפירה   pit, rampart

חצוצרת   cornet

חשד   suspicion

חתול   cat

חתם   to tie up, close, lock, seal

טבור   navel, umbilicus

טבע   nature; <u>hence</u>

דרך הטבע   by way of nature, naturally

טהור   clean, pure

טלטול   moving, exile, migration, homelessness, wandering

טעם   (1) sense, meaning; (2) reason; (3) accent

טרח   being busy, worry, trouble, anxiety

יאש   <u>hithpael and nithpael</u>: to give up, despair

יגון   pain, grief

יגיעה   painstaking, labour

ידה   <u>hiphil</u>: (1) to thank, acknowledge; (2) admit

ידיעה   (from ידע) known, ascertained, definite; <u>hence</u>

ה"א הידיעה   the definite article

יו'ד   the letter <u>yod</u>

יונית   greek

יוצא   (<u>from</u> יצא) transitive; <u>hence</u>

פעל יוצא   transitive verb

יחל   <u>piel</u>: to wait, trust, hope.

יכלת   power, ability, capacity

יסוד   foundation

יצוע   spreading, bed, mattress, couch

יציאה   a going out, departure, separation, removal

יציקה   casting (metal), pouring

יש   there is, there are

ישמעאלים   Ishmaelites, Arabs, Muslims

יתוש   mosquito, gnat

כאב   to be in pain, grieved

כבה   to grow dim, be extinguished, go out

כבוד   honour, glory

הכבוד   (1) the Divine Glory; (2) the soul

כבר   long ago, already, long since

כבש   to press, squeeze; <u>hence</u> to conquer, suppress

כדור   ball, globe, sphere

כובע   helmet

כונה   intention, design, devotion, meaning, purpose

כיון   <u>followed by</u> 'ש: as soon as, since, when

כך   thus, so

כל שכן   so much the more, all the more so

כלה   completion, complete destruction, annihilation

כלום   anything, something, somebody

כלל   to surround, comprise, include; <u>niphal</u>: to be implied, stated in general terms

כלל   general rule, principle

דרך כלל   by way of inclusion, totally, collectively

כמה   how! how many! how much!

כמו   as, like

כמוהו   and like this is (used when providing an analogy)

כנגד   <u>see under</u> נגד

כנוי   (1) surname; (2) attribute, substitute; (3) suffix e.g. יו"ד הכנוי, suffixed <u>yod</u>

כנס   <u>niphal</u>: to be brought in, to enter, be initiated; <u>hiphil</u>: to bring in, introduce, initiate

כפי   <u>or</u> לפי according to, in proportion to

כפל   to repeat, double; <u>pass. pt.</u> כפול repeated

כפל   repetition, a doubling

כרח   force, unwillingness

על כרח   against or without one's will

כתיב   the Biblical text as it is written (as against the prescribed traditional reading קרי (<u>q.v.</u>))

לאה   to labour (in vain), be tired

לאו   no, not

לחה   moisture

לחלח   to moisten; <u>nithpael</u>: to be moistened

למ׳ד   the letter <u>lamed</u>

למוד = לימוד   teaching, study, learning

לפי <u>or</u> כפי   according to, in proportion to, because

לפיכך   therefore

לקא <u>or</u> לקה   to be smitten, affected, punished, stricken

לקט   to pick up, to gather

לשון   tongue, language

לשון יחיד   singular

לשון רבים   plural

על לשון   in the language (of)

לשון המקרא   the language of the Bible, i.e. Biblical Hebrew

לשון נקבה   feminine gender

לשון זכר   masculine gender

לשון צווי   imperative

לשן   <u>hiphil</u> to slander, speak evil of

מבול   flood (of Noah story); decay, destruction

מגד   fortune, precious goods, <u>esp</u>. good fruit

מדה   dimension, measure, proportion; manner, way, character, nature, condition; rule, norm

מדרגה   step, rank, embankment; <u>adv</u>. qualitatively

מהירות   quickness, speed

מהמרות   mounds, debris

מוחלט   irrevocable, confirmed, absolute

מוטל (נטל <u>from</u>) <u>hophal part</u>.: to be thrown, lying; <u>hence</u> flat

מוסיף (<u>abbrev</u>. מ׳) he adds

מוצא שפתיו (<u>hiphil part. of</u> יצא) <u>lit</u>. bringing forth from the lips, <u>hence</u> his utterance

מור to exchange, substitute; <u>hophal</u>: to be exchanged, substituted

מורכב complex, compound

מזל station, constellation

מחבר author

מחוז territory, region, province

מחיה support, provision, living

מחשבה thought, plan

מיוחד (<u>from</u> יחד) <u>pual pass. part</u>. unique, distinguished;

שם המיוחד the divine name, Tetragrammaton

מיוחס <u>pl</u>. מיוחסות (<u>from</u> יחס to connect, be connected) <u>pual pass. part</u>. of traceable genealogy, of distinguished birth, well-connected

מין kind, species; sect (especially applied to Jew-Christians)

כמין something like, in the shape of, of the nature of, after the manner of

מישור plain, level

מכסה tent cover; <u>hence</u> concealment

מכשול hindrance, stumbling block

מלה <u>pl</u>. מלות word

מלוכה kingship, rulership, office, authority

מלמד <u>piel part</u>. it teaches, illustrates; teacher, instructor

ממון	accumulation, wealth, value
ממזרות	the legal condition of a mamzer; bastardship
ממש	substance, reality
מנאפת	(<u>from</u> נאף) lewd, unchaste
מנה	divide, distribute; <u>hithpael and nithpael</u>: to be appointed, designated, ordained
מנהג	manner, conduct, usage
מנהיג	leader, director
מנע	to withhold, refuse, restrain
מס	tribute, tax
מעלה	ascent, step
למעלה	above
מצוה	command
מצות עשה	a positive command
מצוה לא תעשה	a negative command
מצח	forehead
מצע	mattress, bed
מקור	infinitive, verbal root
מקרה	accident, chance
מרמה	fraud, guile, deceit
מרק	cleanse, scour
משגב	secure, height, retreat, stronghold
משורר	singer, psalmist, poet
משחה	anointing, official installation
שמן המשחה	the anointing-oil
משכן	dwelling, <u>esp</u>. the desert sanctuary, the Tabernacle
משל	<u>hiphil</u>: to compare
משל	simile

דרך משל	figuratively, metaphorically
משקל	weight; form, paradigm
מתכת	metal (molten)
נאה	suited, becoming, handsome
נבואה	prophecy, inspiration
נגד	towards, opposite
כנגד	with reference to
נגון	playing on musical instruments; musical accents, mu
נגע	<u>hiphil</u>: to reach
נוכח (<u>from</u> יכח)	in the presence of; second person (number)
לנוכח	with reference to
נו׳ן	the letter <u>nun</u>
נוסף (<u>from</u> יסף)	that which is added; <u>hence</u> paragogic
נוצרים	Christians
נזק	<u>hiphil</u>: to hurt, injure, damage
נחה	quiescent
נחמה	consolation, relief, comfort
נכר	to recognise, favour
נס <u>or</u> נסא	flag, sign; miraculous event
נסמך	(<u>lit.</u> supported, joined) <u>hence</u> a word in the constru state
נקבה	<u>see under</u> לשון
נקוד	pointed (with a vowel point)
נקודה	a vowel point
נקף	to circle, bore; <u>hiphil</u>: to surround
נשב	to blow
נשוא	subject <u>or</u> predicate

סבא   to drink freely

סבה = סיבה   cause

סבך   to interweave, interlace

סבל   to carry a load, endure, sustain

סבלה   load, burden

סחורה   traffic, goods; <u>hence</u> business

סכם   <u>hiphil</u>: to harmonise, agree

סמוך   (<u>lit</u>. supported, joined) <u>hence</u> in the construct state (<u>see</u> נסמך)

סמיכות   <u>or</u> סמיכה construct state

ספק   to supply, furnish, provide

עבר   past tense

עגולה,pl. עגולות (<u>from</u> עגל to be round) celestial bodies (spheres)

עדין   at the same time, yet

עולם   the world

עולם הזה   this world

עולם הבא   the world to come

עומד   (<u>lit</u>. standing) <u>hence</u> intransitive

פעל עומד   intransitive verb

זמן עומד   present tense

עור   <u>polel</u>: to wake up, stir up, exhort

עזרה   temple court, enclosure

עזרת הנשים   the women's court

עזרת ישראל   the men's court

עיקר   root, radical (letter); essence, reality, main object

עלה   to go up; (in late Hebrew the verb in the <u>hiphil</u> has an idiomatic usage: to account to, credit, charge)

עלה ביד	to be successful
עלילה	deed (<u>frequently</u> evil deed)
עליונים	heavenly beings, angels; <u>hence also</u> higher intelligences
עמדה	endurance, permanence, stability, existence
ענין	matter, subject, case, sense, meaning
עסק	to work at, engage in; <u>hithpael</u>: to occupy oneself
עסק	business, worldly occupation, affair, concern
עצם	bone, substance; individual; <u>hence with suffixes</u>
עצמו	himself
עצמם	themselves; etc.
ערב	to be sweet, pleasing (cf. Jastrow pp. 1110f.)
ערבוביא	mixture, confusion, mob
עתיד	standing, ready, designated, future; <u>hence</u> future tense
עתיד לבוא	in the future
לעתיד	in time to come
פאר	<u>piel</u>: to crown, glorify; <u>hithpael</u>: to lord it over, take pride, vaunt oneself
פזור	a scattering, dispersion
פחות	<u>adj. and adv.</u> less, inferior
פטר	firstborn
פיס	<u>hithpael, nithpael</u>: to be appeased, satisfied, persuaded, reconciled
פירוש	(<u>abbrev.</u> "פי or "פיר) explanation, commentary, meaning
פנים	that which is in front of you when you enter; <u>hence</u>, interior, inside

על כל פנים	in any event, anyway
פסוק	division; <u>hence</u> a Biblical verse
פעל	verb
פעל יוצא	transitive verb
פעל עומד	intransitive verb
פ"א הפעל	the first radical (of a verb)
עי"ן הפעל	the second radical
למ"ד הפעל	the third radical
פועל	active participle
פעול	passive participle
שם הפעל	infinitive
פרד	to part, separate from, go away from
פרט	that which is singled out, specification
בפרט	in particular
פרך	tyranny, rigour, harshness, serfdom
פרנסה	provision, maintenance, sustenance
פרסא	Persian, Persian mile
פרש	<u>piel</u>: to specify, explain, interpret
שם המפרש	the specified name, i.e. the Tetragrammaton
מפרשים	commentators
פרשה	portion, chapter or paragraph of the Bible
פשט	the plain meaning of a Biblical text as opposed to דרש (<u>q.v.</u>) (<u>see</u> Introduction)
פתח	to open, begin; <u>hence</u> to introduce
פתיחה	opening, introduction
צואר	neck
בית הצואר	collar

צווי = ציווי   command; <u>hence</u>

לשון צווי   imperative

צוף   to come to the surface, float; <u>hiphil</u>:   to cause to overflow, flood, inundate

צורה   form, shape, figure

צורך   need, necessity

צחות   purity, elegance; <u>hence</u>

צחות הלשון   for the elegance of the language, i.e. poetically

צלע   side, rib, wing of a building

צנוע   discreet, retired, chaste, decorous

צפף   to touch closely, press;   to squeeze into

צרך   to be necessary; <u>hiphil</u>:   to require, demand

קבלה   Tradition

קבע   insert, drive in, fix; <u>hence</u>

שנה קבועה   fixed sleep, i.e. regular sleep

קדם   to precede, anticipate; <u>hiphil</u>:   to be early, quick, hasten to do a thing

קודם   antecedent, before

קוף   <u>hiphil</u>:   to bring close, encompass

קיום   preservation, continued maintenance or existence; basis, foundation

קיטור   vapour, smoke

קים = קיים,<u>f.</u> קימת = קיימת   existing, enduring, lasting; forever

קלון   degradation, disgrace

קצר   to be short; <u>hence</u>

דרך קצרה   by way of brevity, i.e. elliptically (<u>see</u> Introduction)

קר	cold
קרוב	near; <u>hence</u>
זמן קרוב	a short time
קרה = קורה	cooling, cold; <u>hence</u>
קרת רוח	(cooling of the spirit) satisfaction, pleasure, contentment
קרי	the text which is to be read according to the Massoretic notes as against what is written (כתיב <u>q.v.</u>)
קריאה	calling, exclamation; <u>hence</u>
ענין קריאה <u>or</u> לשון קריאה	vocative
קרירות	cold, coldness
ראה	to see; <u>hiphil</u>: to show, enlighten, convince
ראוי	<u>pass. part.; plur. fem.</u> ראוית fit, worthy, seemly
רב = רוב	multitude
ברב	for the most part
רבוי = ריבוי	increase, plenty, amplification; plural
רגל	<u>hiphil</u>: to lead, conduct
רגל	foot pilgrimage; <u>hence</u> festival
רגש	to tremble, shake, stir; <u>hiphil</u>: to stir up; to feel, perceive
הרגשה	sense, feeling, sensation
רוחין	width, relief, ease, comfort
רוה	to be saturated, satisfied
רומח	a spear
רחוק	far, distant; far-fetched
ריס העין	eye-lid
רמז	gesture, hint, intimation, allusion

רפה	to be loose, lax; <u>piel</u>: loosen, let hang down; <u>hence</u> (with יד) to withdraw the hand from
רקח	to spice, perfume
רשת	a net
שבש	<u>hithpael</u>: to be entangled, confused, perplexed, confounded
שגח	<u>hiphil</u>: to look at, consider, care for, supervise, provide
שדל	<u>hithpael</u>: strive, struggle
שוח	to bow down, bend, sink
שוחה	pit, pitfall
שורש	root, radical
שטיח	rug, mat, spread
שטף	to flood, inundate
שית	foundation
שכינה	Shekinah, the Presence (of the Divine Glory)
שכל	insight, understanding, intelligence
שלך	bird of prey, cormorant
שם	(1) name; (2) noun
השם	the divine name, God
שם המפרש	(the special name) the Tetragrammaton
שם השם	the divine name
שמא	lest, perhaps
שמירה	watching, guarding
שנוי	change, variation
שעור	proportion, standard, size, quantity, limit
שפוע = שיפוע	slope

שפיכה	a pouring out
שפלות	humility
שפע	flow, run, overflow; <u>hiphil</u>: to give in abundance
שקט	rest, at ease, quiet
שקל	form, paradigm
שקק	<u>hithpolel</u>: desire, be eager for
שרב	heat of the sun, dry heat
שתק	<u>hiphil</u>: to calm, silence
שתת	to lay the foundation of, start, begin
תאוה	desire, appetite
תהלה	praise, song (of praise)
תואר	<u>or</u> תאר look, appearance, attribute; adjective
ת"ו	the letter <u>tau</u>
תוחלת	hope, expectation
תוך	middle; inside
מתוך	immediately, from, through, because of
תועלת	profit, use, benefit
תוקף	strength, power; mainstay
תחבולה	design, plan (usually of the wicked)
תחל	<u>see under</u> תחלה
תחלה	beginning, start, first stage; <u>adv.</u> at first, in the first place; <u>denom. vb.</u> תחל <u>hiphil</u>: to begin
תחלואינ	diseases
תחת	under, beneath, instead
תחת ש'	since
תחתוני	lower things; <u>hence</u> earthly things, earthly creatures (<u>opp.</u> of עליונים <u>q.v.</u>), lower intelligences

תִינוֹק   child, infant

תכונה = תיכונה middle watch; <u>hence</u>

חכמי התכונה   astronomers

תכלית   end, perfection; destruction

תכן   to arrange in order; <u>niphal</u>: to be weighed, to be right, correct

תמורה   exchange, substitution, <u>i.e.</u> opposite

תנועות   (<u>from</u> נוע to move) movements; <u>hence</u> vowels

תפארת   beauty, crown, glory

לשׁוֹן תפארת   majestic or poetical language

תקומה   rising, resurrection, restoration

תרבות   growth, education

תרבות רעה   bad manners, depravity

תרגם   to translate, explain, interpret